SCENIC RAIL GUIDE to
Central & Atlantic Canada
WITH CONNECTING ROAD ROUTES

D0763616

SCENIC RAIL GUIDE to
Central & Atlantic Canada
WITH CONNECTING ROAD ROUTES

By BILL COO

GREEY
dePENCIER
BOOKS

Photography by Bill Coo, except where otherwise credited.

Special thanks to VIA Rail Canada Inc., Parks Canada, CN Photo Library, Tourism New Brunswick, Canadian Pacific Corporate Archives, Public Archives of Canada, Greg Butler, Lynn Cunningham, Ed Hailwood, Prue Hemelrijk, and the dedicated and imaginative team at Greey de Pencier Books (Katherine Farris, Annabel Slaight, Pam Raiken, Wendy Pease and Lee Goddard).

Thanks also to my son Michael and to Noel Buckley, who photographed the Labrador Route; to Noel and Craig Andrews, who photographed the Hudson Bay Route; to Ricky Goldenhar and Janet Hollingworth, who photographed the Saguenay Route. Finally, a profound thanks to my wife, Lois, for being so patient with the whole family for decades during our voyages of discovery and for looking after the three dogs and nine cats at our new home, "Kinmount."

This book is dedicated to the late T.J. (Jim) Nevin, who created many of the Ontario, Québec and Atlantic Canada tours that are still being enjoyed by tourists from all over the world.

Designed by Ron Butler

Typesetting by Trans Canada Graphics and Colour Separations by Graphic Halftone

Printed by Friesen Printers

Cover photo courtesy of Photo CN

Canadian Cataloguing in Publication Data

Coo, Bill, 1932-
   Scenic rail guide to central and Atlantic Canada, with connecting road routes

Includes index.
ISBN 0-919872-76-X

1. Railroad travel — Canada, Eastern.*
2. Canada, Eastern — Description and travel — Guide-books.*
I. Title.

FC38.C66	917.13'044	C83-098006-7
F1009.C66		

ISBN 0-919-872-76-X   Printed in Canada

Contents

Foreword

I hope this guide will help you take the trip of your life — and I'd like to take this opportunity to thank the many readers who found my first book, the *Scenic Rail Guide to Western Canada*, of such use in planning their routes through to the Pacific. I've repeated myself a bit in the introduction to this guide, just to cover the basics of train travel, because they're much the same wherever you go. But every train journey has its own special character, and no two are really alike. I know, because over the past 40 years (including 29 years with CPR, CNR and VIA), I've logged at least 500,000 miles. (Yes, miles! Railways are one of the last holdouts in a country that's going metric.)

My interest in trains began when, as a youngster, I spent my summer holidays on Lake Ramsey, near Sudbury. Our cottage was within a few yards of the Canadian Pacific main line, and every morning I would wander up to the shining rails to watch the parade of thundering steam engines shaking the ground and covering me with cinders. My favourite was the Dominion, with its beautiful Tuscan red and black Royal Hudson at the front. This train included coaches, sleeping cars, a diner and, at the rear, a gorgeous Mount observation car, complete with a brass-railed observation platform and colourful canopy.

As you'll see when you read on, I'm still a great train enthusiast. I love train travel and recommend it because you can relax and let the scenery roll by, drink and dine in a civilized manner, doze or sleep whenever you want, and concentrate on a good book if you are feeling reclusive. Or you can chat with fellow passengers from all over the world or with a crew who are as knowledgeable, though perhaps not as keen, about trains as I am. But most of all, a train ride anywhere is both an instant geography lesson and a journey into history, maybe even an adventure in pioneering. Imagine being late because of a moose on the tracks!

To help you make the most of this guide, I've included all scheduled rail services between major points, as well as the must-see things that aren't accessible by rail. I believe the way to truly discover this land is to leave your car at home and combine rail travel with side trips using rental cars. You can see on pages 10 to 15 how simple it is to arrange.

With this method of travel — and this book — you can easily visit the best of central and Atlantic Canada, from Apohaqui to Zephyr, including such very special spots as Gaff Topsail, Kamouraska, Moonbeam, Seahorse, Mongoose, Eureka, Paradise and Tonkas Falls. Where *did* those names come from? You'll learn that, too.

This guidebook tells you everything I've learned about Canada from aboard the train — or at least as much as the editors have given me space to say. For instance, I've included: where to ride narrow-gauge, mixed trains; *the* places to see icebergs, whales, snow geese and the most spectacular canyons and waterfalls east of the Rockies; a road that disappears every 12 hours; plus descriptions of wildlife, railway lines, historical highlights and natural phenomena.

But first, a map to get you oriented, and then some practical tips.

The Toronto-bound LRC crossi▪
the Rideau River at Smiths Fa

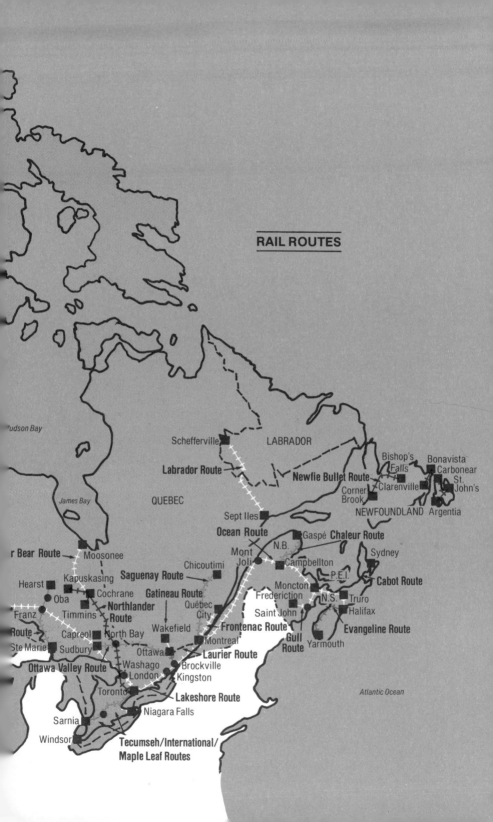

RAIL ROUTES

Hudson Bay

Schefferville   LABRADOR

Labrador Route

Bishop's Falls   Bonavista
Carbonear
Newfie Bullet Route   St. John's

QUEBEC   Corner Brook   Clarenville

James Bay   NEWFOUNDLAND   Argentia

Sept Iles

Ocean Route

r Bear Route   Moosonee   Mont Joli   Gaspé   **Chaleur Route**

N.B.   Sydney

Kapuskasing   Chicoutimi   Campbellton

Hearst   **Saguenay Route**   P.E.I.   **Cabot Route**

Oba   Cochrane   Moncton

Franz   **Northlander**   **Gatineau Route**   Fredericton   N.S.   Truro

Timmins   **Route**   Québec   Halifax

Route   City   Saint John

Capreol   North Bay   Wakefield   **Frontenac Route**   **Evangeline Route**

Ste Marie   Sudbury   Montreal   **Gull**   Yarmouth

Ottawa   **Route**

Ottawa Valley Route   Washago   **Laurier Route**

London   Brockville

Kingston

Toronto   **Lakeshore Route**   Atlantic Ocean

Sarnia   Niagara Falls

Windsor   **Tecumseh/International/**
Maple Leaf Routes

Introduction

Photo CN

Information and reservations

A timetable is your first tool for planning your trip. Try your travel agent, or write or phone the following:

VIA Rail Canada
P.O. Box 8116
1801 McGill College Ave.
Suite 1300
Montréal, Québec
H3A 2N4 (514) 286-2311

Algoma Central Railway
Passenger Sales
P.O. Box 7000
129 Bay St.
Sault Ste. Marie, Ontario
P6A 5P6 (705) 254-4331

Ontario Northland Trans-
portation Commission
Passenger Services
195 Regina St.
North Bay, Ontario
P1B 8L3 (705) 472-4500

Greater Winnipeg Water
District Railway
598 Plinquet St.
Winnipeg, Manitoba
R2J 2W7 (204) 233-1456

Quebéc, North Shore &
Labrador Railway
Passenger Services
100 Retty St.
P.O. Box 1000
Sept Iles, Québec
G4R 4L5 (418) 968-7539

National Museum of
Science and Technology
Steam Train Excursions
2380 Lancaster Rd.
Ottawa, Ontario
K1A 0M8 (613) 998-4566

Reservations are required on some trains. Schedules may be seasonal or restricted to specific days of the week. Be sure to check the days and dates of operation for the trains of your choice, especially when making connections between services. Timetables also outline the procedure for buying tickets, conditions for advance payments, cancellations and refunds.

Baggage

If there's a baggage car on your train, the timetables will tell you. Full-fare passengers can check up to 150 pounds through to their destinations and take a reasonable amount

of personal hand baggage with them. Check baggage at least 30 minutes prior to departure time.

Pets

Pets are allowed to travel on trains, but only in the baggage car. Seeing-eye dogs, of course, can ride in the passenger sections.

Customs and immigration

The International (page 103) and Maple Leaf (page 106) routes both cross the Canada/U.S. border. No passport is required for citizens of either Canada or the U.S. but proof of citizenship may be.

Stopovers

Stopovers are a distinct advantage of rail travel, but be sure there is a train operating on your chosen departure date; some may operate only two or three days a week.

Rental cars

There are several companies that rent cars at reasonable rates. You can book in advance or take your chances that one will be available when you arrive. When traveling by VIA, inquire about the special rates car rental companies sometimes offer VIA customers. There is often a car rental outlet in, or close to, the railway station.

Canada's national parks

These parks have been created for the benefit, education and enjoyment of Canadians and foreign tourists. The trips in this guide take you to Terra Nova, Gros Morne, Cape Breton Highlands, Kejimkujik,

Fundy, Forillon and La Maurice national parks. You may want to write for free — and excellent — detailed guides published by Parks Canada. Specify your choices to Parks Canada, Ottawa, Ontario K1A 1G2.

Road guides
All you require to follow the road routes in this publication are up-to-date maps of the provinces involved. Free maps can be obtained by writing to individual provinces or can be bought at local bookstores. Environment Canada publishes terrific booklets entitled *Ecotours*, which describe the flora and fauna of the various Canadian regions.

City guides
Most cities and towns publish comprehensive, and often free, guides to the attractions of their area. Write in advance or pick up the information at a local tourist office or Chamber of Commerce.

Red-winged blackbird

Package tours
Several reliable tour operators specialize in package tours on the passenger trains in this book. Pick up their brochures from your travel agent or write:

VIA Tours
P.O. Box 8116
1801 McGill College Ave.
Suite 1300
Montréal, Québec
H3A 2N4

Four Winds Travel
175 Fifth Ave.
New York, N.Y. 10010

Horizon Holidays
of Canada
37 Maitland St.
Toronto, Ontario
M4Y 2R9

UTL Holiday Tours
22 College St.
Toronto, Ontario
M5G 1Y6

These tour operators should also know about booking on the Polar Bear Express (page 123), as well as scheduled bus and air tours to the Agawa Canyon (page 128).

Photography
Most of the photos in the railway section of this book were taken from the train (I don't believe in false promises!). Taking pictures through the window requires special care, but you can do it. For colour transparencies, you'll need a colour compensating filter (No. CC30-R) with exposure increases as recommended for this filter on daylight-type film. An exposure meter is recommended for inside shooting. If you don't have a meter, increase exposure one full stop. To avoid reflection, try to hold your camera as close to the glass as possible. Avoid halation by shooting away from the sun. Lessen the effects of lateral blur by shooting at a 45° angle rather than straight out of a side window.

11

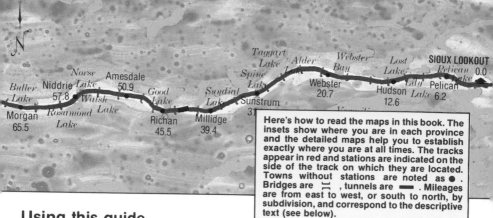

Here's how to read the maps in this book. The insets show where you are in each province and the detailed maps help you to establish exactly where you are at all times. The tracks appear in red and stations are indicated on the side of the track on which they are located. Towns without stations are noted as ●. Bridges are ≍ , tunnels are ▬ . Mileages are from east to west, or south to north, by subdivision, and correspond to the descriptive text (see below).

Using this guide

The Scenic Rail Guide to Central and Atlantic Canada is divided into the trips listed on the contents page. Each chapter includes an overview of the area, followed by the main points of interest given in mileage order. Individual maps follow the route mile by mile. The guide is written from east to west and south to north. If you're traveling the other way it's still easy to follow. Simply hold the maps facing the direction of travel.

A profile at the end of each route gives the history of the railway line, plus the mileage location, population, elevation and name origin (where available) for each station.

How to determine where you are

By tradition, railway subdivisions run from east to west and south to north, with mile 0 always at the east or south terminal of each subdivision. Most of the subdivisions are about 125 miles long, as this was the average distance a steam-powered freight train could travel in 12 hours. Some subdivisions are 250 to 335 miles long, reflecting the faster speeds of modern trains.

There are several ways to find out exactly where you are at any given moment on a train and to pinpoint interesting sites. On most routes white rectangular mileboards along the way indicate the mileage from the last major division point. On some routes these are attached to telegraph poles, on others they are right beside the track, on metal signposts. Between Montréal and Kingston the mileboards are on old concrete markers, which have been there since 1856.

Another way is to find the number on the signal masts and add a decimal point before the last digit (that is, signal 742 is located at mileage point 74.2). Or you can check the station names. A mile before each station or siding there is a sign beside the track giving the name of the upcoming station. On CPR routes, this signboard is usually black on white; on CNR routes it is usually black on yellow. Stations with passenger service have prominent nameboards at each end and sometimes in the centre, too; sidings, junctions or passing tracks generally have a nameboard beside the track as well (see below).

Children on trains

For children of any age, a train trip is a wonderful experience: ever-changing scenery, lots of room to move and friendly people to meet. For the very young there are cut-out trains, colouring books and morning playtimes in the lounge car of the Ocean. For school-age children a train trip offers an unparalleled and fun opportunity to study history, geography and how the rest of the world lives, while meeting children from other countries. A super book for kids is *All Aboard! A Cross-Canada Adventure* (Greey de Pencier Books, 1979). It's a highly readable account of a child's journey across Canada by train, illustrated with memorable colour photographs. An excellent souvenir.

The friendly wave

You often see crews of passing trains and section men waving as a train goes by. Railwaymen are a jolly bunch, but this is more than mere friendliness: they're checking each train's running gear. The "highball" wave is an assurance that everything is in order. Often residents near the tracks check trains, too, and get right into the spirit by waving the proper signals.

Night travel

Some of the best train travel is at night. The locomotive's powerful headlight brightens the track ahead, the signals change from green to red, and cities and towns light up the horizon. Somehow, space acquires a whole new meaning after hours of traveling with only an occasional glimpse of a lonely trapper's cabin.

Station stops

When a train is late arriving at any station, the crew makes every effort to depart as quickly as possible. In such cases, a station stop may be shorter than that shown in the timetable. Station stops are ideal for getting some exercise, seeing the sights (if there's time) and sending or receiving telegrams.

Meal sittings

To avoid lineups, passengers on most trains are given their choice of meal sittings for lunch and dinner. Those with diet restrictions should tell the steward or waiter.

How fast is the train traveling?

You can calculate this by measuring the time in minutes and seconds it takes your train to travel between any two mileboards. Then the table below will give you your train's average speed.

Time per mile	MPH
0 min. 36 sec.	100
0 " 38 "	95
0 " 40 "	90
0 " 42 "	86
0 " 45 "	80
0 min. 48 sec.	75
0 " 51 "	71
0 " 55 "	65
1 " 0 "	60
1 " 5 "	55
1 min. 10 sec.	51
1 " 20 "	45
1 " 30 "	40
1 " 40 "	36
2 " 0 "	30

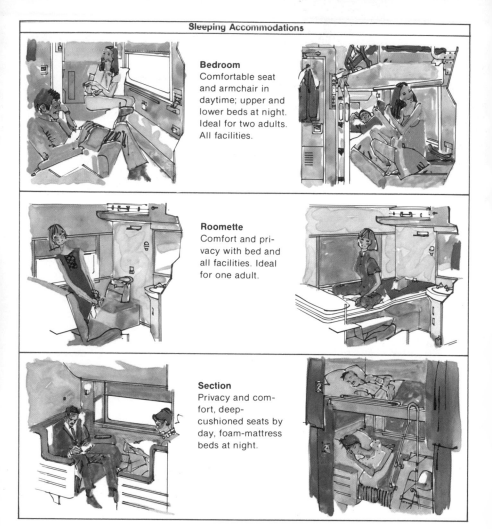

Bedroom
Comfortable seat and armchair in daytime; upper and lower beds at night. Ideal for two adults. All facilities.

Roomette
Comfort and privacy with bed and all facilities. Ideal for one adult.

Section
Privacy and comfort, deep-cushioned seats by day, foam-mattress beds at night.

Sleeping car names

Types of sleeping and dining cars on VIA trains are identified by their names.

"E" cars (for example, Evangeline) contain four sections, eight roomettes and four bedrooms.

"Green" cars (for example, Green Lane) contain six sections, six roomettes and four bedrooms.

"Bay" cars (for example, Fortune Bay) contain 10 roomettes and five bedrooms.

Special facilities on the Ocean

This is the flagship passenger train to Atlantic Canada and there are three ways to travel on it. At the front are day coaches for those traveling short distances. In the middle are the Dayniter cars, with generous stretchout seats, leg rests, pull-down trays and overhead lights. Pillows and blankets are available at a nominal charge from the attendant. At the rear are sleeping cars with upper and lower berths, roomettes and bedrooms with wash and toilet facilities. Folding doors between some bedrooms provide a huge room by day and privacy at night, ideal for families.

For meals, the Ocean features a coffee shop and a takeout counter/lounge adjacent to the day coaches. A dining car serving full-course meals is located at the approximate centre of the train and is available to all passengers, as are the licensed lounges. Complimentary bingo games are held in the dining car most evenings and there are small prizes to add to the fun.

Who's who on the railway

On all railway passenger trains the train conductor is the "captain of the ship" and responsible for its safe and efficient organization. Look for the gold bars on the left sleeve of his uniform. Each bar represents five years of employment, and most conductors have many years of service. Trainmen and baggagemen assist the conductor, one handling the entraining and detraining of passengers, the other your baggage. The Ocean staff also includes a sleeping car conductor, passenger services assistant, dining car stewards, waiters and chefs, sleeping car porters, Dayniter attendants and lounge car stewards/waiters. These people are all there to serve you, so do not hesitate to ask for their assistance.

Languages

Bilingual services are available at most major VIA stations and on most trains. On the Ocean, consult the passenger services assistant. Most dining cars are also staffed with people who can serve you in English or French. The other railway operations usually provide service in English only (except in Québec).

Alcoholic beverages

Trains must conform to the laws and regulations of the province through which they are traveling. All provincial regulations prohibit the consumption of alcohol in coaches,

Dayniters and in open areas of sleeping cars. Roomettes and bedrooms are exempt from restrictions.

Freight trains

On your rail trip you will pass many freight trains. The railways are the lifeline of Canada, carrying many commodities in an enormous variety of specialized cars.

How trains are powered

Most passenger and freight trains are hauled by one or more diesel-electric locomotives; the diesel engine generates electricity, which powers the traction motors for a smooth ride. Some trains consist of self-propelled rail diesel cars (RDCs); in these, diesel engines power the units through a torque-converter. If you are really interested in train cars and equipment, write for *Rail Canada Volume 4*, by D.C. Lewis (Inter-Hobbies Distributors, R.R.1 Martintown, Ontario K0C 1S0).

More reading

If you are interested in further information on the passenger trains described or the routes followed, here's a list of books concerning the trains and their runs.

Newfie Bullet Route
Narrow Gauge Railways of Canada, by Omer Lavallée (Railfare Enterprises, 1979)

Evangeline Route
Train Time, by M.A. Gibson (Lancelot Press, 1973)

Ocean Route
Iron Roads, by D.E. Stephens (Lancelot Press, 1972)
Canadian National Railways, by G.R. Stevens (Clarke, Irwin & Company, 1960)

Tecumseh Route
Railways of Canada, by N. & H. Mika (McGraw-Hill Ryerson, 1972)

Northland Route/Polar Bear Route
Steam into Wilderness, by A. Tucker (Fitzhenry & Whiteside, 1978)
Coach Trains and Travel, by P.C. Dorrin (Superior Publishing Company, 1975)

Black Bear Route
Tracks of the Black Bear, by D. Wilson (Green Tree Publishing Company, 1974)
Algoma Central Railway, by O.S. Nock (Adam and Charles Black, 1975)

Labrador Route
Railroads of Canada, by Robert F. Legget (Douglas, David and Charles, 1973)

Hudson Bay Route
The Battle for the Bay, by G. MacEwan (Western Producer Book Service, 1975).

A CN Marine ferry is dwarfed by an iceberg

The Newfie Bullet Route

An offshore odyssey aboard four different trains carrying you past Newfoundland's ponds, coves, bays and barrens, recapturing the days of the original "Newfie Bullet"

St. John's to Port-aux- Basques

The first Newfie Bullet steamed out of St. John's on the evening of June 29, 1898, hauling two baggage cars, two coaches, two sleepers and a single diner. Arriving 27 1/2 hours later at Port-aux-Basques, its passengers transferred to the S.S. *Bruce* for an overnight voyage across the Cabot Strait to North Sydney.

The final Bullet departed Port-aux-Basques on the morning of July 2, 1969, having taken on passengers from the *William Carson*. Its three diesel units hauled a baggage car, four coaches, two diners and eight sleepers. At 8 a.m. on July 3, it sighed to a halt at the St. John's station. The passengers — myself included — took their photographs and slowly walked away. That run marked the end of an era, and the last opportunity to cross Newfoundland by rail, on a

547.8-mile stretch of narrow-gauge track only three feet, six inches wide, through communities such as Kelligrews, Tickle Harbour, Come By Chance, Goobies, Joe Batt's Arm, Gaff Topsail, Kitty's Brook, Curling, Black Duck, Codroy Pond and Red Rocks.

Throughout its 71-year history, the Bullet was variously known as the Overland, the Foreign Express (since it was the first leg of a sea link to mainland Canada) and the Caribou (for the great herds it passed in the wild interior). But the Bullet was the definitive nickname, and the one that stuck, due to the train's ridiculous rate of speed. People used to swear they could hop off one of the forward coaches and pick a cupful of blueberries before the caboose came into sight, and 25 mph was good going on the flat. Certainly it was one of North America's most

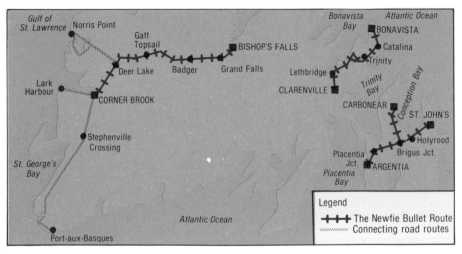

Legend

┿┿┿ The Newfie Bullet Route
〰〰〰 Connecting road routes

A mixed train climbs the hill above Spaniard's Bay on its way to Carbonear

unusual trains, and the subject of richly varied folklore. What other railway employed a "wind-sniffer" to control traffic on a gusty stretch of track? Lauchie McDougall, who lived at mile 533, was paid $20 a month to conduct a weather watch, with only his nose to guide him. If he gave an all clear, the Bullet went through; if not, it was chained down while the storm ran its course. Delays could reach 56 hours, freight cars were blown into the Gulf of St. Lawrence, and tons of ballast were puffed away from under the track. If that wasn't enough, the barren plateau around the Topsails was noted for its 15-foot snowdrifts. In 1903 and again in 1941, trains were marooned there for 17 days.

Moose posed another hazard. Once a pair of them attacked a section gang, totally demolishing a track car. On another memorable occasion, seven beasts charged the Bullet head on, but came out second best. Along the shores of Conception Bay, water routinely overflowed the roadbed. Crews would place pebbles on the rails to gain sufficient traction, a practice known as "rockin' up the grade." Station agents (with or without the aid of Screech, a lethal drink that's sure to cure all ills) have reported ghost trains passing in the night. Even the sea-link transport was fraught with peril. Many ships have been caught for days in pack ice, and during WW II, the S.S. *Caribou* was sunk by a German submarine. It's plain to see that travel from and within Newfoundland has always been (and still is) a bit of an adventure.

The Newfoundland Railway was first proposed in 1868 by Sandford Fleming, who touted St. John's as a point of arrival for British immigrants. Certainly British money backed the first stage of construction in 1881, but not everyone saw the railway's advantages. During a riot known as the Battle of Foxtrap (a village you pass at mile 17), locals armed with pitchforks and broomsticks routed the workers, who had to be rescued by the St. John's militia. Locomotives were bought second-hand from Prince Edward Island, but one went overboard while being shipped across. Still, the first section of track reached Harbour Grace in 1884, where a somewhat premature last spike was driven by the future King George V, then a crew member on a visiting British warship. Another section was built between Whitbourne and Placentia by the colonial government, but it wasn't until 1889 that matters were placed in the hands of an experienced contractor. This was Robert Reid, who had enjoyed success laying CPR track north of Lake Superior. Reid got things moving, but his terms were hard. Workers received $1 for a 10-hour day and were expected to build their own tarpaper shacks and buy their own food, which they cooked over open fires along the right-of-way. Sundays were devoted to mending and washing clothes or baking the next week's bread. Most men were too exhausted to go out on the town, even if there'd been one to go to. The railway was built with pick, shovel and wheelbarrow; rock cuts were drilled and blasted by hand through almost impassable terrain. Newfoundland's rivers and valleys run from north to south, and the

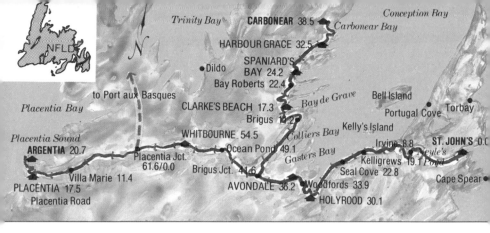

east-west railway crosses them all. Grades are steeper than in the Rockies, and the sharpest curves appear on the steepest grades. Near St. Andrew's, the Bullet goes uphill and down at the same time, and around three curves at once. There's a bridge on the average every four miles, but not a single tunnel from coast to coast.

While it lasted, the Bullet was a way of life — a chance to make friends, have a drink and tell tall tales. The buses that replaced it in 1969 make better time, but they aren't quite the same. Still, you can ride a latter-day Bullet over 200 spectacular miles from St. John's to Placentia Junction, and Bishop's Falls to Corner Brook, filling in the "missing links" by rented car or Roadcruiser bus.

POINTS OF INTEREST

St. John's to Carbonear (St. John's and Carbonear subdivisions)

Mile 0: Historians agree that the railway shouldn't have been built across the barren Topsails Plateau, but Robert Reid insisted, on the theory that its quarry would be a good source of freight traffic. In fact, granite from that remote site was used for three purposes only: to build the St. John's station (opened on January 7, 1903); to form the base of a statue in front of the station; and for cobblestone paving on Water Street, when streetcar tracks were first installed in 1899.

Mile 1-30: After leaving the suburbs of St. John's, the train climbs into densely wooded country dotted with marginal farms and fish-laden lakes. Between miles 13 and 16, look north to Kellys and Bell islands. The former was the haunt of seventeenth-century pirates; the latter, the site of rich iron-ore deposits that were mined between 1893 and 1966. Here you begin an abrupt

descent to Conception Bay, down a very steep grade that causes the brake shoes to produce clouds of smoke. Between miles 18 and 30, you follow the bay, past rocky beaches lined with fishing boats. Salt spray will sweep over the train if there's a wind from the north, and boats have been known to blow up onto the tracks. These waters are noted for their cod, capelin, lobster, squid and giant (the record is 622 pounds) bluefin tuna. Look ahead at mile 29 for a good view of the Butter Pots, weathered rock formations looming over the village of Holyrood.

Mile 30-41: To the north, just past Holyrood station, you can see wooden racks used for drying cod. Between miles 31 and 33, the train climbs high above Holyrood Bay, circling the Butter Pots. Look to the north, under the highway bridge, for a view of falls on the North Arm River before you enter the Harbour Grace Barrens — a wild, desolate region of grotesquely shaped rock broken only by moss, blueberry bushes and stunted spruce. Once it was heavily wooded, but early settlers burned 3,000 square miles of timberland. A dome-shaped mountain appears to the north at mile 36; as the train curves south you can compose an excellent photograph. Avondale station is still occupied by a railway family. Just past it, look south to see some of the Bullet's original wooden coaches, now a playground for local children. At Brigus Junction, the train turns abruptly north past an old boxcar used as a storage shed.

Mile 1-13: Look ahead and to the east between miles 5 and 6 to see the train winding above the trees, with a sparkling lake and rolling hills in the background. In the 1800s, Brigus was a major sealing port, employing 2,000 men. It's also the birthplace of Bob Bartlett, a renowned sealer who captained Robert Peary's polar expeditions. Look east at mile 12.5 for a superb view of Cupids on Bay de Grave. This was the site of a very early outpost, established by John Guy, who arrived with 39 English settlers aboard the *Endeavour* in 1610. Guy named his settlement Sea Forest Plantation and built a fort, sawmill, gristmill and shipyard. But his colony fell victim to marauding pirates and hostile fishermen 18 years later and it was officially disbanded.

Mile 17-29: Look east at mile 18 as you climb high above Clarke's Beach for views of several churches overlooking Bay de Grave. The sight of Bay Roberts, to the east between miles 21 and 22, is stunning, as is the climb above Spaniard's Bay. Between miles 25 and 26, the view eastward features rock-strewn hills, church steeples, forested slopes, neat houses and sparkling lakes. Then you suddenly enter another barren area, passing Riverhead to the west at mile 27. At mile 29, look east and ahead toward Harbour Grace, where some of the finest Newfoundland dogs are raised by prize-winning kennels, including that of Robert and Megan Nutbeam. These dogs weigh 20 pounds at birth, can grow to 180 pounds, and are often able to pull 50 times their own weight. In the early 1800s, thousands were used throughout the island to haul wood, pull catches of fish and deliver mail.

Mile 32-38: Harbour Grace was fortified in 1612 by the notorious pirate Peter Easton, who built additional strongholds at Kelligrews and Ferryland, plundered ships in the region for many years and retired, fabulously wealthy, to become the Marquis of Savoy. For a time, Harbour Grace was the site of Newfoundland's only runway. Wiley Post left from here on his round-the-world journey in 1931, and Amelia Earhart took off the next year on her solo flight to Ireland. The Conception Bay Museum, built on the site of Easton's fort, chronicles these early feats. Look east at mile 36 for a view across the bay to Carbonear, with its shocking pink station. While the train switches cars for a return to Brigus Junction, you'll have time to visit a restaurant and try some local delicacies (cod tongues and figgy duff), stroll the waterfront to see unusual birds (stearins and sea pigeons) and hear the marvelous accent (a blend of Irish, English and Huguenot). You may even find, hidden away in a private garden, what is said to be the grave of an Irish princess abducted by Easton's lieutenant, Gilbert Pike.

POINTS OF INTEREST

Brigus Junction to Argentia (Argentia subdivision)

Mile 42-61: Continuing west across the Harbour Grace Barrens, you follow the shoreline of Ocean Pond, past one of the Avalon Peninsula's typical stunted forests. These small, bushy-topped spruce were used as stovepipe cleaners by resourceful fishermen. Look south at mile 54 to see some of the Newfie Bullet's steel coaches,

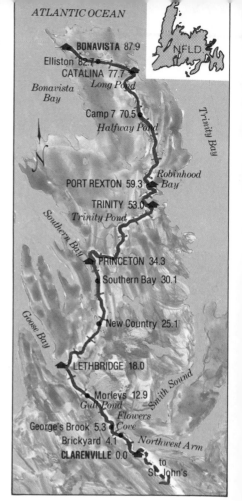

baggage cars and sleepers rusting quietly away. (Others, painted white and converted to work cars for section gangs, can be seen at several points en route.) Whitbourne, the site of Bond Memorial Park, was the home of Sir Robert Bond, prime minister of Newfoundland from 1900 to 1909, who built a unique estate, including a chain of small lakes surrounded by exotic trees and flowerbeds. Look back at mile 55 for a good view of the town, with its red freight sheds, white station and black-steepled church on the hill. At Placentia Junction the track divides, one branch heading southwest toward Argentia, the other northwest to Tickle Harbour and beyond.

Mile 0-20: The Argentia line was the route taken by Lord Beaverbrook in August 1941, to meet Churchill and Roosevelt in Placentia Bay for the signing of the Atlantic Charter. It's also the route of the "Trouter Train," which operates once a year on the Victoria Day weekend, carrying anglers from all over North America to their favourite fishing spots. For the first few miles, you'll see an extraordinary array of fishing shacks on both sides of the track, and some passengers will probably detrain with their tackle. At Villa Marie the terrain becomes unexpectedly rugged and mountainous as the track twists high above the northeast arm of Placentia Sound. The best views occur between miles 15 and 17, overlooking the town of Dunville. Placentia, first inhabited by fishermen in the early 1500s, was officially claimed by the French in 1662. By 1692 they'd erected Fort Royal and set to battling the English up and down the island until 1713, when they ceded Placentia to Britain and decamped to Cape Breton, there to build Fortress Louisbourg. Castle Hill National Historic Park preserves the remains of the French fortifications and interprets this era for visitors. Argentia, where the station is a combined rail/ferry terminal, was the site of a U.S. naval base during WW II, but it's now a summer base for the CN Marine ferry to North Sydney.

John Cabot made his first sighting of the "new found land" in 1497

POINTS OF INTEREST

Clarenville to Bonavista (Bonavista subdivision)

Mile 0: Clarenville, beautifully situated on the Northwest Arm of Trinity Bay, was once a prosperous lumbering centre. During WW II, it was the birthplace of the "Splinter Fleet" — wooden ships built for coastal service. In 1955 it became the North American terminal for the transatlantic telephone cable from Oban, Scotland.

Mile 1-53: The train curves east along Shoal Harbour, passing Church Siding at mile 0.8. An old brickyard appears at Flowers Cove, mile 4.1. Look west between miles 17 and 19, as you follow the shore of Goose Bay, to see the ancient station and freight sheds. Southern Bay lies placidly to the west between miles 28 and 30. At mile 35, the train sweeps up a long hill, then into a severe curve at mile 38, with Indian Lookout to the west. The terrain grows increasingly wild over the next 15 miles. At mile 50, the track descends in a helical loop, dipping under itself while curving around a pond in the narrow valley, then following a ledge high above Trinity Harbour between miles 51 and 53. Here you can look east to a town where wooden trawlers are built by hand, without the aid of blueprints. Some of its white colonial homes, situated on the harbour's three arms, have beaches at both front and back doors, and fragrant briar roses lining well-kept yards. A local man, Dr. Peter Beamish, has established a whaling museum and takes passengers on boat trips to study these mammoth creatures in Trinity Bay. This settlement is especially rich in history. It was the site of both North America's first courtroom proceedings

(1615) and the first administration of smallpox vaccine (1798).

Mile 54-88: The train circles Trinity Bay as far as mile 56, then cuts across a neck of land to Port Rexton, on Robinhood Bay, and through a vast, windswept plateau to Catalina, discovered by a British sea captain in 1499. Icebergs should be visible in these waters well into the summer months. Bonavista, the end of track, depends almost entirely on its fisheries. Catches include cod, tuna and swordfish. Several miles to the north, at Cape Bonavista, there's a stone statue of John Cabot, thought to have landed here in 1497, and a lighthouse that once contained a light brought from Scotland's Inchcape Rock. Nearby Spillars Cove is noted for a double grotto called the Dungeon, formed by centuries of saltwater erosion.

POINTS OF INTEREST

Bishop's Falls to Corner Brook (Bishop's Falls subdivision)

Mile 267-294: For 30 miles the train follows the Exploits River valley, a route favoured by the Beothuk Indians on their migratory hunting expeditions. The Beothuks were a peaceful tribe whose practice of decorating their bodies with ochre paint led to the expression "redskin." Many were senselessly murdered by European settlers, and the last of their race, a woman named Shanawdithit, died in 1829. The river is

lined with forests of birch, cherry, mountain ash, maple, aspen, alder and wild raisin; watch for birds such as yellow warblers and water thrush. The Exploits River bridge is the longest (927 feet) structure on the railway; it's seen to the south near Bishop's Falls. Mile 268.5 was the site of a second narrow-gauge railway — the Grand Falls Central — which operated a 22-mile passenger service between Grand Falls, Bishop's Falls and Botwood. At Grand Falls, look south to see the giant Abitibi-Price paper mill, which began operation in 1909. Two British publishing magnates, Lords Northcliffe and Rothermere, founded the town to supply their firm with newsprint, which accounts for its very English atmosphere. Look north at mile 278 to Rushy Pond; then south at mile 284 to the remains of a Beothuk encampment on an island in mid-river.

Mile 295-310: Badger is a thriving logging community at the junction of the Exploits River and Badger Brook. The Trans-Canada Highway swings north here, to avoid crossing the great Northern Barrens, but the track plunges straight ahead toward the Topsails, ominous peaks that dominate the Newfoundland interior. Smaller heights of land have even more blood-curdling names (Skull and Misery hills). At Millertown Junction, on Joe Glodes Pond, the 20-mile Millertown Railway heads south to Buchans Junction, joining with the 19-mile Buchans Railway. These lines carry lead, zinc and copper ore to Botwood, a journey involving four different tracks in less than 90 miles. (Until 1957, there was a fifth track — the Harpoon Tramway — a roller-coaster bush line that carried only logs.)

Mile 311-373: Now you climb through a wild and desolate region, practically devoid of vegetation, which once sheltered some 10,000 caribou. Their numbers have been depleted, but you still may see them in the distance. Quarry, at mile 324.9, provided stone for the St. John's station. The railway's highest point, 1,566 feet above sea

level, is marked by a sign to the south at mile 328.5. Between miles 329 and 333, you'll see the soaring Topsails — Mizzen and Gaff to the south, Main to the north. Snow fences indicate the abominable conditions that prevail throughout the winter along this barren stretch of line, forcing CN to spend $500,000 in the 1950s to raise the track an average of four feet to lessen drifting. The long descent to Howley, through a forest of black spruce and balsam fir, has produced its share of runaway trains. See if you can spot the wreckage of an old freight on the south side. Grand Lake, the province's largest, appears to the south at mile 357.6. It's crossed on a drawbridge, followed at mile 364 by a dam that controls its water level. Look north here to see the spillways. To the south, between miles 367 and 372, can be seen the Humber Canal and Deer Lake, where huge wooden flumes on the hillside carry Grand Lake's water to a generating plant that supplies electricity to Corner Brook.

Mile 373-405: For some 17 miles you follow the shores of Deer Lake; then, for another 17, the Humber River. At times it's a broad and placid stream, offering excellent salmon fishing. Then it will suddenly become a rushing torrent squeezed into narrow gorges. Look south at mile 389 toward Bowater Park, the home of 593, the Newfoundland Railway's only surviving steam locomotive. Marble Mountain, with its 1,500-foot ski lift, lies to the south at mile 398. Shellbird Island, in mid-river, is reputed to be the site of buried pirate treasure. Nearby Breakfast Mountain has a curious rock pattern (the "Old Man of the Mountain") on its side. Now you approach the city of Corner Brook, site of the immense Bowater pulp and paper mill, opened in 1925, and for many years the world's largest such operation. Just before you arrive at the station, look north for a truly spectacular view of the looming Long Range Mountains.

Boat-building at Trinity, Newfoundland

The Newfie Bullet Route

St. John's and Argentia Subdivisions — CNR St. John's/Placentia Jct./Argentia

The segment from St. John's to Brigus Junction was built by the Harbour Grace Railway, and opened for traffic in November 1884. The line from Placentia Junction to Placentia was built by the Placentia Railway. It opened for traffic in October 1888 and was extended to Argentia by the Reid-Newfoundland Company in 1921.

Miles	Stations	Population	Elev.	Origin of Station Names
0.0	St. John's (Nfld.)	150,700	—	The city was allegedly discovered in 1497 on the feast of St. John the Baptist
8.8	Irvine	—	—	—
19.1	Kelligrews	—	—	—
22.8	Seal Cove	—	—	—
30.1	Holyrood	1,610	—	Holyrood House, Edinburgh, Scotland
33.9	Woodfords	—	—	—
36.2	Avondale	937	—	Avondale, County Wicklow, Ireland
41.6	Brigus Jct.	118	—	French family Bregou
49.1	Ocean Pond	—	—	—
54.5	Whitbourne	1,268	—	Sir Richard Whitbourne (1579-1628), governor of Trepassey, Newfoundland from 1618 to 1620
61.6/ 0.0	Placentia Jct.	—	—	Plascencia, Spain
11.4	Villa Marie	—	—	—
17.5	Placentia	2,209	—	Plascencia, Spain
20.7	Argentia (Nfld.)	493	—	From the latin "argentum," meaning "silver," in commemoration of the opening of a local silver mine

Carbonear Subdivision — CNR Brigus Jct./Carbonear

The line from Brigus Junction to Harbour Grace was built by the Harbour Grace Railway, and opened in November 1884. It was taken over by the Reid-Newfoundland Company and extended to Carbonear in 1898.

Miles	Stations	Population	Elev.	Origin of Station Names
0.0	Brigus Jct. (Nfld.)	118	—	French family Bregou
11.2	Brigus	912	—	
17.3	Clarke's Beach	997	—	Family name common to the region
22.4	Bay Roberts	4,072	—	French family name
24.2	Spaniard's Bay	1,568	—	Acknowledges the involvement of Spain in the Newfoundland fishing industry
32.5	Harbour Grace	2,937	—	In dispute. Probably a contraction of Havre de Grace, the original name of the port of Le Havre, France
38.5	Carbonear (Nfld.)	5,026	—	Several alleged origins: the Portuguese coastal town Carvoeiro; Carboneras in southern Spain; and Carbonnier, a French family name

Bonavista Subdivision — CNR Clarenville/Bonavista

This line was built by the Reid-Newfoundland Company between 1909 and 1911, and opened on November 8, 1911.

Miles	Stations	Population	Elev.	Origin of Station Names
—	Clarenville (Nfld.)	2,087	—	Clarence Whiteway, son of Sir William Whiteway (1829-1908), once prime minister of Newfoundland
0.0	Clarenville Jct.	—	—	—
4.1	Brickyard	—	—	—
5.3	George's Brook	—	—	—
12.9	Morleys	—	—	—
18.0	Lethbridge	452	—	—
25.1	New Country	—	—	—
30.1	Southern Bay	—	—	—
34.3	Princeton	150	—	—
53.0	Trinity Jct.	639	—	—
55.8	Bailey	—	—	—
59.3	Port Rexton	454	—	—
70.5	Camp 7	—	—	—
77.7	Catalina	1,129	—	Spanish Cataluna
82.7	Elliston	540	—	Rev. William Ellis, who conducted the first Methodist service in the community in 1912
87.9	Bonavista (Nfld.)	4,299	—	In dispute. Either from Cap de Bonne Viste (Cartier, 1534) or after Boa Vista, one of the Cape Verde Islands (Gaspar Corte Real, 1500)

Bishop's Falls Subdivision — CNR Bishop's Falls/Corner Brook

This line was built by the Newfoundland, Northern and Western Railway, and opened for traffic in the fall of 1897. It was taken over by the Reid-Newfoundland Company in 1898. The first through passenger train from St. John's to Port-aux-Basques left on June 30, 1898. The final run of the legendary "Newfie Bullet" left Port-aux-Basques on July 2, 1969.

Miles	Stations	Population	Elev.	Origin of Station Names
267.3	Bishop's Falls (Nfld.)	4,504	—	In commemoration of a visit by Anglican Bishop John Inglis (1777-1850) to Newfoundland
271.9	Cruisers	—	—	—
276.2	Grand Falls	8,729	—	Describes the falls on the Exploits River
281.0	Red Cliff	—	—	—
294.2	Badger	1,160	—	Common family name
310.0	Millertown Jct.	186	—	Scottish lumbering firm, Lewis Miller & Co.
319.2	Caribou	—	—	Herds of caribou abound in the region
332.9	Gaff Topsail	—	—	—
345.8	Kitty's Brook	—	—	—
356.8	Howley	—	—	—
367.1	Northern	—	—	—
373.5	Deer Lake	4,546	—	Area of Newfoundland renowned for its herds of caribou
381.0	Pynns	—	—	—
387.2	Pasadena	1,850	—	—
397.4	Russell	—	—	—
405.3	Corner Brook (Nfld.)	24,000	—	For the Corner brook (named by Captain James Cook) that flows through the city

The lighthouse at Lobster Cove is connected by tunnel to the home of the lighthouse keeper

Newfoundland Road Routes

Port-aux-Basques to Corner Brook

The ferry from mainland Canada arrives at Port-aux-Basques, a base for European fishermen since the sixteenth century. Here the Trans-Canada Highway leads west past the beaches of J.T. Cheesman Provincial Park and climbs toward the Long Range Mountains, western Newfoundland's dominant geographical feature. Glaciers disappeared from these very ancient peaks only 10,000 years ago, and you can observe the evidence of their retreat as you drive. Be careful as you approach 1,700-foot Table Mountain on your right, where gale-force winds have often closed the Route and blown freight cars off the tracks. In fact, the railway used to employ a local man, Lauchie MacDougall, known as "the human wind gauge" because of his uncanny ability to sense when a big blow was on the way, without using scientific instruments of any kind. No one knows exactly how he did it, but he managed to pass the secret along to his wife, who continued to warn of impending storms until 1972. Curving north toward Mummichog, you might wish to detour west on Routes 407 and 406 in a loop around the Codroy

Valley, a prosperous farming area sheltered by the Anguille Mountains. Rejoining the Trans-Canada, you turn northeast through a long stretch of birch and balsam forest to Flat Bay Brook, a popular salmon stream, and one of many that pour down into St. George's Bay. Then you can stop at Barachois Pond Provincial Park, with its hiking trails and views of Erin Mountain, or swing west to Stephenville and follow Route 460 to the Port au Port Peninsula, Newfoundland's only French-speaking area. Settled in the 1700s, this was long considered France's most vital North American fishing base. It's joined to the mainland by two narrow beaches separated by a salt-water pond, and features yet another provincial park. Retracing your route back to Highway 1, continue to Blue Ponds Provincial Park, named for its distinctively coloured waters, fed by subterranean springs. From that point, it's a very short drive to the thriving industrial city of Corner Brook.

Corner Brook to Gros Morne

The Trans-Canada Highway from Corner Brook leads northeast along Deer Lake to Route 430, your turn-off to the 750-square-mile Gros Morne National Park. (You may want to detour east on Route 422 to Squires Memorial Park, where in spawning season salmon can be seen jumping the Humber River's Big Falls.) When you enter Gros Morne, Route 431 forks left across the Lomond River, an excellent fishing spot, to Glenburnie. Turn left just past Winterhouse Brook and you'll travel down a strangely lunar gulch, com-

Looking north over Bonne Bay Big Pond toward snow-covered Gros Morne Mountain

posed of yellow-ochre rock, that leads to the isolated fishing community of Trout River, where you can dig for clams at low tide and enjoy sweeping views of the Gulf of St. Lawrence. Retrace that route to Woody Point, where a 20-minute ride aboard the Bonne Bay ferry takes you to Norris Point and Neddie's Harbour. These waters reach 750 feet deep, chilled by the Labrador current. In the early 1900s, the bay was a supply stop for ships of the Royal Navy — you can still see the great iron mooring rings — but today it's frequented by charter boats that take you fishing for cod, tuna and Atlantic salmon. At the information office on Route 430 you'll learn about the park's many nature walks and hiking trails. Some are placid strolls along the beach; others, highly challenging climbs into the starkly beautiful high country that's home to caribou, lynx, bear, rock ptarmigan and the park's symbol, the arctic hare. But even from the road, you should be able to catch a glimpse of moose, beaver and a host of shore birds. Continue through Rocky Harbour to view fishing displays in the lighthouse at Lobster Cove, past stands of the windblown, stunted trees called tuckamore. To the north of Sally Cove are two spectacular ice-age fjords. The first, Western Brook Pond, is now completely severed from the sea, but you can take a boat trip beneath its brooding cliffs, or continue to St. Pauls Inlet, connected to the gulf by a narrow waterway, which is sometimes filled with harbour seals. Past Cow Head, where Jacques Cartier is said to have anchored in 1541, you'll arrive at Shallow Bay, with its famous cliffs of breccia —

jagged limestone and shale that contain a wealth of fossils. Now you must decide whether to visit the even more deserted beaches farther north, or retrace your route back down Route 430 for a close look at 2,644-foot Gros Morne, Newfoundland's second-highest peak, which stands vigil over the untamed glories of Atlantic Canada's newest and largest wilderness park.

Corner Brook to Bottle Cove

This route follows Route 450 along the south shore of Humber Arm, one of three main branches of the Bay of Islands, a heavily forested area first settled in 1779. Many descendants of the original residents remain, commuting to work in Corner Brook's paper mills or living as freelance fishermen in a series of villages that retain all the flavour of Newfoundland's more remote outports. The road is a literal cliffhanger, skirting the base of the Blomidon Mountains and the Lewis Hills. Look for the small white church at Benoit's Cove before arriving at Frenchman's Cove, where you can catch a boat across to Woods Island in mid-bay, or try your hand at fishing with a Newfoundland jig. The smallest boat will take you out far enough to lower a barbed lure into the water and pull it up in short, sharp jerks — a 500-year-old technique that's virtually guaranteed to land you a 10-pound cod. Then it's on past the copper mine at York Harbour to Blow Me Down Provincial Park, where a lookout trail and tower afford wonderful views of Tweed, Guernsey and Pearl islands and the windswept beach at Bottle Cove.

25

The Cabot Route

*Through coal-mining country and over the Canso Causeway
to scenic Cape Breton, land of sparkling lakes, Highland customs
and legendary giants*

Truro to Sydney

For 63 years, the 12-hour rail journey from Halifax and Truro to Sydney was broken by the stormy waters of the Strait of Canso. Trains had to be loaded onto a fleet of ice-breaking ferries for the two-mile trip between Mulgrave and Point Tupper, then reassembled on the opposite shore, an operation taking an hour or more. This was one of the few places in Canada where train passengers could (and did) get seasick.

Construction of the 4,500-foot-long Canso Causeway in the 1950s greatly simplified the trip. Ten million tons of rock were blasted from Cape Porcupine and dumped into the strait, which is more than 200 feet deep in mid-stream, forming an 800-foot-wide base and a surface that accommodates

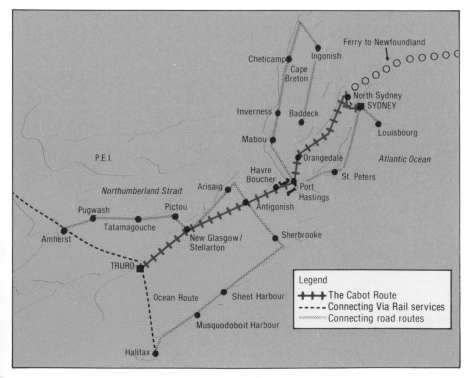

The Jackpine Coastal Walk along the Cabot Trail

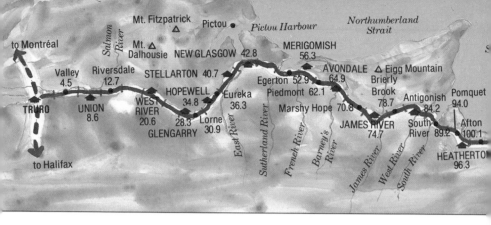

a two-lane highway, a single rail line and a pedestrian walkway. The causeway also prevents ice from entering the strait, creating a 13-mile ice-free harbour, the largest deep-water port in the world.

Beautiful Bras d'Or Lake, virtually tideless and highly reminiscent of a Scottish loch, is Canada's finest unpolluted body of contained salt water, with surrounding hills that slope into picturesque valleys. Scottish settlers found in Cape Breton an echo of their homeland and their influence is evident in the names of its towns and villages: New Glasgow, Glengarry, Heatherton, Iona and McKinnon Harbour. Each summer the flash of tartan and the skirl of pipes at numerous Highland gatherings remind visitors of this Celtic heritage.

POINTS OF INTEREST
Truro to Havre Boucher (Hopewell subdivision)

Mile 1-33: This pleasant countryside, marked by rolling hills, peaceful rivers and verdant valleys, is ideal for farming, hunting and fishing. In 1817 the West River Farming Society was formed to encourage agricultural excellence. It imported Ayrshire cattle, held livestock shows, offered prizes for the best wheat and sponsored regular information-sharing meetings. You can appreciate the area's beauty from Gordon Summit, 571 feet above sea level, at mile 23.6.

Mile 34-43: Coal, steel and railroads all played important roles in the history of Stellarton, New Glasgow, Trenton and Pictou. Coal was discovered near Stellarton in 1798 and mined continuously until recent times. The Foord seam was the world's thickest: 48 feet. Canada's first stationary steam engine went into service here in 1827 and a year later the first iron rails were cast. An

extremely early steam engine, the Sampson, built in 1838 by Timothy Hackworth of Newcastle, England, is on display at New Glasgow's Pictou County Historical Museum. The Stellarton Miners Museum exhibits both early mining equipment and another vintage steam locomotive, the Albion, built in 1854. In the nineteenth century, New Glasgow became a noted shipbuilding centre, while nearby Trenton developed into a steel town.

Mile 52-84: Between miles 52 and 56 you have a good view to the north of Northumberland Strait and Merigomish Harbour. The latter is the site of Big Island, long used by Micmac Indians as a burial ground. In 1827 the Glasgow Colonial Society of the Church of Scotland sent 300 books to Merigomish, thus creating one of Canada's first public libraries. The train crosses Barney's River at miles 65.9 and 66.1, then follows the canyon of the Piedmont Valley, past fens and marshes like those of eastern England. Watch for Sugarloaf Mountain looming 750 feet above Antigonish, a town founded by Loyalists who fled the United States following the American Revolution. Between miles 83 and 84 look south to see the distinctive dome of St. Ninian's Cathedral, built of local blue limestone between 1868 and 1875. Its façade bears the Gaelic inscription Tigh Dhe (House of God). Antigonish is the home of St. Francis Xavier University, founded in 1853; Canada's oldest Highland Games, held annually since 1863; an arrestingly named weekly newspaper, The Casket; and a brick rail station with a well-preserved interior.

Mile 89-106: South River is noted for its dairy herds, which can be seen grazing peacefully on nearby hills. Pomquet was settled almost exclusively by Acadians, descendants of immigrants from St. Malo, France. Mixed farming keeps Heatherton flourishing, while Tracadie (mile 104.1), is famous for its lobster — watch for fishermen at work on St. Georges Bay, to the

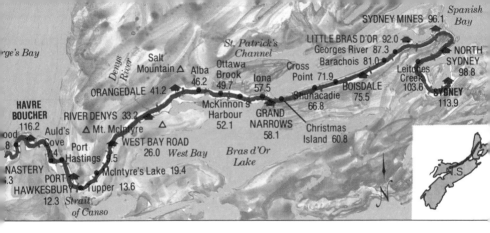

Spanish Bay

SYDNEY MINES 96.1
LITTLE BRAS D'OR 92.0
Georges River 87.3
NORTH SYDNEY
Barachois 81.0
Cross Point 71.9
Leitches Creek 103.6
98.8
SYDNEY 113.9
BOISDALE 75.5
Shunacadie 66.8
Christmas Island 60.8
GRAND NARROWS 58.1
Iona 57.5
Ottawa Brook 49.7
McKinnon's Harbour 52.1
St. Patrick's Channel
Bras d'Or Lake
West Bay
Alba 46.2
ORANGEDALE 41.2
Salt Mountain △
Denys River
rge's Bay
RIVER DENYS 33.2
Mt. McIntyre △
WEST BAY ROAD 26.0
HAVRE BOUCHER 116.2
Auld's Cove
Port Hastings
McIntyre's Lake 19.4
NASTERY
PORT HAWKESBURY
Tupper 13.6
12.3 Strait of Canso

north. Look south at mile 106 for a monastery founded in 1825 by Trappist monks. Augustinian monks, its occupants today, tend their fields in silence, communicating only in sign language. A modern chapel on the grounds contains paintings and stained-glass windows depicting the life of Saint Augustine.

POINTS OF INTEREST
Havre Boucher to Sydney (Sydney subdivision)

Mile 4-51: The brooding waters of Canso Strait appear to the north, at mile 4, and are followed to mile 8. After passing the fishing village of Auld Cove, settled by Irish and Scots, the train swings north to cross the Canso Causeway. Look south to see the ugly gash on Cape Porcupine created by the removal of rock to build the causeway. The swing bridge at mile 8.7 may be open to allow passage of a ship. The train curves sharply south at mile 9, following the harbour. At Port

Hawkesbury, look south toward Mulgrave, where giant supertankers depart for destinations all over the world. The former station at mile 19.4 is now a private home. From mile 35 you'll catch glimpses to the south of Bras d'Or Lake. This beautiful 450-square-mile lake, really an inland sea, is surrounded by hills.

Mile 57-113: This is one of the most scenic sections of the Cabot route. At Iona look north to see the enormous Saint Columba Church, seemingly too large for the population. Nearby is the Nova Scotia Highland Village, which depicts the struggles and triumphs of the Scottish settlers who came to this area in the early nineteenth century. The Barra Strait, which divides Bras d'or Lake in two, is crossed on a 1,697-foot steel bridge at mile 57.7. To the south you'll see the tiny ferry that links Iona with Grand Narrows. This is a favourite stop for fishermen in search of trout or cod. Between miles 59 and 92, the train runs close to St. Andrews Channel; look north at

The Cabot passing Union station

29

mile 60.8 to Christmas Island, burial place of Micmac Chief Noel. At mile 70 is 26-mile-long Boularderie Island, named after Chevalier de la Boularderie, to whom it was granted in 1719, in recognition of his distinguished service in defence of Port Royal.

The coal mines of the Sydney area are visible from mile 96. Operations began at Sydney Mines in 1766, and today some shafts extend for several miles under the ocean floor. Watch for cormorants, puffins, guillemots and razorbills hovering over the CN Marine ferry terminal at North Sydney. Ferries leave from here for Port-aux-Basques and Argentia, Newfoundland At mile 104, look east for your first view of Sydney's harbour. The town was first settled in 1785 by Loyalists from New York State, later joined by immigrants from the Scottish Highlands. Sydney experienced a boom after the Dominion Iron and Steel Company established its blast furnaces here in 1899. Huge mansions were built on the surrounding hills and electric interurban railways linked the town with nearby communities, including Glace Bay, where giant Marconi telegraph towers beamed messages to Europe.

The Cabot Route

Hopewell Subdivision — CNR Truro/Havre Boucher
The segment from Truro to New Glasgow was built by the Nova Scotia Railway, and opened on May 31, 1867. The segment from New Glasgow to Havre Boucher was built by the Halifax and Cape Breton Railway and Coal Company between 1879 and 1880, and opened in December 1880.

Miles	Stations	Population	Elev.	Origin of Station Names
0.0	Truro (N.S.)	12,500	61	(See Bedford subdivision. page 63)
4.5	Valley	344	110	—
8.6	Union	—	222	—
12.7	Riversdale	25	321	—
16.6	Campbell	—	416	—
20.6	West River	85	447	Nearby river
28.3	Glengarry	51	392	Glen in Inverness-shire, Scotland
30.9	Lorne	—	355	Marquis of Lorne, governor-general of Canada from 1878 to 1883
34.8	Hopewell	399	203	Ship that brought Ulster colonists here in 1761
36.3	Eureka	321	153	Eureka Milling Co., first local industry
37.0	Ferrona Jct.	150	141	From Latin "ferrum," meaning iron. Named by the Nova Scotia Steel and Coal Co., which manufactured pig iron here
40.7	Stellarton	5,357	62	Bed of coal known as "stella," which yields oil
42.8	New Glasgow	10,500	31	Named in 1809 by early Scottish settlers after Glasgow, Scotland
46.2	Academy	—	222	—
52.9	Egerton	—	69	Francis Egerton, the last Duke of Bridgewater, known as the "father of British inland navigation"
56.3	Merigomish	191	20	From the Micmac word "mallegomich," meaning "hardwood grove."
62.1	Piedmont	300	263	Foot of range of hills ("pied" and "mont")
64.9	Avondale	96	154	River Avon in Scotland
70.8	Marshy Hope	83	417	James Mappel, an early settler who kept hoping that the marsh would improve
74.7	James River	169	251	Rev. James Munro, first Presbyterian minister
78.7	Brierly Brook	—	152	Early settler John Brailey
84.2	Antigonish	5,489	17	From the Micmac word "nalegitkoonechk," meaning "where branches are torn from the trees."
89.2	South River	—	24	Nearby river
94.0	Pomquet	160	26	From the Micmac word "pogumkek," meaning "raining along"
96.3	Heatherton	327	81	Named by an act of Parliament (1879)
100.1	Afton	221	132	River Afton in Scotland
106.3	Monastery	385	13	Nearby Trappist monastery of Petit Claivaux, built in 1825
108.8	Linwood	—	217	Named by an act of Parliament (1884)
116.2	Havre Boucher (N.S.)	499	20	Captain François Boucher, who was caught by the ice here in 1759, and had to stay until the spring thaw

Sydney Subdivision — CNR Havre Boucher/Sydney
The segment from Havre Boucher to Sydney was built by the Intercolonial Railway between 1890 and 1891, and opened on January 1, 1891. Line changes were made between 1906 and 1915.

Miles	Stations	Population	Elev.	Origin of Station Names
0.0	Havre Boucher (N.S.)	499	20	(See Hopewell subdivision)
7.4	Auld Cove	225	19	Mrs. Alexander Auld, 1785 settler
9.5	Port Hastings (Cape Breton Island)	326	16	Sir Charles Hastings Doyle, lieutenant-governor of Nova Scotia from 1867 to 1873. Formerly Plaster Cove
12.3	Port Hawkesbury	3,427	9	Admiral Edward Hawke, first Baron Hawkesbury (1727-1808). Formerly Ship Harbour
13.6	Tupper	—	37	Sir Charles Tupper (1821-1915), a father of Confederation. Formerly Rocky Ridge
19.4	MacIntyre's Lake	—	138	Lake nearby
26.0	West Bay Road	125	216	From the Micmac word "wolnamkeak," meaning "sandy cove"
33.2	River Denys	97	76	Sir Nicholas Denys, Sieur de Fronsac, who, in 1654, was appointed governor of Cape Breton, P.E.I. and part of Newfoundland
41.2	Orangedale	110	12	—
46.2	Alba	—	18	Latin for "white." Large deposits of white plaster rock are nearby. Formerly Boom
49.7	Ottawa Brook	—	56	—
52.1	McKinnon's Harbour	59	12	Family of early settlers
57.5	Iona	180	15	Historic and sacred isle in Scotland, which it supposedly resembles
58.1	Grand Narrows	98	15	Where the Bras d'Or Lakes narrow
60.8	Christmas Island	151	25	Micmac Chief Noel is buried on the island opposite
66.8	Shunacadie	—	15	Micmac word for "place of cranberries"
71.9	Cross Point	—	25	—
75.5	Boisdale	165	12	Town in Scotland, home of first settlers (1823)
81.0	Barachois	—	30	From the Acadian "barre à cheoir," meaning "lagoon" or "pond," or French "barachoix," meaning "sandbar"
87.3	Georges River	250	22	—
92.0	Little Bras d'Or	101	20	French for "golden arm." Formerly French Village
96.1	Sydney Mines	36,400	75	Formerly called The Mines
98.8	North Sydney	8,319	40	Formerly called North Bar
103.6	Leitche's Creek	94	12	Early settlers called Leech.
113.9	Sydney (N.S.)	85,800	7	Thomas Townsend, first Viscount Sydney (1733-1800).

Nova Scotia Road Routes

Balmoral Mills on the Sunrise Trail

Glooscap Route

Routes 104 and 2 lead northwest from Truro into a land of Indian legend and tidal wonders, situated between the Minas Basin and Chignecto Bay, two forks of the Bay of Fundy. The basin is the site of the world's highest tides, rising and falling as much as 50 feet twice daily. Passing through three separate Economies (Upper, just plain Economy and Lower), you reach the spot where Glooscap, a figure in Micmac Indian folklore, was supposed to have thrown clumps of earth at his pet beaver, creating the Five Islands. Just east of Parrsboro, you can see the footprints of a prehistoric dinosaur, visit the Glooscap Park and Campsite and buy blueberries in season from roadside stands before exploring the town's early nineteenth-century streets. Parrsboro Harbour is also a good place to view the tides, which occur roughly six hours apart. This area is a rockhound's dream come true, and the local museum has a large display of semiprecious stones. If you continue west on Route 209, you'll reach Spencers Island, where the ghost ship *Mary Celeste* was built in 1861. This peninsula offers splendid scenery at Cap d'Or and a four-mile sandbar at Advocate Beach. The North Shore roads can be rather rough, so you may wish to return to Parrsboro, then head up Route 2 to the Miners' Museum at Springhill, where you can descend a 900-foot shaft. Turn off onto Route 302 to visit Nappan's experimental farm and nearby Maccan, the best place to see a phenomenon known as a tidal bore, in which the tide comes rushing upstream on top of the river water. Joggins, farther west on Route 242, is famous for its 300-million-year-old fossilized trees and plantlife, set in the towering sandstone cliffs of Chignecto Bay. From this point, a short drive eastward, through marshy flatland that's a haven for migrating birds, brings you to the town of Amherst.

The Cabot Trail

The nineteenth-century Cabot Trail was described as "the worst road in the Dominion." Today it's one of Nova Scotia's most popular tourist routes — so popular that you'd be wise to plan your trip for a weekday. Your first stop is the fishing village of Chéticamp, settled in 1785. Its attractions include the Acadian Museum, St. Peter's Church and a large community of rug hookers, whose work is much admired.

Three miles north is the western entrance to 370 square mile Cape Breton Highlands National Park; the information centre here offers detailed guides to its many facilities. Pleasant Bay, surrounded by Atlantic Canada's largest sugar maple stand, was settled in 1819 by Scots driven from their homes by the Highland Clearances. About four miles east is the Lone Shieling, a re-creation of the sort of stone hut used by early Scots immigrants when tending flocks of sheep.

At the village of Cape North, you can swing north through the Sunrise Valley to the foot of Sugarloaf Mountain, where John and Sebastian Cabot are said to have landed in 1497, then continue on to Bay St Lawrence.

Back on the trail, the picturesque fishing village of Neil's Harbour is worth a stop, as is Ingonish, set in an area particularly reminiscent of the Scottish Highlands. At Ingonish Beach you leave the park and proceed to Cape Smokey, where the adventurous can ride a ski lift up the north face of this massive headland. St. Ann's is the site of North America's only Gaelic college, founded in 1939. Visitors are welcome at the Highland crafts centre and a museum containing the clothes of Angus MacAskill, the Cape Breton giant. Baddeck, on the shores of beautiful Bras d'Or Lake, commemorates its most famous resident at the kite-shaped Alexander Graham Bell Museum.

Marine Drive

From Antigonish, Route 7 swings past Lochaber Lake to Sherbrooke, where the Sherbrooke Village restoration depicts daily life in the late nineteenth century. Costumed guides lead you through some 20 buildings where craftspeople demonstrate blacksmithing, quilting, weaving and wooden boat building. Try them yourself if you're in a pioneer frame of mind! Or, if you're a fishing enthusiast, this stretch of the St. Mary's River is renowned for its Atlantic salmon. As the road curves west to Liscomb Wharf, you begin to savour views of sheltered coves that offer swimming, scuba diving and fishing boats for hire, and hills and meadows covered with wild flowers and fresh with sea air. Next come Necum Teuch ("beach of fine sand") and Popes Harbour, the most picturesque of the South Shore villages. At Tangier, you can buy delicious smoked salmon and mackerel before visiting the Fisherman's House Museum at Jeddore Oyster Pond. Musquodoboit ("rolling out in foam") Harbour features a museum, located in the former CNR station, that traces the history of Nova Scotia's railways. Then, a turn south on Route 207 leads you past the beach at Lawrencetown, popular with surfers, to Dartmouth and Halifax.

Ceilidh Trail

Just across the Canso Causeway to Port Hastings, Route 19 swings north along Cape Breton's western shore, an area settled 200 years ago by Highland Scots, whose descendants keep alive the ancient Gaelic tongue, extending you *ceud mile failte* (a hundred thousand welcomes). *Ceilidh*, by the way, means gathering — and if you're lucky, there'll be one in progress when you arrive. At Creignish, a mountain road leads to superb views of St. George's Bay, followed by a somewhat baffling series of hamlets named Judique. A shore road to the west winds past tiny fishing wharves where you can buy fresh lobster in May and June, dig for clams, go beachcombing on deserted stretches of powdery sand or watch nesting birds in salt-water marshlands. A quarry on Port Hood Island provided the stone for Fortress Louisbourg, built in the early eighteenth century. At this point, a second shore road leads to even finer beaches, where you can swim in waters warmed to 70°F. by the Gulf Stream. Or, if you remain on Route 19, you'll pass through rich dairy farming country to Mabou, where stately blue herons stand motionless in the harbour. Next you drive through a more heavily forested area to Inverness, once an active coalmining centre, and on to Dunvegan, named for the Clan Macleod's seat on the Isle of Skye, before reaching Margaree Harbour, with its lovely sand beach at the mouth of a famous salmon river.

The Sunrise Trail

Driving east from Amherst on Route 366, your first stop is Tidnish, where an ill-fated railway was begun in the 1890s to transport oceangoing ships overland from Baie Verte to the Cumberland Basin. Four thousand labourers were employed at tremendous cost, but the project was abandoned for lack of funds, and all that remain are portions of the roadbed and a lonely culvert bridge. Now the road leads past a series of lovely beaches (with the warmest salt waters north of the Carolinas) to join Route 6 just outside Pugwash, the site of an annual Gathering of the Clans, where street signs are printed in both English and Gaelic. Here you can charter deep-sea fishing boats, try your luck in nearby trout and salmon streams, or tour a working salt mine before continuing to Wallace, whose quarries provided the sandstone for Ottawa's Parliament Buildings. At Tatamagouche, an Indian word meaning "meeting place of the waters," the Sunrise Trail Museum contains clothing worn by Anna Swan, a nineteenth-

Dusk falls in Peggy's Cove

Photo CN

century giant born in the town of New Annan who toured for many years with P.T. Barnum's circus. She stood almost eight feet — but found herself an equally tall husband and retired happily to the United States. Detour south at this point on Route 311 to see the Balmoral Mills gristmill on Matheson's Brook, built in 1830 and painstakingly restored to working order; then back on Route 326 through Denmark, the site of a steam-powered 1894 sawmill. Follow Route 6 through River John and past more delightful beaches to Pictou, settled in 1773 by Scottish colonists. Its Micmac Museum is located next to an ancient Indian burial ground. This is the centre of Nova Scotia's lobster fisheries, and, just north, at Caribou, there's a ferry to Wood Islands on Prince Edward Island. Now follow Routes 106 and 104 through the Stellarton-New Glasgow region (see page 28) before taking Route 245 along the forested north shore through Arisaig's Provincial Park to Malignant Cove (named for a British man-of-war wrecked nearby), then Route 337 to the lighthouse at Cape George and down to Antigonish.

The Lighthouse Route

Route 433 leads from Halifax to Peggy's Cove, Canada's most-photographed fishing village, where sightseers can outnumber residents 10 to one. But *every* settlement along Nova Scotia's South Shore holds its own special charm. The tiny coves of St. Margarets Bay,

from Indian Harbour to Glen Haven, were hotbeds of rumrunning in Prohibition days. At Tantallon, Route 3 passes a chain of lovely beaches en route to the Aspotogan Peninsula, which you can loop around by taking Route 329 through Bayswater and Deep Cove. Plan to spend time in Chester, settled in 1759. A favourite haunt of wealthy Americans, it comes complete with a ghost ship in the harbour. It's also the embarkation point for Tancook Island, famous for spicy sauerkraut. Across the western arm of Mahone Bay you can see Oak Island, where a mysterious shaft is said to guard a money pit filled with pirate treasure. Then it's on to Lunenburg, renowned as the home of the schooner *Bluenose*. Don't miss the local Fisheries Museum, and be sure to sample some of the area's hearty German recipes — dishes with names like hodge-podge, hugger-in-buff and Solomon Gundy. Route 332 swings south to The Ovens, a park with peculiar rock formations and seaside caverns, the site of a mini gold strike in 1861. Take the car ferry to La Have, first settled in 1632, and the nearby Risser's Beach Provincial Park, with its sweeping sand dunes. Then continue north to Bridgewater, where you can trace the history of Lunenburg County at the Des Brisay Museum and tour the restored Wile Carding Mill. From this point, you can follow Route 103 to Liverpool and Yarmouth, or turn north toward the Annapolis Valley on Route 10, stopping at New Germany to view the nineteenth-century frame church of St. John in the Wilderness.

The Evangeline Route

Picture-postcard seascapes and apple orchards in the verdant Annapolis Valley — your chance to sample Digby scallops and join the Order of Good Cheer

Halifax to Yarmouth

The 216-mile route of the Dominion Atlantic Railway through the lush farmland and picture-postcard apple orchards of the Annapolis Valley, and along the French shore of the Bay of Fundy, is steeped in history. The Flying Bluenose was inaugurated in the summer of 1891. It included Canada's first Pullman parlour car, the Haligonian. A second Pullman, the Mayflower, was added the following year to this crack train, which connected with steamships sailing from Yarmouth to Boston. The service proved so successful that in 1904 a sea link to New York was added, and that same year the Flying Bluenose acquired a sister train, the New Yorker.

Several engines of this period were painted a distinctive black and magenta, with gold trim. In 1923 the original cars were replaced by the Annapolis Royal and Grand Pré buffet-observation-parlour cars that featured brass-railed platforms and colourful awnings. Until 1956, passengers on DAR trains 95 to 98 enjoyed the solid comfort of cars 6613 and 6614, each containing 22 revolving parlour seats, an open observation area that allowed riders to savour the sea air, and a 12-seat dining room that offered fresh Digby scallops daily. Even after the DAR was taken over by the CPR, the dining rooms continued to use DAR silver and china emblazoned with the "Land of Evangeline" crest.

Today, the rail diesel cars on this run are the finest in Canada, and passengers can still board ships at Yarmouth for Bar Harbor and Portland, Maine.

The DAR realized that local history would attract tourists and so in 1917 built a beautiful 14-acre park at Grand Pré near the place from which the Acadians were expelled in 1755, an event immortalized in Longfellow's poem "Evangeline." The park's gardens, statuary and chapel were complemented by a rustic log train station, now gone. Today the site is a national park.

A highlight of this route is Annapolis Royal, that ancient capital of Acadia described by Champlain in 1604 as "one of the most beautiful ports which I have seen on these coasts, where 2,000 vessels could be anchored in safety." As you walk its historic streets, past houses where soldiers once caroused, princes dined and colonial governors were born and raised, you can almost hear the roar of cannons that shook the town for decades, as French and English battled for possession.

POINTS OF INTEREST
Halifax to Kentville (Halifax subdivision)

(From Halifax to Windsor Junction the Evangeline travels over CN's Bedford subdivision. Please refer to page 52 for points of interest for this portion of the route.)

Mile 1-31: The wilderness area en route to Windsor includes several lakes, so watch for beaver dams. Mount Uniacke is named for Richard Uniacke, an Irish adventurer who became Nova Scotia's attorney general in 1797. He built a magnificent colonial-style home on his 5,000-acre estate in 1813 — look north at mile 13 to see if you can catch a glimpse of it. The 253-foot bridge high above the St. Croix River at mile 24.6 provides an excellent view over the rugged valley, where you may be able to see the 550-foot radio tower on the Canadian Forces Base at

High tide conceals the stilts holding up the houses in the colourful village of Bear River

Newport Corner.

Windsor, on the Avon River, is the hometown of Judge Thomas Chandler Haliburton, creator of the itinerant clockmaker Sam Slick, whose homespun wit charmed readers all over the world. Haliburton's house can be seen to the south, as can the Fort Edward blockhouse, the oldest such structure in Canada, built in 1750. Flora Macdonald, who befriended Bonnie Prince Charlie, wintered here with her husband in 1779.

Mile 31-45: The Avon River is crossed on a 3,000-foot dam and causeway that, in 1970, replaced a steel bridge. The Bay of Fundy tides, highest in the world, rise to 50 feet here, filling the Avon and Meander rivers in a matter of minutes. Falmouth, which lies exactly halfway between the equator and the North Pole, is noted for its 200 acres of greenhouses, which produce flowers, fruit and vegetables year round.

At Hantsport, look north to see gypsum being loaded for bulk export to the United States. The *Otis Mack*, a small red tug, can sometimes be spotted grounded on the mud flats at low tide. Photographers should keep their cameras ready for the next 12 miles as the train curves high above the river; it was here that several miles of track were washed away by the Saxby Gale in 1869.

A lighthouse appears close to the track to the north at mile 41.8. At mile 42, look north again, across the Minas Basin to Blomidon, home to Glooscap of Micmac legend. According to legend, Glooscap's smile brought sunshine and his anger, thunder. Swinging on a wide curve to the north, the train crosses the Gaspereau River at mile 44.4, before reaching Horton Landing.

A 10-foot-high iron cross, painted black, marks the spot at mile 45 where, in 1755, 2,000

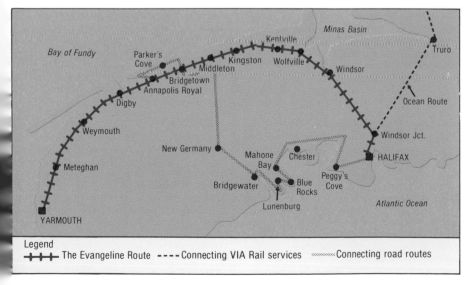

Legend
+++ The Evangeline Route ---- Connecting VIA Rail services ⬝⬝⬝⬝⬝ Connecting road routes

Ferries, freighters and fishing boats head out into the Bay of Fundy from Digby Gap

Acadians were herded into small craft, then loaded onto passenger ships that dispersed them to New England, Louisiana and the West Indies, after which their settlement at Grand Pré was burned to the ground.

Mile 46-49: To the north, at mile 46.2, is beautiful Grand Pré National Historic Park. It contains a chapel built to commemorate the Church of St. Charles, where the expulsion order was read to the Acadians; a statue of Longfellow's heroine Evangeline; a bust of the poet himself; a wooden church erected by Loyalist settlers in 1804; an Acadian log house from Falmouth believed to be more than 200 years old; and a marker honouring Sir Robert Borden, prime minister during World War I. To the north, at mile 49, you can see remnants of dikes built by the Acadians to transform marsh into farmland. Made of stone and log packed with clay, the dikes contained hinged wooden doors that prevented sea water from sweeping in during high tide, but allowed the marshes to be drained when tides were low.

Wolfville, once known as Mud Creek, is very much a New England-style college town, home of Acadia University. One of its best-known residents is realist painter Alex Colville. At one time the DAR operated a ferry, the *Kipawo*, named for the towns it serviced *Ki*ngsport, *Parr*boro and *Wol*fville.

Mile 50-58: Locally grown apples and potatoes are shipped from Port Williams. The Cornwallis River is very narrow here, forcing large cargo ships to turn around in an unorthodox way: they ram their bows into the mud banks and are reversed by the changing tide. This area was originally settled by Micmacs.

Just before arriving in Kentville, look south to the Cornwallis Inn, once owned and operated by the DAR, where elegant guests used to enjoy buffet suppers and concerts on what is now an asphalt parking lot. The upper floors of the Kentville station contain the DAR's headquarters.

The surrounding town gives little hint that it was once known as the Devil's half acre because of a large number of low-life pubs.

POINTS OF INTEREST
Kentville to Annapolis Royal (Kentville subdivision)

Mile 1-45: The first apples were planted here by the Acadians in 1634. Today, the 100-mile-long, 10-mile-wide strip along the Annapolis Valley from Windsor to Digby is one of the world's most celebrated apple-producing areas. Soil and weather conditions are ideal for the cultivation of many varieties, including Delicious, Spy, McIntosh, Courtland, Russet and Gravenstein.

Besides apple-processing, Coldbrook is noted for roses grown in large greenhouses. Berwick, birthplace of Alfred Fuller, founder of the Fuller Brush Company, has streets shaded by stately elms, maples and hemlocks. The Aylesford area contains a number of beef, dairy and hog farms, peat moss fields (mile 14.2), and pear and plum orchards. Near Auburn you'll see extensive cranberry bogs. Watch to the north here for St. Mary's Church, built in 1790. Its walls are plastered with powdered mussel shells.

A few miles to the south, near Kingston, you may see ponderous Argus aircraft taking off from Greenwood anti-submarine air base. The train parallels Kingston's main street, affording a good view of a typical Nova Scotia town. Nearby Wilmot was settled in 1783 by Loyalists from New York State. The region around Bridgetown, today characterized by prosperous farming and dairy operations, was first settled by the French in 1654. They were followed in the mid-eighteenth century by New Englanders and, later, Loyalists, so that the town contains splendid examples of New England and American Gothic architecture.

Mile 46-58: Here the valley becomes dramatically more scenic. To the north, winding rivers and fields of grazing livestock are framed by North Mountain. At mile 46.2, you cross Bloody Creek, so named for the battles fought here by British, French and Micmacs to gain control of Acadia. Look south at Tupperville to a century-old schoolhouse, now a small museum. Round Hill is the burial place of Colonel James DeLancey, a Loyalist who led raids into New York State during the American Revolution.

Annapolis Royal is a study in contrasts: a sleepy town with many historic structures hard by the Annapolis River power project, which is harnessing the power of the Fundy tides. There are many places to visit here: Schoolmaster McNamara's house, built in the 1780s; the O'Dell Inn and Tavern, a Victorian stagecoach stop; the art exhibits at the Pickels and Mills Building, constructed in the 1870s; Champlain's View, a waterfront walkway; and Fort Anne National Historic Park. Don't leave without joining the Order of Good Cheer, North America's oldest social club, founded by Champlain in 1606.

POINTS OF INTEREST
Annapolis Royal to Yarmouth (Yarmouth subdivision)

Mile 1-25: This portion of the route offers some of Nova Scotia's loveliest scenery and longest bridges. After crossing Allen's Creek on a 486-foot trestle at mile 0.3, look back and to the north for an excellent view of Annapolis Royal, Granville Ferry and Fort Anne. While crossing Moose River at mile 7.7, look south to four churches clinging to the hillside, most built by Loyalists who settled the area in 1784. The oldest is St. Edward, a blue wooden structure dating from 1788. Its interior plaster was made from burnt clam shells, and its original boxed pews with doors remain. It's now used only one Sunday a year.

Clementsport, an old sea village, contains a number of early captain's houses. Cornwallis Station is a Canadian Forces training centre. Easily the most spectacular bridge on this portion of the route is the 14-span, 1,640-foot structure over the Bear River at mile12.9. It curves to the north, offering good picture-taking opportunities. Watch here for wading herons, eagles soaring overhead and ospreys diving for striped bass. Between here and the 285-foot bridge over the Big Joggins River at mile 16.5 are superb views to the north of Annapolis Basin and Digby Gap. Watch for a host of fishing boats and the sleek *Princess of Acadia* linking Digby and Saint John.

Digby is known to gourmets the world over for its Digby scallops. Every day 50 or more draggers set out early in the morning, returning at sundown with fresh scallops, pollock, haddock and cod. Also worth a try are Digby chicks, a

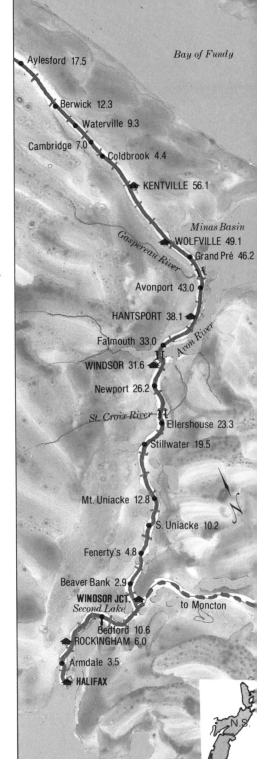

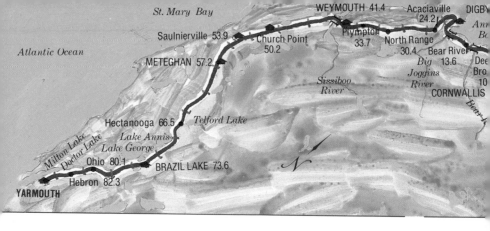

The Nova Scotia, a DAR business car

type of smoked herring. Digby is the site of the stately Trinity Church, built by shipwrights to resemble an upside-down sailing vessel. The Pines Hotel, to the north at mile 20.4, was once operated by the DAR; now it's provincially owned. To the north, at mile 24.2, look across a valley to see the hillside church at Marshalltown, the hometown of renowned primitive painter Maud Lewis. The town sits on a strange ridge, or esker, produced by glacial action many centuries ago. At one time Weymouth was the terminus of a 17-mile wooden-tracked railway built by an early settler who bought 10,000 acres of forest, then constructed the rail line to ship out lumber. To the south are stores and homes built on wooden pilings that allow tidal waters to flow underneath.

The Sissiboo River is crossed at mile 41.6 on a 13-span, 1,224-foot bridge. The station at mile 50.2 serves Church Point and St. Bernard, both several miles to the north; the former boasts a charming church, the latter, a cathedral. Meteghan, on St. Marys Bay, is noted for its shipbuilding. At mile 68.3, the train crosses the Salmon River, a misnomer, since fishermen are more likely to catch tommycod. In the vicinity of

Hebron you'll see herds of Jersey and Guernsey cattle. Also look for white, pink and blue lupins growing in the fields. At mile 83, north across Doctor Lake, is the Yarmouth Inn, also once owned by the DAR.

Mile 86: Leif Ericsson is believed to have first landed at what is now Yarmouth in A.D. 1007, carving an inscription — the Viking equivalent of "Kilroy was here" — in a stone on display at the Yarmouth County Historical Museum. The first settlers, Puritans from Sandwich, Massachusetts, arrived here in 1761, leading to the development of an enterprising community that by 1870 was Canada's leading seaport and shipbuilding town. Visit the harbour, where you'll see herring seiners coming and going, and take time to drop by the Firefighters' Museum.

The Evangeline Route

Halifax Subdivision — CPR Windsor Jct./Kentville
Kentville Subdivision — CPR Kentville/Annapolis Royal
Yarmouth Subdivision — CPR Annapolis Royal/Yarmouth
The segment from Windsor Junction to Windsor was built between 1855 and 1858 by the Windsor Branch Railway, and opened for traffic in 1858. The segment from Windsor to Annapolis Royal was built by the Windsor and Annapolis Railway Com-

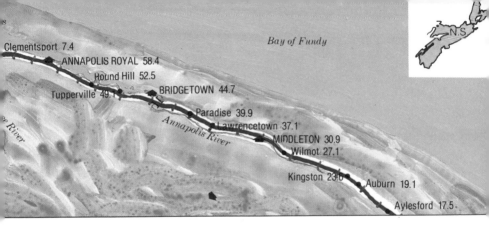

pany between 1865 and 1869, and opened for traffic in 1869. The segment from Annapolis Royal to Yarmouth was built by the Western Counties Railway Company between 1873 and 1879, Yarmouth to Weymouth in 1876, Weymouth to Digby in 1879, and Digby to Annapolis Royal in 1891.

The whole route became the Dominion Atlantic Railway on July 22, 1895 and was leased to the CPR on January 1, 1912. DAR trains operate over the CN Bedford subdivision between Halifax and Windsor Junction.

Miles	Stations	Population	Elev.	Origin of Station Names
0.0	Windsor Jct. (N.S.)	667	128	Windsor, England, on the River Thames
2.9	Beaver Bank	220	229	A nearby stream is full of beavers
4.8	Fenerty's	—	254	—
10.2	S. Uniacke	65	449	—
12.8	Mt. Uniacke	230	523	Richard J. Uniacke, Irish settler (1808)
19.5	Stillwater	167	412	Calm lakes nearby
23.3	Ellershouse	408	258	Francis V. Ellerhausen, German settler (1864)
26.2	Newport	419	119	Lord Newport, a friend of Lieutenant-Governor Jonathan Belcher
31.6	Windsor	3,626	28	Windsor, England
34.6	Shaw's Bog	—	—	—
38.1	Hantsport	1,444	50	Abbreviated form of Hampshire, England
43.0	Avonport	235	57	River Avon in Scotland
44.9	Horton Landing	—	44	—
46.2	Grand Pré	2,401	28	French for "the great Prairie," a translation of the Micmac "mskegoo-a-kadik"
49.1	Wolfville	3,073	28	Elisha de Wolfe, a member of one of the founding families
50.9	Port Williams	805	31	Sir William F. Williams (1800-1883), governor of the province
56.1	Kentville	5,198	35	Duke of Kent (1767-1820), father of Queen Victoria
0.0	Kentville	5,198	35	(See Halifax subdivision)
4.4	Coldbrook	335	74	Brook of very cold water nearby
7.0	Cambridge	688	71	City in England
9.3	Waterville	878	94	A descriptive name chosen by the residents in 1871
12.3	Berwick	1,701	138	Berwick-on-Tweed, England
17.5	Aylesford	738	100	Fourth Earl of Aylesford, lord of the bedchamber to George III
19.1	Auburn	383	95	Reminiscent of Auburn in Oliver Goldsmith's "Deserted Village"
23.6	Kingston	1,434	86	Located within Kings County
27.1	Wilmot	615	70	Montague Wilmot, lieutenant-governor of Nova Scotia in 1763
30.9	Middleton	1,823	70	Midway between Kentville and Annapolis Royal
37.1	Lawrence-town	509	82	Colonel Charles Lawrence, governor of Nova Scotia from 1753 to 1760
39.9	Paradise	354	50	From the Indian word "nesogwaakade," meaning "place of eel weirs"
44.7	Bridgetown	1,037	27	Bridge connecting Granville with Annapolis
49.1	Tupperville	153	—	Sir Charles Tupper, a father of Confederation
52.5	Round Hill	256	32	Translation of "le pré ronde"
58.4	Annapolis Royal (N.S.)	738	30	Amalgamation of the name of Queen Anne of England and the Greek word "polis," meaning "city"
0.0	Annapolis Royal (N.S.)	738	30	(See Kentville subdivision)
7.4	Clements-port	424	68	Request of local residents (1856). Formerly Moose River
9.1	Cornwallis	—	65	Colonel Edward Cornwallis, governor of Nova Scotia in 1749
10.4	Deep Brook	5,565	—	Nearby stream
13.6	Bear River	—	42	Corruption of Louis Hébert, an apothecary who explored the area with Champlain in 1604
20.2	Digby	2,542	43	Admiral Robert Digby (1732-1815) brought a shipful of Loyalist settlers here in 1783
24.2	Acaciaville	245	—	Nearby vale of acacia trees
30.4	North Range	92	302	Nearby range of hills
33.7	Plympton	291	292	—
41.4	Weymouth	584	60	Weymouth, Massachusetts
50.2	Church Point	288	154	St. Mary's Church, built by French settlers
53.9	Saulnierville	743	123	French Acadian family Saulnier
57.2	Meteghan	1,269	131	From the Amerindian word "matogan," meaning "blue stone," found on the sandbar in the river
66.5	Hectanooga	96	170	From the Amerindian word "hektanigank," meaning "start of portage"
73.6	Brazil Lake	87	211	Nearby lake
80.1	Ohio	—	157	Chosen by two settlers who intended to go to Ohio U.S.A., but instead settled here and called their farms Ohio
82.3	Hebron	440	82	In dispute. Either Hebron, Connecticut, home of early settlers, or after Hebron, Palestine (Hebrew for friendship or associate)
86.0	Yarmouth (N.S.)	7,801	258	Yarmouth, Massachusetts, home of early settlers. Formerly called Cap Fourchu (cloven cape)

The Gull Route

Photograph a covered bridge in the beautiful Kennebecasis River Valley before crossing the famous Reversing Falls, created by the world's highest tides

Moncton to Fredericton

Ground-breaking ceremonies for the European and North American Railway took place in Saint John on September 14, 1853, complete with an artillery salute and a two-mile-long parade. On March 17, 1857, the first passenger train steamed rather tentatively over a mere 3½ miles of track from Saint John to Coldbrook, but by 1860 the line extended all the way through Moncton to Shediac, on the Northumberland Strait. In those days, American railways ran only to Bangor, Maine, so that passengers had to take a train from Halifax to Saint John, then a stagecoach to Bangor or steamship to Portland. A rail route was completed in 1888, but it was to be another three decades, and then only on summer weekends, before people could ride all the way from New York City to Halifax in a sleeping car aboard the Down Easter or the Pine Tree-Acadian.

The Gull began service on March 30, 1930, as a daily train linking Boston, Portland and Bangor to Fredericton, Saint John and Halifax, with a sleeping car to Halifax and a buffet-lounge-sleeper to Saint John. During the summer months, passengers could travel one way by steamship between Saint John and Boston, creating one of North America's first rail-cruise options.

POINTS OF INTEREST
Moncton to Saint John (Sussex subdivision)

Mile 0-64: The Gull follows the twisting Petitcodiac River for 30 miles, crossing it at mile 16.8. Note Petitcodiac's combination house and station, its wide porch shaded by huge trees. An octagonal log house lies just to the west at mile 28.2. Sus-

sex, a quiet market town, used to bottle a ginger ale containing mineral water from local springs and was, for 60 years, the site of a military base. The scenery becomes more spectacular between miles 47 and 64 as the Gull follows the eastern bank of the Kennebecasis River. Norton, mile 54.3, is well known for its trout fishing and moose hunting. One of the best views occurs to the west at mile 59.5: a 147-foot covered bridge, built in 1917, with Bloomfield's church in the background. This is one of 20 such bridges in the immediate area, but the only one visible from the train.

Mile 65-86: Hampton, to the east, is a beautiful English-style village with one of Canada's oldest churches. See if you can spot its lych-gate, which shelters the casket during a burial service. The town station now houses a crafts cooperative that sells pottery, textiles and leatherwork. The Hammond River is crossed at mile 70.8 on a 309-foot bridge. At Rothesay, the Kennebecasis River flows a mile wide and is dotted with pleasure boats. Fine summer homes were kept here by wealthy residents of Saint John. The station, built in 1858 and restored with the assistance of Heritage Canada, once included a magistrate's office and an upstairs apartment with four fire-

Gulls seeking shelter as the fog rolls into Saint John harbour

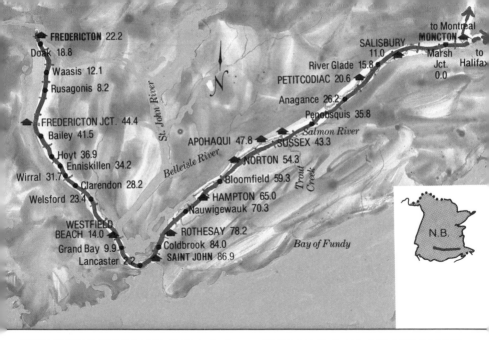

FREDERICTON 22.2
Doak 18.8
Waasis 12.1
Rusagonis 8.2
FREDERICTON JCT. 44.4
Bailey 41.5
Hoyt 36.9
Enniskillen 34.2
Wirral 31.7
Clarendon 28.2
Welsford 23.4
WESTFIELD
BEACH 14.0
Grand Bay 9.9
Lancaster 2.2

St. John River

N

Belleisle River

APOHAQUI 47.8
NORTON 54.3
Bloomfield 59.3
HAMPTON 65.0
Nauwigewauk 70.3
ROTHESAY 78.2
Coldbrook 84.0
SAINT JOHN 86.9

SALISBURY 11.0
River Glade 15.8
PETITCODIAC 20.6
Anagance 26.2
Penobsquis 35.8
Salmon River
SUSSEX 43.3

to Montreal
MONCTON
Marsh   to
Jct.   Halifax
0.0

Trout Creek

Bay of Fundy

N.B.

places. Today, it houses a crafts studio and art gallery. Look north between miles 78 and 82 for views of Kennebecasis Bay. As you approach Saint John, look for St. John's Anglican Church on a hilltop to the south. Begun in 1824, this is the city's oldest stone building, constructed of stone quarried in England and used as ballast on the voyage across.

Mile 86.9: Saint John was first visited by Champlain in 1604, followed by Charles de la Tour, who established a fortified trading post in 1631. The first permanent English settlement dates from 1762, but the town got its real start in 1783,

with the arrival of more than 4,000 American Loyalists. Two years later it was incorporated, making it Canada's oldest city. (It also instituted Canada's first police force in 1826, two years before Sir Robert Peel created London's famous "bobbies.")

A disastrous fire in 1877 destroyed more than half the city core, leaving 15,000 people homeless. This was the fourth major blaze in half a century, and resulted in an almost complete rebuilding program, using brick instead of wood.

Today, you can follow the Loyalist Trail

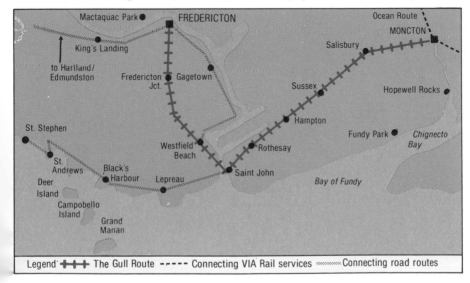

Mactaquac Park •   FREDERICTON   Ocean Route
                                                   MONCTON
    King's Landing   Salisbury
to Hartland/
Edmundston   Fredericton • Gagetown   Sussex   Hopewell Rocks •
              Jct.
St. Stephen   Hampton
                                                      Fundy Park •   Chignecto
 St.   Bay
 Andrews   Black's   Westfield   Rothesay
Deer   Harbour   Beach
Island   Lepreau   Saint John   Bay of Fundy
 Campobello
 Island
       Grand
       Manan

Legend: ┿┿┿ The Gull Route ----- Connecting VIA Rail services ∞∞∞ Connecting road routes

through downtown Saint John, past eighteenth-and nineteenth-century homes, stores, churches and burial grounds. Be sure to visit Loyalist House (1817) and Barbour's General Store (1867).

POINTS OF INTEREST
Saint John to Fredericton (McAdam and Fredericton subdivisions)

Mile 1-44: Look south across the harbour at mile 1 to see a boulder on the Market Slip that marks the spot of the Loyalist landing. Just beyond, at Reid's Point, is a Celtic cross erected in memory of hundreds of Irish immigrants who died of cholera in 1847. Look carefully to the north at mile 1.8 while crossing the 1,265-foot Reversing Falls Bridge, where twice daily the Bay of Fundy tides force the Saint John River to change direction in a rocky gorge. The spectacle occurs in three phases: at low tide, the river drops 14½ feet over a ledge; when water levels are equal, the falls disappear and the whole surface becomes calm as a millpond; and at high tide, a 28½-foot wall of onrushing water creates rapids that flow upstream.

Between miles 6 and 14, along Grand Bay, the Saint John River is clearly visible to the north. Called "Woolastook" by Indian tribes, it was once part of a prehistoric sea. Archeological excavations along its banks have revealed evidence of a 5,000-year-old civilization. Today it follows a winding 450-mile course through dense forest and pastoral farmland. At mile 14, look north up Long Reach, flanked by wooded hills. Its beaches are an excellent place to collect seashells and sand dollars. Between miles 20 and 22, the Gull follows the Nerepis River's narrow gorge before crossing the placid Oromocto River at mile 44 and swinging north at Fredericton Junction toward New Brunswick's capital.

Mile 22.2: Fredericton was first settled in 1731 by Acadians, who named their village Ste-Anne's Point. The Loyalists arrived in 1783, and soon the homes of wealthy merchants and lumber barons sprang up along the river bank. Today the city resembles both Stratford and Cambridge, England, and can best be appreciated on a heritage walking tour. Christ Church Cathedral, completed in 1853, is one of North America's finest examples of Gothic architecture, and comes complete with resident ghost. The Legislative Building contains more than 400 hand-coloured Audubon engravings, a set of Hogarth

Tourism New Brunswick

Fiddleheads, highly-coveted delicacies that grow in the spring in New Brunswick

Quoddy Head lighthouse on Campobello Island

prints and a 1783 copy of the Domesday Book. The Beaverbrook Art Gallery houses an excellent collection, including works by Krieghoff, Dali, Turner, Graham Sutherland and several members of the Group of Seven. It's one of many bequests to both city and province by Lord Beaverbrook, the former Max Aitken, who came to Fredericton as a child. He amassed a considerable fortune before departing for England, where he became a noted politician and newspaper tycoon. If you're in a more frivolous frame of mind, you might visit the York-Sunbury Museum in the Military Compound, which contains (among other, more sensible exhibits) a 42-pound frog, whose owner, an 1880s hotelkeeper, fattened it up on a diet of whisky and buttermilk.

The Gull Route

Sussex Subdivision — CNR Moncton/Saint John

This line was built by the European and North American Railway between 1858 and 1860, and opened on August 1, 1860.

Miles	Stations	Population	Elev.	Origin of Station Names
—	Moncton (N.B.)	82,900	50	(See Springhill subdivision, page 63)
0.0	Marsh Jct.	—	—	—
2.1	Bend	—	—	Bend in nearby Petitcodiac River
2.9	Fundy	—	—	From the French word "tendu," meaning "split"
11.0	Salisbury	1,077	102	John Salisbury, an associate of Governor Edward Cornwallis
15.8	River Glade	289	82	Clump of trees on Petitcodiac River
20.6	Petitcodiac	1,472	96	From the Micmac word "epetkutogoyek," meaning "river that bends backward"
26.2	Anagance	145	61	From the Maliseet word "oonegansook," meaning "little portage stream"
35.8	Penobsquis	407	92	From the Maliseet "penobsqsips," meaning "stone brook"
43.3	Sussex	3,840	71	Duke of Sussex, son of George III. Formerly called Pleasant Valley
47.8	Apohaqui	342	73	Maliseet word for "junction of two streams." Formerly Studville
54.3	Norton	1,097	52	Norton, Massachusetts. Formerly called Finger Board
59.3	Bloomfield	88	35	—
65.0	Hampton	1,705	27	A shire town of Kings County.

Miles	Stations	Population	Elev.	Origin of Station Names
70.3	Nauwigewauk	150	23	Maliseet word "nahwijewauk." Formerly called Hammond River
78.2	Rothesay	1,011	22	Prince of Wales, Duke of Saxony, Cornwall and Rothesay, later Edward VII
84.0	Coldbrook	507	14	From the Maliseet word "moosowtik," meaning "moose path"
86.9	Saint John (N.B.)	116,300	18	Champlain landed here on June 24, 1604, the feast day of St. John the Baptist

McAdam Subdivision — CPR Saint John/Fredericton Jct.

This line was built by the European and North American Railway in 1871, and leased to the CPR in 1890.

Miles	Stations	Population	Elev.	Origin of Station Names
—	Saint John (N.B.) (VIA)	116,300	18	(See Sussex subdivision)
0.0	Mill Street	—	—	—
2.2	Lancaster	—	—	—
3.0	Saint John (CP)	—	—	—
9.9	Grand Bay	—	65	—
14.0	Westfield Beach	1,048	25	—
23.4	Welsford	424	85	Major Augustus Welsford, who was killed during the Crimean War (1853-1856)
28.2	Clarendon	—	185	George William Frederick Villiers, fourth Earl of Clarendon, and Britain's foreign secretary from 1853 to 1858 and 1868 to 1870
31.7	Wirral	124	—	Wirral Peninsula, Cheshire, England
34.2	Enniskillen	78	113	Formerly called Adare Settlement, after Adare, Ireland
36.9	Hoyt	325	57	William Hoyt, early settler
41.5	Bailey	—	29	Loring Woart Bailey (1839-1925), a University of New Brunswick professor
44.4	Fredericton Jct. (N.B.)	630	71	Frederick, bishop of Osnaburg, second son of George III. Formerly called Hartt's Mills

Fredericton Subdivision — CPR Fredericton Jct./Fredericton

This line was built by the Fredericton Railway Company in 1890, and leased to the CPR.

Miles	Stations	Population	Elev.	Origin of Station Names
0.0	Fredericton Jct.	630	71	(See McAdam subdivision)
8.2	Rusagonis	339	38	—
12.1	Waasis	—	59	—
18.8	Doak	—	125	Robert Doak, Scottish settler (c. 1812)
22.2	Fredericton (N.B.)	47,500	41	(See McAdam subdivision)

New Brunswick Road Routes

The world's longest covered bridge, at Hartland

Saint John to St. Stephen

Proceeding west on Route 1, you arrive at Lepreau. To the south, at Point Lepreau, is Atlantic Canada's first nuclear power plant; upstream the Lepreau River offers exciting white water canoeing. Twelve miles farther on you reach the junction of Route 776. Turn south here to Blacks Harbour, the location of the mainland terminal for the car and passenger ferry to Grand Manan Island, the largest of the three Fundy Isles. (On a clear day you should be able to see the others — Deer Island and Campobello, site of Franklin Roosevelt's beloved summer retreat — during the 18-mile, two-hour trip to Grand Manan.) This 55-square-mile, sparsely populated island has a number of attractions. Its stark beauty has been compared to that of the Isle of Skye and life here is slow and simple — no neon, no fast food and no pollution. Grand Manan is famous for its wildlife: more than 275 species of birds have been spotted here. The Allan Moses Bird Collection, housed in the Grand Manan Museum, features more than 300 rare or extinct species; and seals and whales, including the almost-extinct right whale, are frequently visible from the shoreline. Unusual rock formations abound here too. Grand Manan's major industries are fishing and the harvesting of dulse, a type of edible seaweed. Campers can stay at Anchorage Provincial Park; hotel and guest house accommodation is available as well.

Back on the mainland, return to Route 1 and proceed west to St. George. On your way you'll pass Lake Utopia, said to be the home of a fearsome sea monster, although more than a century's reported sightings don't deter fishermen, boaters and water-skiers. St. George itself is the site of a concrete fish ladder on the Magaguadavic River that speeds the journey of Atlantic salmon to their upstream spawning grounds; also located here is one of Canada's oldest Protestant graveyards.

From St. George you can detour south to Letete, from which free government-run ferries make the 20-minute trip to Deer Island, site of the world's largest lobster pounds. Or you can continue to St. Andrews, reached by turning south from Route 1 to Route 127. Founded in 1784 by Loyalists, it contains homes predating that year because some of the first settlers disassembled their houses in Maine and shipped them in by barge. The town contains a great number of well-preserved buildings: of 350 structures in the central area, 280 were built before 1880 and 14 date to the eighteenth century. The harbour is still guarded by a century-and-a-half-old blockhouse, the only survivor of a trio built to guard against American invasion during the War of 1812. Also of note here is Greenock Presbyterian Church, completed in 1825, on whose exterior is a carved oak tree, emblem of Greenock, Scotland, birthplace of its builder, Christopher Scott. The town contains many fine old cottages that have been in the owners' families for decades, and two historic hotels: the Shiretown Inn, built in 1881, and the Algonquin, erected in 1888.

Eighteen miles away lies St. Stephen, known as the Gateway to Atlantic Canada.

Each August it celebrates with its neighbour, Calais, Maine, a friendly relationship that dates back to before the War of 1812, during which inhabitants of the two towns refused to fight one another. The Charlotte County Historical Society Museum and Duncan McColl United Church are worth a visit. St. Stephen is noted as the home of Arthur Ganong, a confectioner who invented the chocolate bar. Nearby Oak Bay Provincial Park offers camping facilities and excellent swimming.

Saint John to Edmundston

The fastest way to reach Fredericton is via Route 7, but Route 102, which follows the Saint John River's meandering course, offers a much more scenic drive. Gagetown, once a contender for capital city of the province, is today a sleepy town with several notable attractions. Tilley House, built in 1786 and birthplace of Sir Samuel Tilley, one of the Fathers of Confederation, houses the Queens County Museum. It contains Tilley family memorabilia and exhibits of local artifacts. Gagetown is also the home of the Loomcrofters, a weaving group formed in 1939 and known since as the creators of many fine tartans and other handwoven fabrics. The Loomcrofters Studio is located in a building constructed by the British as a trading post circa 1761.

Oromocto, home of CFB Gagetown, the largest military training base in the Commonwealth, is the site of Fort Hughes, the reconstruction of a 1781 British blockhouse. In the summer, red-coated students act as guides. Also located here is the Chestnut Canoe Company, manufacturer of fine canoes and snowshoes since 1897.

Having passed through Fredericton, you join the Trans-Canada Highway, Route 2. Like Route 102, it follows the Saint John River. Only 15 minutes west of the city you reach Mactaquac Provincial Park, located on a 65-mile-long pond created in the 1960s by the Mactaquac Power Development. This 1,400-acre recreation area has much to offer: hiking and nature trails, all manner of water sports, an 18-hole golf course and excellent camping facilities. Nearby Woolastook Wildlife Provincial Park provides an opportunity to see birds and animals native to New Brunswick in their natural habitat.

Another short drive brings you to Kings Landing Historical Settlement, which recreates life in the province between 1790 and 1870. Its 55 buildings include a blacksmith shop, general store, school, church, tavern and sawmill; costumed guides add to the sense of stepping into another age.

Woodstock is another town with many gracious old homes. A two-storey frame house, built in the 1820s, was the residence of Charles Connell, an eccentric provincial postmaster general who in 1860 substituted his own likeness for that of Queen Victoria on an issue of half a million stamps. People were outraged, and Connell was forced to burn the stamps in front of his house, after which he retired in some disgrace.

Hartland is the site of the world's longest covered bridge, built in 1896. Legend has it that if you cross your fingers, make a wish and run across its 1,282-foot length without exhaling, your wish comes true.

Next you proceed through Florenceville, site of a mammoth McCain food processing plant, to Perth-Andover, a highly religious area where signs on every second barn warn you to "Repent your sins." New Denmark, not surprisingly, is Canada's largest Danish community; the New Denmark Memorial Museum displays tax records, memorabilia and clothing worn by early settlers.

Grand Falls is a predominantly French-speaking town, with Canada's widest main street, originally built as a military parade ground. Here the Saint John plunges through a narrow gorge, dropping 75 feet to a whirlpool that used to be known as "the coffee mill." In lumbering days, logs caught in its swirling torrent were ground to a point like so many sharpened pencils.

St-Léonard is both the centre of a major potato-growing area and home to the Madawaska Weavers, whose hand-loomed fabrics in colourful patterns are in great demand. From this point, it's a short drive to Edmundston, at the junction of the Madawaska and Saint John rivers. Its main industry is a pulp and paper mill, but it's in fact a sophisticated city, with notable religious architecture, especially the Church of Our Lady of Sorrows, in which you'll see beautiful wood carvings of the Stations of the Cross by Claude Roussel.

The Chaleur Route

*A cliff-hanging ride along the Gaspé coast, with views of
the Gulf of St. Lawrence, gannet-covered Bonaventure Island
and the world-famous Percé Rock*

Matapédia to Gaspé

During its 30-year construction, the Baie de Chaleur route was unaffectionately known as the "railway to nowhere" — nowhere being the point in Québec closest to Europe. The line, predicated on the construction of a grain elevator at Gaspé, was continually plagued by scandal. In 1891, the Québec Liberal government was implicated in a series of kickbacks and payoffs involving the line between Matapédia and Caplan, leading to the defeat of Québec's premier, Honoré Mercier.

When the first train arrived in Gaspé on July 17, 1912, there was no sign of the vast grain elevator that was supposed to have been built, establishing the town as a major port. Fortunately, tourism proved a far more realistic proposition. The Baie des Chaleurs became known as the Canadian Riviera — a reputation based on its agreeable climate, inviting beaches and salmon-filled rivers. In the 1920s and 1930s, the Duke and Duchess of Windsor, Jack Dempsey and Bing Crosby vacationed at its gracious villas and stylish hotels. Little has changed since then. The first views of Bonaventure Island and Percé Rock remain stunning, blue herons still soar over placid sandbars and agate collectors treasure stones they've gathered on the shore.

The Gaspé Peninsula, part of the Appalachian mountain chain, was inhabited for 6,000 years by ancestors of today's Micmac Indians. Viking seamen were the first

European visitors, followed by Basque, Norman and Breton sailors who fished the Grand Banks of Newfoundland. Jacques Cartier claimed the region for France in 1534, in a ceremony that included the raising of a huge wooden cross. The British gained possession in 1763; American, Irish and Scots settlers followed, forming the basis of a cultural mosaic that still endures.

POINTS OF INTEREST
Matapédia to New Carlisle (New Carlisle subdivision)
Mile 7-98: Look south across the Restigouche River between miles 7 and 10 to Sugarloaf Mountain and Campbellton. The river was the site of the last naval encounter between French and English in Canadian waters: a 17-day battle in July 1760. Part of the hull of a French ship, the *Marquis de Malause*, is preserved at a nearby Capuchin monastery. Near Nouvelle, the Miguasha Cliff supplies plant and animal fossils to museums all over the world. Carleton, mile 44.4, is a lumbering, fishing and cattle-breeding centre noted for its sandy beaches. At mile 46, look north to see Mount St. Joseph and a hillside shrine venerating the Virgin Mary. Maria, mile 53, is part of a Micmac Indian reservation, with a tepee-shaped church administered by the Oblate Fathers. All its streets are named for birds, and residents pride themselves on their traditional basketwork.

Look north between miles 54 and 55 for views of Mount Maria. The Cascapédia River is crossed on two bridges at mile 60.1. Look north here to the midstream Ile de Cheval. New Richmond is an all-year ocean port in a wooded setting. At mile 70, look south for a view of ominous cliffs towering over rocky beaches, then southwest between miles 71 and 72 to mountains across the

Flocks of gannets fly across from Bonaventure Island to be fed by residents and tourists on the beaches of the Gaspé coast

47

curving bay. Now the Chaleur follows a twisting course along 100-foot-high reddish cliffs, crossing Rousseau Brook at mile 82.2 and the Little Bonaventure River at mile 84.9. The town of Bonaventure, mile 89.2, has a granite church, built by Acadians in 1860. The Bonaventure River is crossed at mile 90.1 — look south here for a panoramic view of the New Brunswick coastline in the distance. New Carlisle, mile 98, is noted for its fine colonial homes, many churches and a historic court established in 1785 by Nicholas Cox, then lieutenant governor of Gaspé. Settled primarily by Loyalists, it is also the hometown of the Parti Québécois Leader René Lévesque.

POINTS OF INTEREST
New Carlisle to Gaspé (Chandler subdivision)

Mile 0-58: The Chaleur climbs past red bluffs to mile 3. Paspébiac, at mile 3.6, was the Gaspé's first fishing settlement, established in 1767. The white church of St-Godefroi is seen to the north at mile 13 as you cross the Shigawake (Indian for "land of the rising sun") River on a 500-foot bridge. Then comes the descent to Port-Daniel, affording good views of spruce and white birch forests to the north. Watch for black-crowned night herons while crossing the Rivière Port-Daniel Nord on a 524-foot bridge at mile 23. At mile 23.7, you enter the 630-foot Cap à l'Enfer tunnel, the only one on the route. Gascons was the site of an advantageous shipwreck. After saving the crew, villagers helped themselves to silver plate, silk dresses, satin shoes and the payroll for a British garrison. The Chouinard River and Perry Brook are crossed at miles 29.8 and 32.8. Newport (mile 36.9), with its seaside church, is the centre of an area that produces vast numbers of Christmas trees. After crossing the Grand Pabos River at mile 42.5, the Chaleur follows a fine, sandy beach to mile 44. Look south here for swimmers and joggers. The Little Pabos River is crossed at mile 50.7; the Grande River is spanned by a 685-foot bridge at mile 52.9. The town of Grande-Rivière is noted for its crab fisheries. To the south, at mile 58, is the tiny village of Ste-Thérèse-de-Gaspé; from this point, watch for wooden cod drying racks that dot the shoreline.

Mile 62-81: Your first view of Bonaventure Island's 300-foot cliffs occurs to the south at mile 62. This massive rock, once attached to the mainland, was farmed in recent times, although only a few abandoned buildings remain. Now it's a bird sanctuary, the home of some 50,000 gannets (diving birds with six-foot wingspans), as well as kittiwakes, herring gulls, razor-billed auks, murres, sea pigeons and black guillemots. The L'Anse-au-Beaufils River is crossed at mile 65.5 on a 760-foot trestle. Then the Chaleur begins a long, sweeping climb to the north, avoiding the mountains that surround Percé village, before returning to sea level at mile 75. For the next four miles, look south along a golden sand beach for fossilized tree trunks and shrimp boats bobbing in the bay. The Barachois River is crossed on a 473-foot bridge at mile 78.6. Between miles 79 and 82, look southwest for gorgeous views of Percé Rock. This ship-shaped, 400-million-ton limestone block is 1,555 feet long and 288 feet high. Champlain anchored here in 1534, naming it "pierced rock" for a 60-by-100-foot natural arch at the south end. It, too, was farmed in the past, but now it's the domain of fossil hunters, who reach it on foot at low tide. The rock is said to be eroding by some 300 tons a year, but don't be concerned — at that rate, it ought to last another 130 centuries.

Mile 83-104: Look for a dog-shaped rock to the south near mile 83.3 that gave St-Georges-de-Malbaie its original name of Chien Blanc. Prével (mile 89.1), is peaceful now, but during World War II it was the site of heavy guns trained out to sea. A good spot to photograph the train in motion is the 775-foot bridge above the L'Anse-à-Brillant River at mile 89.8. Between miles 90 and 92, look south over Seal Cove. Douglastown, mile 96.7, was the site of an unsuccessful experiment on the part of a Scottish surveyor who attempted to found a model community. The driftwood-laden beaches nearby are broken by the crossing of the St-Jean River on a 549-foot bridge at mile 97.6. Look ahead at mile 101 as the Chaleur follows the Baie de Gaspé, fed by three salmon rivers (the St-Jean, York and Dartmouth). High atop the hill is Gaspé's wooden cathedral, with beautiful stained-glass windows and a huge granite cross, erected in 1934 to commemorate Cartier's landing four centuries before.

Seal Cove, on the Baie de Gaspé

Rivière St-Jean

GASPE 104.2
Baie de Gaspé
DOUGLASTOWN 96.7
Prével 89.1

BARACHOIS 79.3

Grande Rivière

Rivière du Petit Pabos

Petite Rivière

GRANDE-
RIVIERE
53.9

Summit 69.1
PERCE 65.1
Cape Cove 62.3

Rivière Cascapedia

Irishtown
57.7

Rivière Bonaventure

CASCAPEDIA 60.6

MARIA
53.0   NEW RICHMOND 68.9
Black Cape 71.7

RLETON
.4

CAPLAN 78.5

CHANDLER 44.1

Gascons
28.3   NEWPORT
36.9

Golfe du St-Laurent

Marcil
16.2

BONAVENTURE 89.2
NEW CARLISLE 98.0

PORT-DANIEL 22.5

ST-GODEFROI 11.1

Baie des Chaleurs

Gascons, a typical Gaspé coastal hamlet

Miles	Stations	Population	Elev.	Origin of Station Names
22.2	Pointe à la Garde	—	44	Nearby battery garrison
26.4	Escuminac	—	24	Micmac word for "observation post"
35.5	Nouvelle	350	50	Abbé Henri Nouvel (1621-1702), Jesuit missionary
44.4	Carleton	156	56	Sir Guy Carleton (1724-1808), governor of Québec from 1768 to 1778 and governor-in-chief of British North America from 1786 to 1796
53.0	Maria	429	38	Sir Guy Carleton's wife, Maria
57.7	Irishtown	—	140	Early settlers from Ireland
60.6	Cascapédia	513	38	Micmac word for "strong current"
68.9	New Richmond	333	12	(See Bala subdivision, Richmond Hill, page 122)
71.7	Black Cape	182	80	Nearby cape
78.5	Caplan	496	93	Indian settler Jean Caplan
89.2	Bonaventure	1,155	67	Marquis de Bonaventure
98.0	New Carlisle (P.Q.)	1,213	10	Carlisle, town in Cumbria, England

Chandler Subdivision — CNR New Carlisle/Gaspé

This line was built by the Atlantic, Québec and Western Railway, and opened for traffic on July 17, 1912.

Miles	Stations	Population	Elev.	Origin of Station Names
0.0	New Carlisle (P.Q.)	1,213	10	(See Cascapédia subdivision)
11.1	St. Godefroi	400	85	Charles Godefroi Fournier, parish founder
16.2	Marcil	200	179	—
22.5	Port Daniel	204	15	Captain Charles Daniel, contemporary of Champlain
28.3	Gascons	312	123	Shipwrecked sailor from Gascon, France
36.9	Newport	589	48	—
44.1	Chandler	3,842	9	Philadelphia industrialist and local pulp mill owner
53.9	Grande Rivière	4,390	64	To distinguish it from Petite Rivière
61.8	Beck	—	68	—
62.3	Cape Cove	147	70	Between Cap d'Espoir and Cap Malin
65.1	Percé	5,198	105	An offshore rock with a hole in it, through which boats pass
69.1	Summit	—	313	Highest point on the line
79.3	Barachois	515	69	(See Sydney subdivision, page 30)
89.1	Prével	—	232	—
96.7	Douglastown	335	25	Rear Admiral Sir Charles Douglas, who, in 1766, was in charge of the relief of Québec
104.2	Gaspé (P.Q.)	16,200	10	From the Micmac word "gespeg," meaning "the end"

The Chaleur Route

Cascapédia Subdivision — CNR Matapédia/New Carlisle

The segment from Matapédia to Caplan was built by the Baie de Chaleur Railway in 1893. The segment from Caplan to New Carlisle was built in 1910 by the Atlantic, Québec and Western Railway.

Miles	Stations	Population	Elev.	Origin of Station Names
0.0	Matapédia (P.Q.)	596	53	(See Mont Joli subdivision, page 64)
12.7	Cross Point	401	29	Across the river from Campbellton

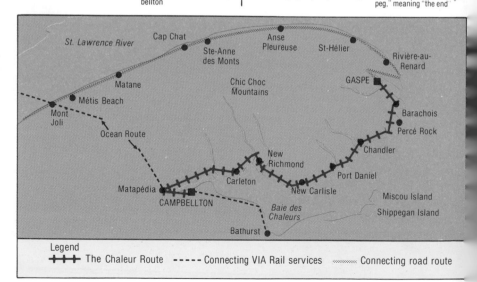

St. Lawrence River

Cap Chat
Ste-Anne des Monts
Anse Pleureuse
St-Hélier
Rivière-au-Renard
Matane
Chic Choc Mountains
GASPE
Métis Beach
Mont Joli
Barachois
Percé Rock
Ocean Route
Chandler
New Richmond
Carleton
Port Daniel
Matapédia
New Carlisle
CAMPBELLTON
Miscou Island
Baie des Chaleurs
Shippegan Island
Bathurst

Legend

+++ The Chaleur Route — — — — Connecting VIA Rail services 〰〰〰 Connecting road route

Sunrise at Percé Rock

The Gaspé Road Route

The Gaspé Peninsula (from the Indian word gaspeg, meaning "where the land ends") is a region of extraordinary variety. Highway 132 leads northeast from Mont-Joli to Parc de Métis, whose formal gardens were part of an estate owned by George Stephen, first president of the CPR. You can visit his 30-room mansion before proceeding to Métis-sur-Mer, the area's oldest resort, which features gracious summer homes and an offshore cluster of spherical rocks that provides good bird-watching.

St-Ulric was the site of an almost fortunate shipwreck in 1806. A coal carrier ran aground nearby, enabling townspeople to salvage several winter's worth of fuel. Matane, situated on a well-known salmon river, is an active fishing centre. An annual festival celebrates the shrimp catch, and an unusual museum, located in a lighthouse, recounts local history. The coastline grows more rugged as you approach Grosses-Roches. Look inland here to see the Chic-Chocs, eastern Canada's highest peaks.

Les Méchins was named for its dangerous offshore reefs, while Capucins, noted for its mussel harvest, takes its name from boulders shaped like hooded monks. Cap-Chat sits on a rocky promontory that, when viewed from the river, resembles a crouching cat. Ste-Anne-des-Monts is noted for a church dedicated to the patron saint of sailors. St-Joachim-de-Tourelle is the site of towering cliffs and a pair of massive granite pillars on the beach. During Prohibition, Marsoui was a haunt of rum-runners. Mont-St-Pierre, a resort town situated between two mountains, features a grove of olive trees. Anse-Pleureuse derived its name from winds that blew mournfully along the shore; at Rivière-la-Madeleine, people believed that similar sounds were the cries of sailors lost at sea. Watch for *vigneaux* (wooden tables used for drying cod) at Grande-Vallée.

Cloridorme was the scene of an attack by a German submarine in 1942, but the torpedo missed its target and exploded harmlessly on a rock. Each fall, thousands of eels leave a freshwater pool near St-Hélier, swimming up the St. Lawrence to spawning grounds in the mid-Atlantic Sargasso Sea. Rivière-au-Renard features an impressive modern church. Cap-des-Rosiers was named by Champlain for its abundant wild roses. Its lighthouse, built in 1858, is the highest of a series that used to guide ships safely down this treacherous coast. Now the highway curves back and enters Forillon National Park — a rugged landscape that's home to more than 160 different species of birds — where you can camp, hike and observe basking herds of pilot whales.

The Ocean Route

Along the route of the Intercolonial Railway, past sandy beaches, marshland sanctuaries teeming with wildlife, migrating snow geese and basking whales

Halifax to Montréal

The Ocean is Canada's longest-running train, having operated continuously under that name since July 3, 1904. It was unusual in that it offered an all sleeping-car service from its inception, placing it in the same class as the Twentieth Century Limited. (Coach passengers were handled by the slower Scotian). Patrons enjoyed gourmet meals in the diner and downed their favourite beverages in plush lounges before retiring. In the late 1960s, Skyview lounge cars, providing unforgettable views of Montréal and Québec City, were introduced and the schedule was reduced to 20 hours point to point.

The Ocean follows a route established by the Intercolonial Railway, a line plagued by conflicting purposes and parish pump politics. In the 1850s, few Maritimers saw the need for a rail link to central Canada. They had their own small, regional lines, and much preferred to travel west on American systems, reached by taking steamships to Portland, Maine. The ICR was perceived as a plot to lure them into Confederation, and many people argued that it would never pay its way.

A good deal of evidence supported that belief. Not a single contractor came within striking distance of his stipulated completion date. The railway took four years longer to build than had been anticipated, with final costs exceeding contracted figures by 40 percent. Ticket clerks pocketed most of the day-to-day revenues, passes were available at the drop of a hat, and special trains ran hither and yon at sweetheart rates. A story spread that contractors were paid by distance, since the line went swinging in half circles, veered off to tiny villages and looped up through Campbellton, miles away from a simpler route along the American border.

In fact, the Intercolonial route is 89 miles longer than the shortest east-west line that passes through Saint John and Sherbrooke. But at least the job was superbly done, thanks to the ceaseless efforts of Sandford Fleming, who served as engineer-in-chief, arguing for iron bridges and steel rails in an age when these were viewed as reckless extravagances. When the first passenger train from Halifax arrived in Lévis on July 6, 1876, pulling the opulent private car belonging to Samuel Tilley, then lieutenant governor of New Brunswick, Fleming commented that the work was "second to none," and he was right.

POINTS OF INTEREST
Halifax to Truro (Bedford subdivision)

Mile 1-11: To the immediate south are the Ocean Terminals, so large that the *Queen Mary* and *Queen Elizabeth* could be berthed end to end. Due to an enormous increase in wartime activity, centralized traffic control was installed on the critical Halifax-Truro link in 1941. One man, seated at a console, could dictate the movements of 80 trains a day by means of electrically operated switches. This system (one of North America's first such installations) made possible the dispatch of an additional 28 passenger trains a day, running at 20-minute intervals, whenever a troop ship docked in Halifax harbour.

At mile 3.4, look south for a lovely view of the Northwest Arm. To the north, at mile 4.3, is a small railway museum. At mile 5, you pass the Fairview Cemetery, the resting place of 125 vic-

Looking south along Halifax Harbour's Northwest Arm and out toward the Atlantic Ocean

tims of the *Titanic* sinking, as well as the site of a common grave for unidentified victims of the Halifax Explosion. Underneath the A. Murray McKay Bridge are the Narrows, leading to the Bedford Basin — where, on the morning of December 6, 1917, the outbound Norwegian vessel *Imo*, loaded with supplies for Belgian relief, collided with the French munitions ship *Mont Blanc*, arriving from New York with 5,000 tons of explosives, acids and benzine. Most of their crews boarded lifeboats and rowed to shore before an explosion rocked the harbour. A whole suburb was blown to bits; the Intercolonial station was reduced to a pile of rubble; freight cars in Rockingham yard went flying two miles through the air; and airborne debris inflicted injuries up to four miles distant. Some 1,600 people were killed and thousands more were wounded; property damage was estimated at

$35 million. That evening, Halifax suffered its worst blizzard in 20 years, so that many of those who survived the disaster itself perished from exposure. It was the largest man-made explosion prior to detonation of the first atomic bomb. No hint of the devastation remains as the Ocean follows the Bedford Basin between miles 5 and 11, but to the north at mile 9.6, a partly submerged tug indicates the ever-present dangers of navigation amid rocks and reefs.

Mile 17-64: Several lakes lined with sandy beaches and charming summer homes appear amid the spruce forest. Kinsac Lake is visible to the east, between miles 17 and 20; Shubenacadie Lake to the west, between miles 25 and 27. North America's first iron railway bridge, erected in 1877, crosses the Nine Mile River at mile 32.4. Its successful completion led to the replacement of wooden bridges throughout the country. The

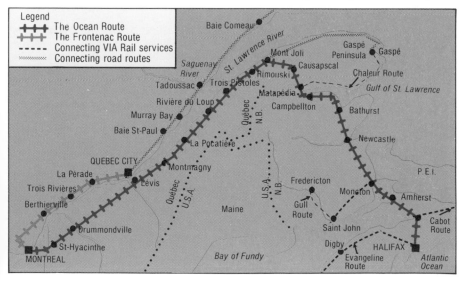

53

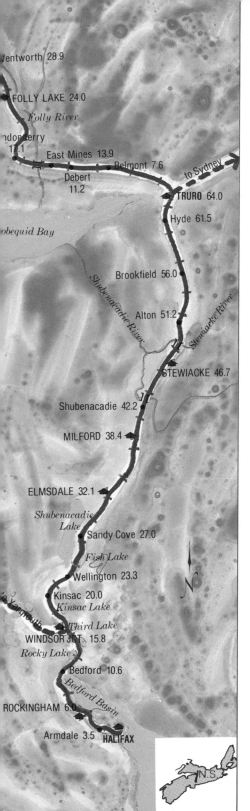

Wentworth 28.9

FOLLY LAKE 24.0

Folly River

ndonderry
17.1

East Mines 13.9

Belmont 7.6

Debert
11.2

to Sydney

TRURO 64.0

Hyde 61.5

obequid Bay

Shubenacadie River

Brookfield 56.0

Alton 51.2

Stewiacke River

STEWIACKE 46.7

Shubenacadie 42.2

MILFORD 38.4

ELMSDALE 32.1

Shubenacadie Lake

Sandy Cove 27.0

Fish Lake

Wellington 23.3

Kinsac 20.0

Kinsac Lake

to Yarmouth

Third Lake

WINDSOR JCT. 15.8

Rocky Lake

Bedford 10.6

Bedford Basin

ROCKINGHAM 6.0

Armdale 3.5   HALIFAX

N.S.

area around Elmsdale and Shubenacadie is noted for extensive clay deposits, dairy farming and lumbering; the Stewiacke River, at mile 48.7, is a popular salmon-fishing stream. Truro's fine old residences contrast sharply with its modern station, housed in a shopping plaza.

POINTS OF INTEREST
Truro to Moncton (Springhill subdivision)

Mile 11-24: Debert was an important military base during World War II, but nowadays the only activities overhead are flights of ducks from a nearby sanctuary. In 1963, archeological excavations revealed evidence of an 11,000-year-old hunting civilization. At mile 11.4, just past the crossing of the Debert River, is the infamous Grecian Bend. Sandford Fleming had originally selected another, more practical route for the roadbed, but he failed to reckon with the influence wielded by James Livesay, who owned an ironworks on the southern slope of Cobequid Mountain, near Londonderry. A three-year battle resulted in the railway's present course — a path immortalized by an outraged Fleming as a "gigantic and conspicuous sweep ... the line describes nearly a half circle." The 464-foot viaduct at mile 14.5 soars 87 feet above water level. Folly Lake, to the north between miles 23 and 24, was formed 10,000 years ago when a melting glacier dammed both ends of a narrow pass. Watch for moose and bear amid the beech, maple and birch forest.

Mile 25-68: One of Nova Scotia's most striking views occurs to the north between miles 25 and 30, as the Ocean winds through the Wentworth Valley high above the Wallace River. Watch for a ski club on the opposite slopes. To the south, between miles 30 and 34, are a series of pastoral valleys, with Sugarloaf Mountain in the background. Oxford's town lake, whose water is both saltier than the ocean and fed by sulphur springs, is the basis of a resort development. The River Philip, crossed on a 415-foot bridge at mile 47.1, flows only 12 miles from the Cobequid Mountains to the Northumberland Strait. It's well known for its trout and salmon fishing. To the north, between miles 51 and 53, is another colourful valley dotted with hemlock trees. Salt Springs is the centre of a rich dairy-farming area; perhaps the cows keep production high by means of a very saline liquid diet.

Springhill's coal mines date from 1872, but tragedy has always stalked the town. An explosion in February 1891 claimed the lives of 125 miners; a further 39 perished in 1956; a fire devastated the town's business district in 1957; and in 1958, 76 more men were lost in the shafts. The Springhill Miners' Museum portrays the residents' courage in the face of recurring disaster.

Oxford Junction station

The mines are closed today, but for many years, coal trains pulling a solitary, soot-encrusted passenger car of the Cumberland Railway and Coal Company would meet the passenger trains at Springhill Junction. Another pleasant valley extends to the south between miles 60 and 68, best viewed while crossing the Little Forks River on a 348-foot bridge at mile 62.9. Maccan was another interchange point with mixed trains of the Maritime Coal, Railway and Power Company, a line which meandered west for 12 miles to River Hébert and Joggins. Coal was first mined here in 1720, and visitors can still see fossilized trees buried in abandoned seams.

Mile 70-87: The terrain changes as the Ocean approaches the Cumberland Basin, first glimpsed to the south at mile 70. Amherst, geographical centre of the Maritime provinces, overlooks the vast Tantramar marshes, which cover 50,000 acres. Once the world's largest hayfield, the area is now a Canadian Wildlife Service sanctuary for Canada geese, marsh hawks, black ducks and blue-winged teal. Its original dikes, built by the Acadians in 1672, are slowly disappearing. Be on the lookout here for mechanical harvesters — huge airboats and pontoon craft, powered by airplane or automobile engines, that skim across the waters threshing wild rice. The Nova Scotia/New Brunswick border at mile 80.1 is marked by the Missaquash River. Look north between miles 81 and 82 to historic Fort Beauséjour, French-built between 1750 and 1755 but captured by the British the same year it was completed, and renamed Fort Cumberland. At Aulac, the Ocean descends to sea level, then crosses the Tantramar River at mile 85.6 on a 500-foot bridge. Sackville is a pleasant town, the home of Mount Allison University, and the site of North America's only harness shop that continues to manufacture old-fashioned horse collars.

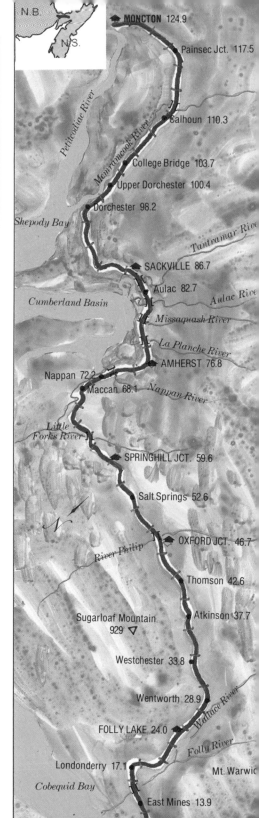

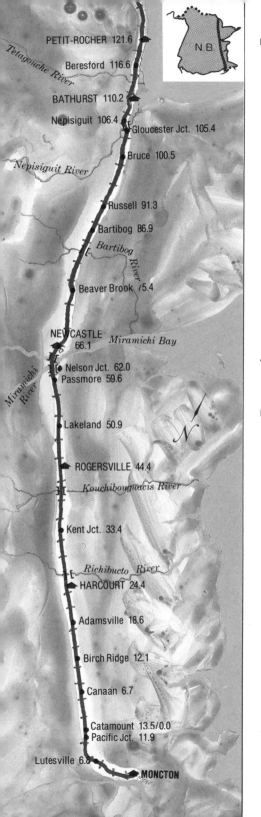

Mile 87-125: The Intercolonial Railway's Dorchester diversion swings south instead of heading due west from Sackville. Once again, Fleming's advice was overruled, because one of the ICR's commissioners, a former premier of New Brunswick, just happened to hail from Dorchester. Look south at mile 97 for a distant view of Shepody Bay. At Dorchester, you should be able to spot the nine chimneys of Keillor House, built in 1813 by an ambitious Yorkshireman. The even larger building on the hill isn't a mansion — it's the Dorchester Penitentiary. Directly to the south, the Memramcook River overflows with water or becomes a mud flat, depending on the tide. At mile 101, you'll see the pillars of an 815-foot covered bridge that used to span the river. Look south between miles 103 and 104 to the village of College Bridge, whose St. Joseph's College was founded by the Acadians. Moncton is a major rail centre and transportation hub. Its Centennial Park contains a steam locomotive and a CF-100 jet fighter; its oldest building is the Free Meeting House, built in 1821. The 350-foot concrete communications tower, visible from the train, is one of the tallest such structures in Canada.

POINTS OF INTEREST
Moncton to Campbellton (Newcastle subdivision)

Mile 62-173: The Miramichi River is bridged on a 1,230-foot structure at mile 62.2, followed by an equally lengthy crossing of the Little Miramichi at mile 63. These waters contain silver Atlantic salmon that attract anglers from all over the world. Newcastle was settled by Basque fishermen, followed by Scottish and Irish lumbermen and shipwrights. Their folklore included the Dungarvon Whooper — a spirit whose eerie cries should not be confused with wind whistling through the pines and tamarack. Nearby Chatham was the home of Joseph Cunard, founder of the famous steamship line. The Nepisiguit River is crossed on a 630-foot bridge at mile 105.5, just before the Ocean arrives at Bathurst, gateway to the Caraquet coast. The city thrives on copper mining and pulp and paper mills. Beresford is noted for its lovely beaches; look east at mile 116.6 to see its modern church. To the east, between miles 122 and 127, you'll glimpse Nepisiguit Bay, crossed each July during a grueling 22-mile marathon row from the Gaspé Peninsula. The town of Jacquet River was founded in 1790 by J. Doyle, who for many years remained its only inhabitant. The river itself is crossed on a 313-foot bridge at mile 139.9. To the north is Chaleur Bay, Cartier's "bay of warmth," where clams are dug on sandy beaches and giant bluefin tuna provide excellent fishing. Heron Island becomes visible between miles 142 and 158.

Look north at mile 156 to a large church against the background of the mountainous Gaspé coast. If you're traveling on a dark and stormy night, you might see the phantom ship of Chaleur Bay — a four-masted vessel with sails ablaze. It's either a mirage or the ghost of a French ship sunk in 1760 during the Battle of the Restigouche. Fine views occur to the north between miles 164 and 173, especially on a clear, sunny day. Campbellton is New Brunswick's third-largest seaport and a vital commercial centre. It's located at the base of Sugarloaf Mountain, a 1,000-foot mass of volcanic rock that offers good skiing at Sugarloaf Provincial Park.

POINTS OF INTEREST
Campbellton to Rivière-du-Loup (Mont Joli subdivision)

Mile 4-105: Look north at mile 4 across the tidal flats to see a tall, beautiful church silhouetted against high, rolling hills. At mile 7.3, the Ocean passes through the only tunnel en route, then crosses the Restigouche River, source of North America's finest Atlantic salmon, at mile 12.3. For the next 35 miles, you'll follow an Indian trail that later became the Kempt military road. The Matapédia River has 222 separate rapids and almost as many salmon pools. Photographic opportunities abound as you follow its valley to Routhierville. A 259-foot covered bridge, to the east at mile 34, links the town to the highway. Causapscal is the centre of a farming and lumbering area. It was here that Lord Strathcona, then president of the CPR, met and married an Indian beauty on one of his many salmon-fishing trips. To the east, between miles 53 and 56, is Lac au Saumon, framed by 700-foot mountains. The nearby town was settled by Acadians from Iles de la Madeleine. Their church, Saint Edmond's, features stained-glass windows designed by Max Ingrand. Look east at mile 60 to a waterfall in the Humqui River, with Amqui's town church in the background. To the east, between miles 63 and 73, is Lake Matapédia, measuring some 15 miles long by five miles wide and dotted with verdant islands. At Val-Brillant, look west to view the twin-spired parish church, then east at mile 76 to the church at Sayabec, perched on a hillside overlooking the lake. Between miles 95 and 99, look north over rolling valleys to the St. Lawrence River as the Ocean descends to Mont-Joli. The Mitis River is crossed at mile 102.1 on a 418-foot bridge; look south here to the tiny village of Ste-Angèle-de-Mérici; then north to the spire of St. Octave's church before arriving at Mont-Joli, a moose and deer-hunting centre known as the Gateway to the Gaspé.

Mile 119-189: At mile 119, look north across the

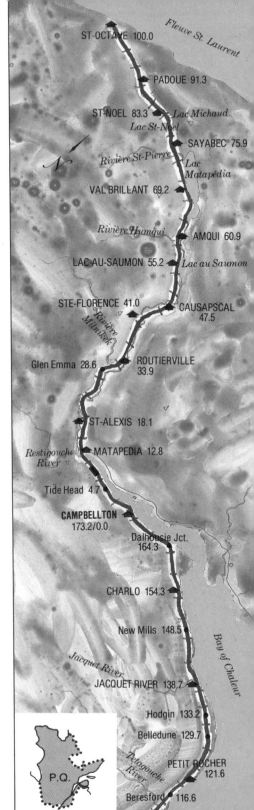

fields toward the shoreline, where a silver dome marks the graves of most of the 1,015 passengers who perished on the night of May 29, 1914, when the 3,650-ton Norwegian freighter *Storstad* collided with the luxurious 14,200-ton CP liner *Empress of Ireland*. The majestic ship sank within 15 minutes, and a mere 464 passengers scrambled to safety. It's known that $1 million in silver bars remain in the hull at the bottom of this treacherous waterway. Look north at mile 123 for a view of Rimouski's harbour and Ile St-Barnabé, named by Champlain in 1604 to honour a martyred apostle. It's hard to believe today that a fire in 1950 destroyed a quarter of the town. A local museum, housed in a restored 1824 church, features works by Québec artists, including Plamondon, Huot, Duguay and Taylor. The Ocean crosses the Rimouski River on a 436-foot bridge at mile 124.3, then follows it closely between miles 126 and 131. Legend tells that when the world was created, the angel assigned to its beautification arrived at Bic at the end of a hot, hard day, and dropped a surplus of mountains and islands. After crossing the Bic River at mile 133.7, you'll see why. Look offshore to Ile du Massacre, which commemorates the killing by Iroquois warriors of 200 Micmacs hiding in a cave; Ile du Bic, the official station for river pilots between 1762 and 1914; and Ile Bicquette, the scene of many shipwrecks, now the home of eider ducks, sea otters and harp seals. To the north, at mile 137, is Cap-à-l'Original, high above Ha! Ha! Bay. Saint Fabien's Church lies to the north at mile 144; the area around St-Simon-de-Rimouski is noted for its natural grottos and unusual rock formations. Trois-Pistoles, founded in 1696 by Jean Riou, is a major tourist resort, with a broad harbour and a lovely three-spired church built in 1857. Furnaces used to extract whale oil in the 1500s have been discovered and restored on nearby Ile aux Basques. Other, smaller islands offer sanctuary to blue

herons, herring gulls and eider ducks. The Trois Pistoles River is crossed on a 541-foot bridge at mile 164.7; look south here to a charming white-painted church. Ile aux Pommes, to the north at mile 168, is the site of apple trees that have survived for more than three centuries; while Ile Verte was used as an observation post to track ships arriving at the mouth of the Saguenay River to trade with the Indians at Tadoussac. Look south at mile 188 to see a huge illuminated cross on the hillside, with Rivière-du-Loup's grand cathedral visible to the north. The river itself is bridged on a 372-foot structure at mile 188.7; look down to see one of eight waterfalls that extend for over a mile, dropping a total of some 300 feet. The five offshore islands, known as Les Pélerins, (the pilgrims) — so called because they resemble a row of hooded figures — contain colonies of cormorants, black guillemots and great blue herons. This stretch of the St. Lawrence is known for its whales. Species that gather here to feed on abundant shrimp and capelin include beluga, minke, pilot, blue and finback.

POINTS OF INTEREST
Rivière-du-Loup to Lévis (Montmagny subdivision)

Mile 11-114: Mile 11 provides a good view of Les Pélerins. At mile 24, the town of Kamouraska is visible to the north. Its islands are the home of black-crowned night herons, best seen during the early hours of dusk. Look north at mile 40 to La Pocatière, with its Bishop's Palace and modern cathedral, with Stations of the Cross sculpted by Médard Bourgault. St-Jean-Port-Joli is noted for the production of fine wood sculptures, an old art that was revived by the Bourgault family in the 1920s; other craftsmen here create mosaics, copper-enamel works, fabrics, paintings and wooden toys. The village

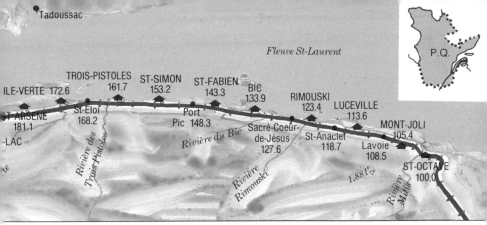

Tadoussac

Fleuve St-Laurent

P.Q.

ILE-VERTE 172.6 TROIS-PISTOLES 161.7 ST-SIMON 153.2 ST-FABIEN 143.3 BIC 133.9 RIMOUSKI 123.4 LUCEVILLE 113.6

ST-ARSENE 181.1 St-Eloi 168.2 Port Pic 148.3 Sacré-Coeur-de-Jésus 127.6 St-Anaclet 118.7 MONT-JOLI 105.4

-LAC *Rivière des Trois Pistoles* *Rivière du Bic* Lavoie 108.5 ST-OCTAVE 100.0

Rivière Rimouski 1,881' *Rivière Mitis*

The St. Lawrence River gleams beyond the skyline of Rivière-du-Loup

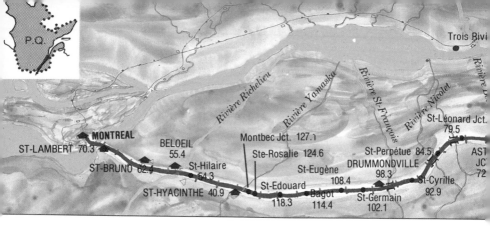

P.Q.

Trois Rivi

Rivière Richelieu   *Rivière Yamaska*   *Rivière St-François*   *Rivière Nicolet*

St-Léonard Jct. 79.5

MONTREAL

ST-LAMBERT 70.3

BELOEIL 55.4

Montbec Jct. 127.1

Ste-Rosalie 124.6

St-Perpétue 84.5

AST JC 72

ST-BRUNO 62.4

St-Hilaire 54.3

St-Eugène

DRUMMONDVILLE 98.3

St-Edouard

St-Cyrille 92.9

ST-HYACINTHE 40.9

118.3   Bagot 114.4   St-Germain 102.1   108.4

St-Romuald
Manseau 53.0
St-Apollinaire 20.0
QUÉBEC CITY 4.3
emieux 57.6
Villeroy
LAURIER 29.4
Chaudière 9.3
LÉVIS 0.0
Ile d'Orléans
Daveluyville 67.6
Val-Alain 40.5
Fortier 34.8
Villeroy 47.0
Trudel 14.1
CHARNY 8.1
Harlaka 110.2
St-Vallier 90.0
ST-CHARLES 101.3
La Durantaye 94.8
Rivière Chaudière
Rivière du Sud

Champlain leaving Québec as a prisoner on Thomas Kirke's ship, 1629

church, built in 1776, is renowned for its beautiful interior. The Trois Saumons River is crossed on a 360-foot bridge at mile 59.5. L'Islet has sent its sailors all over the world, including Captain Joseph-Elzéar Bernier, who in 1909 claimed a large group of Arctic islands for Canada. Offshore, near Cap-St-Ignace, is Ile aux Grues (Goose Island), settled in 1679 but devastated by General Wolfe 80 years later. Each fall, countless snow geese invade its tidal flats. At mile 77.5, the Bras St-Nicholas River is crossed on a 384-foot bridge, followed by a 584-foot structure spanning the Rivière du Sud at mile 77.8. Look north at mile 78 to Montmagny's unusual ten-sided church. Ile d'Orléans and Grosse Ile appear to

The walled section of Québec City   61

A typical early Montréal house

the north between miles 78 and 90. The latter was the site of a quarantine station established in 1832 to control the spread of cholera by European immigrants. In 1837 alone, 5,424 Irish men, women and children perished of typhus aboard their crowded ships or on the island. During the station's 105 years of operation, some 7,000 more immigrants would meet the same dreadful fate. In contrast, Ile d'Orléans is scenic and pastoral, noted for its strawberry fields, gristmills, stone churches, pastel houses and outdoor bake ovens. At St-Charles, the Ocean swings north toward Lévis, descending to the waterfront at mile 110. Next to Lévis station is the ferry to Québec City.

POINTS OF INTEREST
Lévis to Montréal (Drummondville and St-Hyacinthe subdivisions)

Mile 0-8: Look north between miles 0 and 4 to one of Canada's greatest panoramas, a never-to-be-forgotten view of Québec City. It unfolds from east to west: huge grain elevators on the Beauport Flats; the towering spire of Notre-Dame Basilica; waterfront Place Royale, with its funicular to the fortresslike Château Frontenac; the ferry boats linking Lévis and Québec; the Citadel; and the Plains of Abraham. Huge ships sail majestically by as the Ocean climbs from water level at mile 4, up the escarpment to Charny.

Ste-Foy to Charny: Passenger trains from Québec City (Ste-Foy) travel 3.3 miles through the Bridge subdivision to Charny, over the 3,238-foot Québec Bridge, rising some 150 feet above the St. Lawrence. Its main span, the world's longest, is a triumph of engineering skill, but its construction was dogged by tragedy. Work began in 1906, but the following year, on August 29, the south section collapsed, sending 76 workmen to their deaths. A new start was made in 1910, but the centre section gave way on September 11, 1916, with a further loss of 10 lives. The completed structure was opened for traffic on December 3, 1917, and formally christened

by the Prince of Wales on August 22, two years later.

Mile 8-98: The Chaudière River is crossed on a 1,000-foot bridge at mile 8.8. St-Rédempteur's lovely church lies to the south at mile 9. Others are visible to the south at miles 47 and 53. Aston-Jonction's church is seen to the south at mile 72, while the church at St-Léonard-d'Aston appears to the north at mile 79.5. At mile 84.5 is St-Perpétue's former station, converted to house a local firm. St-Cyrille's Church is seen to the north at mile 92.9. Drummondville's many industries depend on power dams built on the St-François River, crossed at mile 97.8.

Mile 40-60: Look south at mile 40.7 to see the Gothic chapel of the St-Hyacinthe Seminary, built in 1927 and modeled on Amiens Cathedral. Between miles 43 and 60, you'll see the pleasant orchards, rolling hills and winding roads of the historic Richelieu Valley. The Richelieu River, flowing 80 miles from Lake Champlain in New York State, is crossed at mile 55, the scene of a tragic accident in 1864, when a Grand Trunk Railway train plunged through the open drawbridge into the water below. Between St-Hilaire and Montréal are the Montregian (Royal) Hills, eight volcanic cones formed 120 million years ago when the entire area was covered by the Champlain Sea. Five hills are visible from the train: Yamaska, St-Hilaire, Rouge, St-Bruno and Mont Royal. In a quarry high on Mont St-Hilaire geologists have discovered 20 minerals that exist nowhere else on earth, as well as an abundance of shells and fossils. Nearby Lac Hertel is surrounded by nature trails.

Mile 70-72: The Victoria Bridge is crossed at 20 mph between miles 70.3 and 72. It carries the Ocean over the St. Lawrence Seaway, affording spectacular views of Montréal. Before a bridge existed here, the Montréal Ice Railway linked Hochelaga and Longueuil during the winter months. Rails were laid on timbers arranged in stone cribs, and steam engines gingerly hauled short trains across the frozen waters. The original railway bridge was a single-track, enclosed tubular structure designed by Robert Stephenson. It opened on December 17, 1859, and consisted of 25 spans totaling 1.7 miles in length. It was considered the eighth wonder of the world, and the then Prince of Wales (who became King Edward VII in 1901) drove its last ceremonial rivet on August 25, 1860. Smoke retention and increased traffic led to the construction of an open-girder, double-track bridge that opened on December 13, 1898. This was called the Victoria Jubilee Bridge, and ran just west of the previous structure. Look east as you reach the bridge to see the Irish Stone, a monument erected in 1859 in memory of immigrants who died of cholera and typhus in the preceding decade.

Looking north, over the Tantramar Marshes, at the Ocean passing Fort Beauséjour on the hill

The Ocean Route

Bedford Subdivision — CNR Halifax/Truro
The segment between Fairview and Rockingham was built by the Intercolonial Railway, and opened for traffic in February 1855. The segment between Rockingham and Truro was also built by the Intercolonial, and opened on December 15, 1858.

Miles	Stations	Population	Elev.	Origin of Station Names
0.0	Halifax (N.S.)		24	George Montagu Dunk, Earl of Halifax (1716-1771), president of the Board of Trade. Formerly called Chebookt, from the Micmac word "chebookt," meaning "great long harbour"
3.5	Armdale		49	The estate of Sir Charles Tupper (1821-1915) on the northwest arm of Halifax harbour
4.3	Southwestern Jct.		40	—
5.0	Fairview Jct.	277.400	25	—
6.0	Rockingham		11	Charles Watson-Wentworth, second Marquis of Rockingham (1730-1782)
10.6	Bedford		44	John Russell, fourth Duke of Bedford, secretary of state from 1748 to 1751. Formerly called Kwebek, an Indian word meaning "head of the tide," and Fort Sackville
12.7	Bedford Quarry		140	
15.8	Windsor Jct.	667	128	Junction with railway line to Windsor
20.0	Kinsac	—	95	Nearby lake
23.3	Wellington	166	80	British general (1792-1852) who defeated Napoleon I at the Battle of Waterloo
27.0	Sandy Cove	176	56	—
32.1	Elmsdale	643	50	Grove of elms nearby
38.4	Milford	—	54	Named by an act of Parliament (1884)
42.2	Shubenacadie	812	58	From the Micmac word "segubunakadie," meaning "the place where the potato grows"
46.7	Stewiacke	1.003	83	From the Micmac word "siktaweak," meaning "oozing from dead water"
51.2	Alton	—	95	—
56.0	Brookfield	807	99	Named by William Hamilton, the first white settler, in 1784. Formerly called Sibumeadook by the Micmacs
61.5	Hyde	—	131	—
64.0	Truro (N.S.)	12,500	61	Town in Cornwall, England. Formerly called Cobequid

Springhill Subdivision — CNR Truro/Moncton
The segment from Truro to the New Brunswick border was built by the Intercolonial Railway between 1871 and 1872, and opened on November 11, 1872. The segment from the border to Painsec Junction was built by the New Brunswick Railway (Eastern Extension) in 1869, and opened on December 13, 1869. The segment from Painsec Junction to Moncton was built by the European and North American Railway, and opened on August 27, 1857.

Miles	Stations	Population	Elev.	Origin of Station Names
0.0	Truro (N.S.)	12,500	61	(See Bedford subdivision)
7.6	Belmont	438	86	Formerly called Highfield. Name changed by an act of Parliament (1873)
11.2	Debert	593	154	Adaptation of the original French colonial name Ville au Bourg, or Ville Burke
13.9	East Mines	80	195	—
17.1	Londonderry	238	335	County in Northern Ireland, home of original settlers
24.0	Folly Lake	68	612	Bad choice of settler Flemming, called "Flemming's Folly"
28.9	Wentworth	129	471	Sir John Wentworth, lieutenant-governor of Nova Scotia from 1792 to 1808
33.8	Westchester	283	316	Westchester County, N.Y., where the early Loyalist settlers came from in 1784
37.7	Atkinson	—	246	—
42.6	Thomson	61	106	—
46.7	Oxford Jct.	214	92	Nearby town. The name Oxford comes from a ford over the River Philip, where oxen once crossed to pasture
52.6	Salt Springs	57	151	In 1813, an attempt was made to mine salt from the local springs
59.6	Springhill Jct.	203	200	Natural water springs are common in the nearby hills
68.1	Maccan	562	31	From the Micmac word "maakan," meaning "the fishing place"
72.2	Nappan	270	28	From the Micmac word "nepan," meaning "good place to get wigwam poles"
76.8	Amherst	10,500	59	Lord Jeffrey Amherst (1717-1797), commander-in-chief of the British forces in North America during the Seven Years War. He became governor-general of British North America in 1761
82.7	Aulac (N.B.)	154	24	Area near lake at the head of Aulac River
86.7	Sackville	5,755	25	George Sackville Germain, first Viscount Sackville (1716-1785).
92.7	Evans	—	232	—
98.2	Dorchester	1,183	22	Lord Dorchester, previously Sir Guy Carleton (1724-1808), governor of Québec from 1776 to 1778 and governor-in-chief of British North America from 1786 to 1796

The Ocean passing through Morrissey Rock tunnel between Campbellton and Matapédia

100.4	Upper Dorchester	—	27	—
103.7	College Bridge	513	29	College-Saint-Joseph (Memramcook Institute)
110.3	Calhoun	89	50	T.B. Calhoun, first postmaster
117.5	Painsec Jct.	105	149	From the French "pin sec," meaning "dry pine." Formerly called Pine Hill
122.6	Humphrey	2,492	65	—
124.9	Moncton (N.B.)	82,900	50	Robert Monckton (1726-1783), General James Wolfe's first brigadier in 1759. Spelling changed in 1786

100.5	Bruce	—	238	—
105.4	Gloucester Jct.	—	93	Princess Mary, Duchess of Gloucester and Edinburgh (1776-1857)
106.4	Nepisiguit	—	101	From the Micmac word "winpegijooik," meaning "river that dashes roughly along"
110.2	Bathurst	15,900	49	Henry Bathurst, third Earl of Bathurst (1762-1834). Formerly called St. Peter's
116.6	Beresford	2,307	33	William Carr Beresford, Viscount Beresford (1768-1854)
121.6	Petit-Rocher	—	83	—
129.7	Belledune	205	94	French for "fine beach"
133.2	Hodgin	—	130	—
138.7	Jacquet River	854	50	James (Jock) Doyle, 1790 settler
148.5	New Mills	158	42	Mills established by William Fleming in 1814
154.3	Charlo	1,617	55	Charles Doucet, early settler
164.3	Dalhousie Jct.	165	82	George Ramsay, ninth Earl of Dalhousie, governor-in-chief of Canada from 1819 to 1828
167.8	McLeod	—	51	Angus McLeod, first postmaster
173.2	Campbellton (N.B.)	8,400	42	Sir Archibald Campbell, lieutenant-governor of New Brunswick from 1831 to 1837.

Newcastle Subdivision — CNR Catamount (Moncton)/Campbellton

This line was built by the Intercolonial Railway, and opened for traffic on July 1, 1876.

Miles	Stations	Population	Elev.	Origin of Station Names
0.0	Moncton (N.B.)	82,900	50	(See Springhill subdivision)
3.6	Gort	—	115	—
4.5	Odlum	—	140	—
6.8	Lutesville	—	214	Jeremiah Lutes, postmaster. Formerly called Moncton Mountain
11.9	Pacific Jct.	—	276	—
13.5/ 0.0	Catamount	—	347	"Felis concolor" (panther or Indian devil)
6.7	Canaan	88	263	Head of the Canaan River
12.1	Birch Ridge	—	300	Ridge of birch trees
18.6	Adamsville	—	300	Michael Adams, New Brunswick surveyor-general from 1878 to 1883
24.4	Harcourt	264	201	William Harcourt, third Earl of Harcourt (1743-1830), British field marshal
33.4	Kent Jct.	127	269	Duke of Kent, later William IV (1830-1837)
44.4	Rogersville	1,061	304	James Rogers, bishop of Chatham from 1860 to 1902
50.9	Lakeland	—	141	—
59.6	Passmore	—	130	—
62.0	Nelson Jct.	—	36	Horatio Nelson (1758-1805), famous British admiral
62.5	Derby Jct.	116	36	Fourteenth Earl of Derby, prime minister of Britain in 1852 and from 1858 to 1859
66.1	Newcastle	6,423	138	Duke of Newcastle, prime minister of Britain from 1754 to 1762
75.4	Beaver Brook	225	333	Beaver dams nearby. Max Aitken (Lord Beaverbrook) chose his name in honour of this town
86.9	Bartibog	639	522	Micmac Chief Bartholomew La Bogue
91.3	Russell	—	496	John Russell, first postmaster

Mont Joli Subdivision — CNR Campbellton/Rivière-du-Loup

This line was built by the Intercolonial Railway between 1874 and 1876. The Campbellton to Mont Joli segment was opened in July 1876, and the Mont Joli to Rivière-du-Loup segment in August 1874.

Miles	Stations	Population	Elev.	Origin of Station Names
0.0	Campbellton	8,400	42	(See Newcastle subdivision)
4.7	Tide Head	797	34	—
12.8	Matapédia (P.Q.)	596	53	From the Micmac word "matapegiag," meaning "river that breaks into branches"
18.1	St. Alexis	75	98	Alexis Boulanger, who donated land for the parish church
19.0	Clark Brook	—	101	—
28.6	Glen Emma	—	207	—
33.9	Routhierville	219	280	—
41.0	Ste Florence	450	354	—
47.5	Causapscal	2,974	454	Micmac word meaning "rocky point"
55.2	Lac au Saumon	1,307	502	Where the Matapédia River widens here was formerly a salmon spawning ground
60.9	Amqui	3,777	526	From the Micmac word "amgoig," meaning "place of amusement"
69.2	Val Brillant	698	537	Abbé Pierre Brillant, first curé in the region (1889)
75.9	Sayabec	1,799	581	Micmac word meaning "filled-up river," often caused by beaver dams

Miles	Stations	Population	Elev.	Origin of Station Names
83.3	St. Noel	906	644	Abbé Noel Chabanel (1613-1649), a martyr at Huronia River
91.3	Padoue	292	715	—
100.0	St. Octave	280	387	Abbé Octave Caron
105.4	Mont Joli	6,698	262	Beautiful view of the St. Lawrence River from the mountain
108.5	Lavoie	—	—	Charles Lavoie, Department of Lands and Forests officer
113.6	Luceville	1,410	—	Luce Gertrude Drapeau, owner of the seigniory
118.7	St. Anaclet	698	—	—
123.4	Rimouski	30,700	—	Micmac or Maliseet word meaning either "land of moose" or "home of dogs"
127.6	Sacré Coeur de Jésus	1,923	—	Named in 1900 after the parish
133.9	Bic	1,154	—	Corruption of French "pic," meaning "distant pointed peak"
140.2	Mountain	—	—	—
143.3	St. Fabien	1,497	—	—
148.3	Port Pic	—	—	—
153.2	St. Simon	528	—	Religious parish (1869)
161.7	Trois Pistoles	4,654	—	In dispute. A crewman sent to fetch fresh water for a stranded ship lost a silver goblet valued at trois pistoles
168.2	St. Eloi	339	—	Eloi Rioux, first missionary in the area
172.6	Ile Verte	1,356	—	Named by Champlain, and an apt description of the area
181.1	St. Arsène	523	—	Arsène Mayrand, local curé
188.8	Rivière-du-Loup (P.Q.)	13,200	—	Large wolf packs were once common in the area

Montmagny Subdivision — CNR Rivière-du-Loup/Lévis

The segment from Rivière-du-Loup to Montmagny was built by the Grand Trunk Railway (East) of Canada between 1858 and 1860. The Grand Trunk also built the line from Montmagny to St. Charles between 1854 and 1855. The final segment to Lévis was built by the Intercolonial Railway, and opened on July 21, 1884.

Miles	Stations	Population	Elev.	Origin of Station Names
0.0	Rivière-du-Loup (P.Q.)	13,200	—	(See Mont Joli subdivision)
6.0	Chemin-du-Lac	—	—	—
11.8	St. Alexandre	891	—	Alexandre A. Taché, archbishop of St. Boniface
16.1	St. André	75	—	André Trudeau, surveyor
19.8	Ste Hélène	222	—	Daughter of Pascal Taché
25.4	St. Pascal	2,491	—	Pascal Taché, seignior of Kamouraska
29.0	Kamouraska	503	—	Amerindian word meaning "where there are rushes on the other side of the river"
31.3	St. Philippe-de-Néri	683	—	—
41.1	La Pocatière	4,246	—	Marie Juchereau, widow of de la Pocatière
42.6	Pointe Rouge	—	—	—
56.3	St. Jean-Port-Joli	1,741	—	The parish name plus a description of the harbour
64.7	L'Islet	772	—	Small rocky island near the village
71.2	Cap St. Ignace	1,199	—	St. Ignatius of Loyola, founder of the Jesuit order
78.1	Montmagny	12,000	—	Charles Huault de Montmagny, governor and lieutenant-general of New France from 1636 to 1648
83.0	St. Pierre	281	—	Pierre Blanchet, founder of the parish church
90.0	St. Vallier	572	—	Jean Baptiste de la Croix de Chevrières de St. Vallier, second bishop of Québec
94.8	La Durantaye	412	—	Olivier Morel, Sieur de la Durantaye
101.3	St. Charles	—	—	Charles des Boues, grand vicar of Pontoise
108.1	Bégin	—	—	—
110.2	Harlaka	—	—	Indian word meaning "whoever can reach it"
114.8	Lévis (P.Q.)	17,819	—	François Gaston, Chevalier de Lévis (1719-1787) of Montréal, who succeeded Montcalm when Québec fell to the British in 1759

Drummondville Subdivision — CNR Lévis/Montbec Jct.
St. Hyacinthe Subdivision — CNR Montbec Jct./Montréal

The segment from Lévis to Chaudière was built by the Québec and Richmond Railway, and opened on November 27, 1854. Most of the route from Chaudière to Montbec Junction was built by the Drummond County Railway between 1890 and 1898. The segment from Montbec Junction to St. Hubert was built by the St. Lawrence and Atlantic Railway between 1848 and 1851, and opened for traffic on October 20, 1851.

Miles	Stations	Population	Elev.	Origin of Station Names
0.0	Lévis (P.Q.)	17,819	—	(See Montmagny subdivision)
1.0	Pointe Lévis	—	—	—
2.4	Hadlow	—	—	Town in Kent, England
4.3	St. Romuald	—	—	—
8.1	Charny	5,175	—	Charles de Charny, son of Jean de Lauzon, governor of New France
9.3	Chaudière	1,655	—	French translation of Algonquian word "asticou," meaning "boiling kettle"
14.1	Trudel	—	—	F.X.A. Trudel, senator from 1873 to 1890
20.0	St. Apollinaire	1,193	—	—
29.4	Laurier	945	—	Sir Wilfrid Laurier, prime minister of Canada from 1896 to 1911
34.8	Fortier	—	—	Pioneer family
40.5	Val-Alain	—	—	—
47.0	Villeroy	198	—	—
53.0	Manseau	742	—	Abbé Martial Manseau, first parish curé
57.6	Lemieux	250	—	Randolphe Lemieux, postmaster-general (1886)
67.6	Daveluyville	1,002	—	Adolphe Daveluy, local merchant
72.0	Aston Jct.	349	—	Aston, town in Yorkshire, England
79.5	St. Léonard Jct.	1,049	—	Saint of the religious parish
84.5	Ste. Perpétue	674	—	—
92.9	St. Cyrille	1,059	—	Cyrille Brassard, first settler
98.3	Drummondville	43,000	—	Sir Gordon Drummond (1771-1854), hero of the Battle of Lundy's Lane during the War of 1812
102.1	St. Germain	1,289	—	St. Germain de Grantham, after Edward Granville Eliot, third Earl of St. Germain (1798-1877), who accompanied the Prince of Wales to Canada in 1860
108.4	St. Eugène	295	—	Eugène Casgrain, local seignior
114.4	Bagot	400	—	Sir Charles Bagot, governor-general of Canada from 1841 to 1843
118.3	St. Edouard	—	—	—
124.6	Ste Rosalie	2,702	—	Dessaules family, with several children named Rosalie
40.6	Montbec Jct.	—	—	Junction of lines from Montréal and Québec
40.9	St. Hyacinthe	40,000	—	Hyacinthe Simon Delorme bought the seigniory in 1753
54.3	St. Hilaire	—	—	After the religious parish
55.0	Otterburn Park	3,506	—	—
55.4	Beloeil	12,274	—	Either Beloeil, Belgium, or descriptive of the beautiful scenery
59.3	St. Basile	4,385	—	Basile Daignault, one of the builders of the parish church
62.4	St. Bruno	15,780	—	Abbé Bruno Leclerc, curé and parish founder (1910)
66.5	St. Hubert	21,741	—	Bishop of Maastricht, the Netherlands
70.3	St. Lambert	20,318	—	Raphael Lambert Closse (1618-1662), sergeant-major at the Ville Marie garrison
—	Montréal (P.Q.)	2.8 million	47	In 1534, Jacques Cartier gave the name Mont Réal to the hill overlooking the city; after the British captured the city in 1760, the name was changed to Montréal

The Saguenay Route

Over soaring bridges and past cascading waterfalls, with stops at isolated fishing camps and breathtaking views of Lac St-Jean and the mighty Saguenay River

Montréal to Chicoutimi

The Saguenay is a land of fabulous wealth and beauty, of staggering industrial potential and scenic grandeur. No wonder that Indians whom Jacques Cartier encountered during his explorations of 1534 and 1535, conferred the title "kingdom" on this richly varied area — both the setting for Louis Hémon's habitant classic *Maria Chapdelaine* and the site of vast hydroelectric plants; of a valley where river and tide meet one another in a Laurentian fjord two miles wide; and of 387-square-mile Lac Saint-Jean, a saucer-shaped indentation left by ice age glaciers, fed today by a dozen waterways. The Saguenay is good clay farming soil and a sportsman's paradise teeming with the famous landlocked salmon called ouananiche. It's a harvest of blueberries that appears in deep pies and sweet wines; modern cities like Chicoutimi, with hills and churches that echo ancient Rome; year-round attractions ranging from winter carnivals to sun-drenched swimming beaches; a region of friendly people who live their lives with infectious gusto.

Your journey to the Saguenay takes you plunging through Canada's second-longest tunnel and over some of its highest trestles, past waterfalls, rapids and rustic log cabins. Stops are made at many of the fishing camps that dot 1,500 lakes and 700 rivers, where moose and caribou roam the adjacent woodlands. And finally, at journey's end, there's Lac Saint-Jean, surrounded by fertile plains and framed by mountains marching into the distance. No one can appreciate these wonders in a hurry — plan to spend at least a day cruising the river and another circling the lake by rented car.

The Saguenay River is a supreme stroke of nature, with incoming 20-foot tides that rush the 65 miles from Tadoussac to Chicoutimi in 45 minutes, creating violent and unpredictable currents as icy cold sea water meets Lac Saint-Jean's warmer outflow. Small boats caught in the maelstrom are secured to rings fixed in the granite bases of Cap Trinité and Cap Eternité, towering more than 1,700 feet above the surface. Atop Cap Trinité is a 25-foot statue of the Virgin Mary, carved of wood and sheathed in lead,

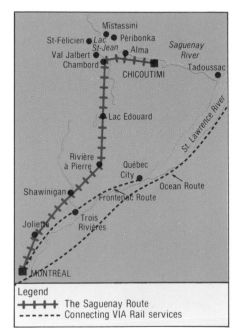

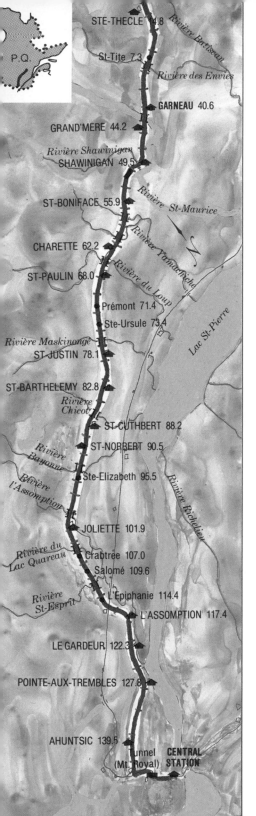

P.Q.

STE-THECLE 4.8
St-Tite 7.3
Rivière Batiscan
Rivière des Envies
GARNEAU 40.6
GRAND'MERE 44.2
Rivière Shawinigan
SHAWINIGAN 49.5
ST-BONIFACE 55.9
Rivière St-Maurice
CHARETTE 62.2
Rivière Yamachiche
ST-PAULIN 68.0
Rivière du Loup
Prémont 71.4
Ste-Ursule 73.4
Lac St-Pierre
Rivière Maskinongé
ST-JUSTIN 78.1
ST-BARTHELEMY 82.8
Rivière Chicot
ST-CUTHBERT 88.2
ST-NORBERT 90.5
Rivière Bayonne
Rivière l'Assomption
Ste-Elizabeth 95.5
Rivière Richelieu
JOLIETTE 101.9
Rivière du Lac Quareau
Crabtree 107.0
Salomé 109.6
Rivière St-Esprit
L'Epiphanie 114.4
L'ASSOMPTION 117.4
LE GARDEUR 122.3
POINTE-AUX-TREMBLES 127.8
AHUNTSIC 139.5
Tunnel (Mt. Royal) CENTRAL STATION

erected in 1881. A third rock formation is Le Tableau ("the blackboard"), an immense slab polished by glacial action to resemble a school slate. Ships carrying bauxite from Guyana, cryolite from Greenland and petroleum coke from Texas ply these brooding waters, en route to the aluminum smelters at Arvida.

Driving through the area around Lac Saint-Jean you'll find numerous wayside shrines, sparkling homes with rocking chairs perched on long verandas and well-kept farms with rakish split-rail fences. Be sure to visit the ghost town of Val-Jalbert at the base of the 275-foot falls on the Ouiatchouane River (yes, they're higher than Niagara). Stop to photograph the twin-steepled stone church and zoological gardens at St-Félicien and the Indian reservation at Pointe-Bleue, where, if you hit the right weekend in July, you can participate in the annual native festival. But there's even more to see: the observatory and reflecting telescope at Dolbeau; the Trappist farm and monastery at Mistassini, where brown-robed monks produce delicious chocolates; the Maria Chapdelaine Museum at Péribonka, where Louis Hémon prepared his beloved classic; and the sculpture park and artists' lane at Alma. Church fanciers should also visit Jonquière's Notre-Dame-de-Fatima, shaped like a vertically split tepee; the dramatic Saint-Raphaël church; and the equally striking Saint Marc's, in Bagotville, which resembles a nun's headdress. In Chicoutimi itself, the Saguenay Museum contains a wealth of historical material; and during the February Carnaval-Souvenir you can watch lumberjack contests, go street dancing in period costume and drink the lethal "caribou" — a mixture of whisky and sweet red wine that's guaranteed to make you forget the cold.

POINTS OF INTEREST
Montréal (Central) to Garneau

Mile 0-5: As your train leaves Central Station, it immediately plunges into the Mount Royal tunnel, built between 1912 and 1918 to bring Canadian Northern Railway trains into downtown Montréal so as to compete with the CP and

One of the grandest fishing lodges,
built of polished logs, is at mile
58.8, near Miquick

St-André 141.3

Lac Quiatchouan

Mink Lake 133.1

Lizotte 130.1

Lac Long 125.1

KONDIARONK 123.9

VAN BRUYSSELS 118.1

Kiskisink 116.9

Lac Kiskisink

Summit 107.2

SUMMIT CLUB 106.2

Lac George

LAC EDOUARD 95.3

TRITON CLUB 90.7

CLUB NICOL 87.9

Pearl Lake 84.2

SANFORD 80.7

Hegadorn 77.0

Iroquois 74.5

St-Hilaire 70.0

Falrie 68.8

Jacques Cartier Club 67.1

Linton 61.9

Miquick 59.1

Laurent 53.4

Lemieux 51.0

Talbot 47.5

Rivière Batiscan

RIVIERE-A-PIERRE 39.9

LAC-AUX-SABLES 23.4

HERVEY 18.7

STE-THECLE 14.8

St-Tite 7.3

P.Q.

Grand Trunk railways. Three miles in length (or, to be exact, 16,315 feet), this is Canada's second-longest tunnel. Its initial cost of $3 million — an immense sum in those days — was more than justified by a subsequent building boom that transformed the city core and climaxed in the Place Ville Marie development. The first passengers to Ottawa and Toronto rolled smoothly through the tunnel on October 21, 1918, drawn by an electric locomotive that's still in use today, transporting commuters over the 17 miles to Deux-Montagnes on Canada's only remaining electrified railway.

Mile 126-114: Here you cross Rivière des Prairies twice, on a 1,416-foot bridge at mile 125.8 and a 1,121-foot span at mile 125.2. The stone houses of L'Assomption, to the south at mile 117, are typical of early French-Canadian architecture, with gabled roofs and chimneys at both ends. At mile 114.7, the Frontenac route leads off toward Trois-Rivières and Québec City.

Mile 107-49: Have your cameras ready here to capture the views from a series of spectacular trestles — but if you're afraid of heights, perhaps you'd better close your eyes. First comes the Lac Quareau River Viaduct, 490 feet long and 55 feet high, at mile 106.5. Note a small power dam to the north. Near Joliette (mile 101.9), you'll see Canada's most northerly tobacco crops growing on land reclaimed from a marshy channel of the St. Lawrence River. The green buildings with red doors are curing sheds. A church, to the north at Ste-Elizabeth (mile 95), is dedicated to John the Baptist. The Chicot River is bridged at mile 87 by a 252-foot trestle running 59 feet above the water. At mile 76.3, a 175-foot-high viaduct crosses the former course of the Maskinongé River. An earthquake in the seventeenth century altered that flow to its present position, at mile 76.1. Look south here for a view of the Ste-Ursule Falls. At mile 65.1, a 1,071-foot trestle carries you 130 feet above the swirling Rivière du Loup, affording a particularly good view of the Laurentian mountains to the north. The East Yamachiche River is crossed on a 616-foot bridge running 90 feet above water level, at mile 58.1, followed by a graceful steel span curving southward over the Laverene Gully, at mile 52.1. Finally, at mile 50.7, a 610-foot tunnel leads to a 367-foot bridge over the Shawinigan River, at mile 50.

Mile 49-41: The St-Maurice River was called Métabérotine by early Indians, meaning "sheet of water exposed to all winds." The waters seem quite placid as you cross a 722-foot bridge at mile 43.5, but look north and you'll see swirling rapids and a power dam. By the mid-1800s there were 80 sawmills on the St-Maurice, and a flume was built so that logs could bypass the angry cascade. Today, 100 million pulpwood logs are floated down to Shawinigan's paper mills each year. The nearby city of Grand-Mère is named for a rock formation, once located on an island in the river,

that resembles the profile of an old woman. When the power dam was constructed in 1916, the rock was dismantled and moved piece by piece to a municipal park.

Garneau to Chicoutimi (Lac St-Jean subdivision)

Mile 0-39: At mile 3, the Hérouxville church dominates the skyline to the east. St-Tite (mile 7.3) is known as "glove town" because of its production of leather goods and western wear. Each September, 80,000 people dressed in 10-gallon hats and cowboy boots gather here for a genuine (though French-flavoured) rodeo. At mile 14.8, the twin-spired cathedral at Ste-Thècle can be

A bearskin on the former Métabetchouan Club

seen to the west; the foaming rapids of the Propre River are bridged at mile 21.6. Near mile 28 you first encounter the swiftly flowing Batiscan River, which you'll follow for the next 70 miles. The train twists and turns along its banks, affording excellent photo opportunities, and crosses over on a 325-foot bridge at mile 30.4. Look west in Rivière-à-Pierre to see a large cross made from local granite erected to mark the fourth centenary of Canada's discovery by Jacques Cartier.

Mile 40-95: Civilization all but disappears as the Saguenay enters the vast Laurentides wilderness area. More than 20 fish and game clubs are located on nearby rivers and lakes, with accommodations ranging from spartan to luxurious. Part of this area lies within the boundaries of Portneuf Provincial Park, so look sharp for moose, bear, wolf, partridge and hare. Created in 1968, the park offers good fishing for speckled trout in a region of rolling hills, lush valleys and tumbling waterfalls. Its stands of red spruce, balsam, fir, maple and birch provide a beautiful fall colour show. Some of the Batiscan's many rapids can be seen to the west at miles 51, 56 and 57; then look west at mile 58.8 to a splendid lodge constructed of polished logs, set against a placid curve in the river. More rapids come into view between miles 63 and 67; watch for old bridge piers in midstream. The less ostentatious Jacques Cartier Club lies to the west at mile 67.1, followed by a hillside statue of Jesus at mile 69.5 and the Iroquois Club, to the east at mile 74.5. Sanford station, to the east at mile 80.7, is typical of small northern stops; the Triton Club, three miles farther on, is built on stilts to avoid spring floods. At mile 93, the train passes over the Batiscan Falls.

Mile 95.3: Lac Edouard was named for a Batiscan Indian hunter. Its 20-mile length teems with speckled trout, pike and pickerel. To the east, you'll see the spire of the nearby town church.

Mile 96-160: Now you enter an area of larger, more

71

placid lakes. Watch for a beaver dam to the east, on Lac Coquille, at mile 104.8. Residents of tho Summit (Sommet) Club, to the west at mile 106.2, may come down to meet the train; note a green and white flag that's put in a holder on the platform to warn the engineer when someone wants to board. Summit is the highest point on the Chicoutimi line. East at mile 117.3, a bearskin graces the former Métabetchouan Club; Club Kondiaronk, to the east at mile 123.9, is served by one of the tiniest stations en route. Between miles 128 and 130 there are good views of Lac au Mirage to the west. Lac-Bouchette is a forestry village in an untamed setting that draws many pilgrims. Services are conducted here by the Capuchin Fathers at the shrine of Our Lady of Lourdes and Saint Anthony, which features a grotto modeled after the one at Lourdes. At mile 157, you first catch sight of Lac Saint-Jean in the distance to the east. Chambord is a farming town that also provides good fishing for salmon, pike and walleye; just across from its station you'll see a religious diorama.

Mile 161-211: Lac Saint-Jean is plainly visible to the north between Chambord and mile 173. One of the waterways that feeds this magnificent inland sea is the 85-mile Métabetchouan River, crossed at mile 164.6 on a 418-foot bridge. Its delta was the sight of a meeting between the missionary Father Albanel and representatives of 20 Indian nations in 1671. Five years later, the first trading post was opened nearby. Look north for a monument to Father Jean de Quen, Lac Saint-Jean's discoverer. The town of Métabetchouan features a pink granite Gothic church and a giant floral clock. Under its former name of St-Jérôme, it was linked to Québec City by the Jesuit's Trail. The soil around Hébertville is particularly fertile, and has been farmed since 1849. A stone church can be seen to the north, built of black granite from the St-Gédéon quarries. Look south at mile 193.7 to see cottages reflected in Lac Samson. Rivière aux Sables is crossed at mile 200.6 — watch for whitewater rafters in its swirling rapids. As you approach the industrial city of Jonquière, amalgamated with Kénogami and Arvida in 1975, you'll become aware of its gigantic paper mills and aluminum smelters. The Alcan complex is the world's third-largest such plant; watch for its smokestacks to the north at mile 204.5. You'll also notice the yellow locomotives of the Roberval and Saguenay Railway, which provides a connection to the deep-water anchorage at Port Alfred on the Saguenay. Your first views of the mighty Saguenay River lie to the north as you descend a steep grade toward Chicoutimi and cross the Chicoutimi River on a 167-foot bridge at mile 209.6. To the north you'll see a power dam; to the south are thundering falls and a 1921 mill that's been converted to house a restaurant and theatre.

The only tunnel on the Saguenay Route

The Saguenay Route

**Mont Royal Subdivision — CNR Montréal/Jct. de l'Est
St. Laurent Subdivision — CNR Jct. de l'Est/Pointe aux Trembles
Joliette Subdivision — CNR Pointe aux Trembles/Garneau**
The segment from Montréal to Jct. de l'Est was built by the Mount Royal Tunnel and Terminal Company, and opened for traffic on October 4, 1918. The segment from Jct. de l'Est to Joliette was built by the Châteauguay and Northern Railway (later the Canadian Northern Quebec Railway) between 1904 and 1905, except for the L'Assomption to L'Epiphanie section, which was built between 1885 and 1886 by the L'Assomption Railway. The segment from Joliette to Garneau was built by the Great Northern Railway of Canada between 1897 and 1901.

Miles	Stations	Population	Elev.	Origin of Station Names
0.0	Montréal (Central) (P.Q.)		47	(See St. Hyacinthe subdivision, page 65)
0.2	South Portal		—	South portal of Mt. Royal tunnel
0.5	Grotto		—	Resembles underground grotto
3.2	Portal Heights		—	North portal of Mt. Royal tunnel
3.7	Mont Royal		—	Nearby mountain named by Jacques Cartier
5.1	Jct. de l'Est		—	—
141.6	Jct. de l'Est		—	Junction for railway toward the east
141.3	Gohier	2.8 million	—	—
139.5	Ahuntsic		—	Amerindian church convert who saw the assassination of Abbé Viel at what is now Sault au Récollet, in 1625
137.5	National Quarries		—	Nearby rock quarry
136.1	Montréal Nord		—	Suburb of Montréal
132.8	Rivière-des-Prairies		—	Early explorer des Prairies, who in 1640 was the first white man to ascend the Ottawa River
127.8	Pointe-aux-Trembles		43	Named by Cartier for the trembling aspens in the area
122.3	Le Gardeur		—	—

72

Miles	Station	Population	Elev.	Origin of Station Names
117.4	L'Assomption	—	62	Named for the seigniory of St. Pierre-du-Portage-de l'Assomption, founded in 1724
114.4	L'Epiphanie	2,910	75	Feast of L'Epiphanie
109.6	Salomé	175	123	—
107.0	Crabtree	1,942	125	Edwin Crabtree, an early settler who built a local paper mill
101.9	Joliette	30,200	197	Barthélemy Joliette (1787-1850)
95.5	Ste Elizabeth	490	171	Elizabeth, mother of John the Baptist
90.5	St. Norbert	125	174	—
88.2	St. Cuthbert	1,532	192	Sieur J. Cuthbert, donor of land for the church in 1766
82.8	St. Barthélemy	468	173	Sieur de Barthélemy, who donated the land for the original village
78.1	St. Justin	372	—	Marie Justine Têtu, wife of Sir Hector Langevin, an associate of Sir John A. Macdonald
73.4	Ste. Ursule	422	361	Seigniory owned by the Ursulines of Trois-Rivières
71.4	Prémont	—	428	—
68.0	St. Paulin	730	540	—
62.2	Charette	624	413	General de Charette
55.9	St. Boniface	2,680	409	—
49.5	Shawinigan	51.500	349	Algonquian word meaning "portage of the beech trees"; A rock in the river separating two falls resembles a seated old woman
44.2	Grand'Mere			
40.6	Garneau (P.Q.)	—	44	François-Xavier Garneau (1809-1866), Canadian historian and author

Lac St. Jean Subdivision — CNR Garneau/Chicoutimi

This line was built by the Québec and Lac St. Jean Railway between 1888 and 1893.

Miles	Stations	Population	Elev.	Origin of Station Names
0.0	Garneau (P.Q.)	—	544	(See Joliette subdivision)
3.0	Hérouxville	1,017	544	Rev. M.S. Héroux, missionary
7.3	St. Tite	3,128	458	—
14.8	Ste Thècle	1,761	512	Curé in charge of the local mission
18.7	Hervey	330	583	—
23.4	Lac-aux-Sables	857	518	Nearby lake (lake of sand)
28.0	Montauban	903	—	Town in France
31.8	Rousseau	—	518	J.A. Rousseau, MLA for Champlain from 1900 to 1908
39.9	Rivière-à-Pierre	817	708	Stream nearby with rocky bed
47.1	Talbot Club	—	—	Fishing club
47.5	Talbot	—	970	—
51.0	Lemieux	—	744	Rodolphe Lemieux, postmaster-general in 1866
52.4	Laurentides	—	717	Nearby Laurentian plateau
53.4	Laurent	—	728	—
59.1	Miquick	—	846	Indian word meaning "bear"
61.9	Linton	77	887	—
62.7	Orléans Fish and Game Club	—	—	Fishing club
67.1	Jacques Cartier Club	—	963	Fishing club
68.8	Falrie	—	—	—
70.0	St. Hilaire	—	—	Elie St. Hilaire, MLA for Chicoutimi from 1887 to 1888
74.5	Iroquois	—	1,197	Indian tribe
76.4	Stadacona	—	1,207	Indian word meaning "wing"
77.0	Hegadorn	—	—	—
80.7	Sanford	—	1,243	—
84.2	Pearl Lake	—	1,131	Nearby lake
84.9	Hirondelle	—	—	—
87.9	Club Nicol	—	—	Fishing club
90.7	Triton Club	—	1,164	Fishing club
95.3	Lac Edouard	447	1,194	Indian hunter named Edward
103.8	Club Gregoire	—	—	Fishing club
106.2	Summit Club	—	1,440	Fishing Club
107.2	Summit	—	1,472	Highest point on the line
110.8	Brooks	—	—	—
116.9	Kiskissink	—	1,303	Indian word meaning "little cedar lake"
117.3	Métabetchouan Club	—	—	Fishing club
118.1	Van Bruyssels	53	1,286	—
123.9	Kondiaronk	—	1,401	—
125.1	Lac-Long	—	1,364	Nearby lake
130.1	Lizotte	—	1,311	—
133.1	Mink Lake	—	—	Nearby lake
141.3	St. André	—	—	André Néron, first settler
143.0	Lac-Bouchette	1,685	1,135	Nearby lake
147.3	Bilodeau	—	—	—
155.2	Blackburn	—	—	—
159.5	Chambord	1,755	551	Henri, Comte de Chambord (1820-1883), last of the Bourbon family and pretender to the French throne
165.4	Desbiens	1,673	390	—
169.0	Métabetchouan	3,016	359	Indian word meaning "where the river meets the lake"
173.2	Déchène	—	—	A.M. Déchène, MLA for L'Islet from 1896 to 1902
174.6	St. Gédéon	—	353	Gédéon Ouimet, Québec premier from 1873 to 1874
181.4	Hébertville	1,362	518	Abbé Nicolas-Hébert, curate of Kamouraska in the 1850s
183.2	Saguenay Power	—	525	Nearby power dam on the Saguenay River
191.5	Moquin	—	—	—
201.5	Jonquière	—	487	Jacques-Pierre de Taffanel, Marquis de la Jonquière, governor of New France from 1749 to 1752
204.3	Arvida	—	363	Arthur Vining Davis, Aluminum Company of Canada official
205.1	Ha Ha Bay Jct.	129,000	341	Adaptation of an old French term meaning a blind alley. When early French explorers discovered the bay was not a continuation of the river, they are reported to have cried "Ha ha!"
210.9	Chicoutimi (P.Q.)		21	"Shkoutimeou," a word of Montagnais origin, meaning "farther on it is still deep," probably referring to the Saguenay River

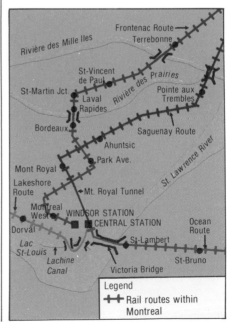

Legend

+ + Rail routes within Montreal

The Frontenac Route

Montréal to Québec City

The Frontenac links three of Canada's most historic cities: Québec City, founded in 1608, Trois-Rivières, founded in 1634, and Montréal, founded in 1642. Early French settlers in this region lived in fear of attack by both English marauders and the Iroquois; today, passengers can enjoy the beauty of the region, as they pass peaceful villages, each with its distinctive church, backed by the Laurentian Mountains. For many years, the CPR morning train from Montréal, complete with diner and parlour cars and later with dome cars, was *the* way to travel to Québec City.

POINTS OF INTEREST

St-Martin Junction to Lorette

Mile 4-83: The ominous guard towers of Archambault prison are visible to the north at mile 4.5, contrasted at mile 10.1 by tranquil Terrebonne, seen as the train rumbles across the 628-foot bridge that spans Rivière des Mille-Iles. The town of Mascouche appears to the north at mile 14.7. This is a major tobacco-growing area — watch for green curing sheds. Between here and Berthierville you'll also see solid fieldstone houses built in the nineteenth century, and hundreds of coniferous trees, part of a 35-million tree nursery operation.

Many rivers and creeks are crossed in this stretch — six between St-Barthélemy and Maski-

nongé, including Empty Bottle Creek at mile 54.2. The Maskinongé River, crossed at mile 57.5, is home to fighting muskellunge that weigh up to 90 pounds. Look north at mile 62 as you cross the Rivière du Loup, which flows for 90 miles from high in the Laurentians.

Trois-Rivières, originally a fur-trading post, has become "the newsprint capital of the world," although a disastrous fire almost destroyed the city in 1908. Take a few minutes to appreciate the Italianate station waiting room. With its polished pewlike seats, marble floor, white stucco walls and wrought-iron chandeliers and wall sconces, it resembles a chapel.

Mile 83-153: Look north at mile 83.5 as the Frontenac slowly crosses the St-Maurice on a 1,120-foot bridge — frequently this magnificent river is choked with logs. To the south, at mile 88, the octagonal Basilica of Our Lady of the Cape Shrine can be seen. The chapel here has been a place of pilgrimage since 1909.

In 1609 Champlain met the Hurons at Batiscan, persuading them to become allies of the French. The wide Batiscan, crossed at mile 102.5, is often the scene of summer canoe races. In the winter Ste-Anne River, bridged by a six-span, 908-foot structure at mile 106.8, is dotted with hundreds of colourful huts occupied by fishermen hoping for a good catch of tommycod — the patient sportsman can be rewarded with as many as 45 on a good day. An annual contest offers prizes for the best-decorated huts.

Portneuf (mile 125), is the site of an old Huron village. At mile 125.9, as the train crosses the Portneuf River, look north to peaceful farmland and sturdy stone houses. As the Jacques-Cartier River is crossed at mile 134.9, you can see Pinkney Mountain, Hart Hill and Snow Mountain to the north. Look north at Lorette to a church on the hill that stands in quiet contrast to the jets from Québec City's airport that roar overhead.

The Frontenac Route

Montréal Terminals Subdivision — CPR Windsor Station/Montréal Ouest
Park Avenue Subdivision — CPR Montréal Ouest/St. Martin Jct.
Trois-Rivières Subdivision — CPR St. Martin Jct./Lorette

The line between St. Martin Junction and Québec City was started in 1874, and was opened for traffic on February 8, 1879 by the Québec, Montréal and Occidental Railway. It was originally incorporated in 1853 as the North Shore Railway Company. Passenger trains from Montréal to Québec City via Trois-Rivières travel over CN tracks (Bridge subdivision) to Ste Foy station.

Miles	Stations	Population	Elev.	Origin of Station Names
0.0	Montréal (P.Q.)		47	(See St. Hyacinthe subdivision page 65)
2.0	Westmount		152	West slope of Mont Royal
4.7	Montréal Ouest		158	Western part of Montréal
5.9	Breslay		—	—
6.1	Park Avenue		—	Station on Park Avenue
8.4	Jacques Cartier Jct.	2.8 million	98	Former junction with Jacques Cartier Union Railway and Montréal Tramways
9.8	Bordeaux		76	Bordeaux, France
10.2	Laval des Rapides		75	François de Montmorency Laval (1623-1708), first bishop of Québec
12.8/ 0.0	St. Martin Jct.		107	Parish of St. Martin, founded in 1769
4.9	St. Vincent de Paul		71	—
10.6	Terrebonne		60	Seigniory with fertile soil
14.3	Mascouche		63	Amerindian word meaning "smooth plain"

Logs jam the St. Maurice River

Miles	Stations	Population	Elev.	Origin of Station Names
17.8	Cabane Ronde	—	59	—
22.8	L'Epiphanie	2,910	75	The feast of L'Epiphanie
27.0	Vaucluse	1,473	76	Vaucluse, France
30.0	Lavaltrie	1,473	85	Seraphin Margane, Sieur de la Valtrie (1643-1699), who was granted the seigniory in 1672
35.7	Lanoraie	1,362	68	De la Noraye, the original owner of the seigniory
44.0	Berthier (Berthierville)	4,249	36	Alexandre Berthier, captain of the Regiment de l'Allier de Carignan, who bought the seigniory in 1673
47.6	St. Cuthbert	1,532	38	Sieur James Cuthbert, who donated land for the church here in 1766
52.3	St. Barthélemy	468	33	Sieur de Barthélemy, who donated the land for the original village
57.7	Maskinongé	1,001	49	Algonquian word meaning "pike"
60.3	Lavoie	—	—	Charles Lavoie, Department of Lands and Forests official
61.7	Louiseville	3,995	42	Commemorates the visit, in 1880, of Princess Louise, wife of the Marquis of Lorne, governor-general of Canada from 1878 to 1883
67.1	Yamachiche	1,202	33	Algonquian word meaning "muddy river"
74.5	Pointe-du-Lac	2,737	68	Site on the point at the lower end of Lac St. Pierre
79.2	Bureau	—	—	—
82.3	Trois-Rivières	97,600	51	Meeting of three rivers: St. Maurice, Bécancour, St Laurent
84.9	Cap-de-la-Madeleine		51	Ste Marie Madeleine de Châteaudun a diocese of Rouen. France
95.1	Champlain	548	46	Samuel de Champlain (1567-1635), who founded Québec City in 1608
102.1	Batiscan	936	33	Montagnais word meaning "light mist."
107.2	La Pèrade	1,032	38	Thomas de Lanouguère (1644-1678), acting governor of Montréal alleged to have signed himself as Tarieu de la Pèrade
115.7	La Chevrotière	126	103	Sieur N. Chavigny de la Chevrotier, granted the siegniory in 1652
125.0	Portneuf	1,320	192	French for "new port"
129.6	St. Basile	—	198	Basile Daignault, one of the builders of the parish church
134.3	Pont Rouge	3,342	358	A red-coloured bridge was built here in 1769
146.5	Bélair	723	189	—
152.4	Lorette (P.Q.)	11,694	88	Loreto, Italy

North Shore Road Route

This 410-mile trip along Highways 360 and 138 follows the St. Lawrence River from Québec City to Sept-Iles, passing through the cradle of New France. Your first stop, a short jog off the highway, is Montmorency Falls, which tumbles 274 feet. In wintertime, frozen spray builds up a massive cone of ice known as "the sugarloaf." Near Château-Richer, be sure to stop at a roadside oven for freshly baked bread and the delicious French Canadian meat pies called tourtières. On the horizon ahead you'll see the twin spires of Sainte-Anne-de-Beaupré, dedicated to the mother of the Virgin Mary. The first chapel on this site was built in 1658, and today's basilica, completed in 1970, attracts more than one million people a year — the devout, the curious and those in search of miraculous cures. Whatever your religion, this magnificent shrine merits an unhurried stay.

If you wish, visit the nearby 243-foot Saint Anne Falls before joining Highway 138. The parish church at St-Joachim, to the south, contains a wealth of eighteenth-century wood sculptures. A slight detour leads you to Cap-Tourmente, a stopping place each spring and fall for 100,000 snow geese on their way between the U.S. east coast and Baffin Island. Rejoining the highway, which turns inland and climbs over the next 25 miles, you detour south once more to Petite-Rivière, a shipbuilding village where an off-shore cross becomes visible during tidal changes. This region's maple groves are spectacular in the fall, attracting painters and photographers to the artists' colony at Baie-St-Paul, surrounded by the 4,000-foot-high Laurentian mountains. Be sure to visit the local art gallery, housed in an early eighteenth-century mill.

Now you follow the shoreline on Highway 362 to St-Joseph-de-la-Rive, where parchmentlike paper is produced in an old schoolhouse by mixing ferns, leaves and wildflowers into the pulp. At this point, a ferry will take you across to Ile aux Coudres, with its massive windmills, wayside chapels, plum orchards, placid stone farmhouses and a cross commemorating the first mass celebrated in Canada, on September 7, 1535. Back on the mainland, Les Eboulements ("the landslides") was the site of a devastating earthquake in 1663. From the lighthouse at Cap-aux-Oies, the westernmost point to which Atlantic salt water flows, you can see frolicking beluga whales. At St-Irénée, stop to view the parish church and colourful mariners' houses.

Montmorency Falls, just east of Québec City .

The village of Tadoussac lies at the junction of the St. Lawrence and Saguenay rivers. The Tadoussac chapel (see page 2), built in 1747, is the oldest in North America

You rejoin Highway 138 at La Malbaie, a popular resort town once frequented by the Rockefeller family. Here you can see where Champlain anchored his ship at high tide, only to find himself aground the following morning. Enraged, he christened the place *malle baye* ("bad bay"). Because of its English-speaking presence (the town is also known as Murray Bay), La Malbaie contains several Anglican churches, a rarity in largely Catholic rural Québec.

Continue now to Cap-à-l'Aigle, watching for soaring eagles en route. As you approach Port-au-Persil, you'll see a waterfall, an old inn and a pottery school. The church at Baie-Ste-Catherine has a unique altar: a gilded cedar stump. Here you must take a short ferry across the Saguenay River. As you wait, try fishing for speckled trout right from the dock, and watch for dolphins upstream. Tadoussac, on the far bank, features one of the oldest (1747) surviving chapels in North America, a re-creation of Canada's first trading post (1600) and sand dunes

where summer skiers schuss down a 365-foot hill. This area is renowned for its sea trout and duck hunting. Escoumins is the site of an ochre mine; at St-Paul-du-Nord, watch for distinctive red cliffs and offshore boulders that resemble reclining cows. Forestville has been a wood processing centre since the mid-1840s; its pulp and paper mill features an immense flume system that utilizes the current from a nearby dam. Look for the many barges waiting in the river to transport logs south to Québec City.

At Chute-aux-Outardes, a mile-long pine pipe carries water from a dam to a nearby generating station. Stop to photograph the 104-foot covered bridge at Pointe-aux-Outardes before proceeding to Baie-Comeau, founded in 1936 by American publisher Robert R. McCormick, who built a newsprint plant to supply his presses. Today the town is best known for its hydro-electric development. Godbout features a canning plant for periwinkles (small marine snails), a forest products mill and an Indian cemetery on the shoreline, which is slowly being eroded by the encroaching waters. A seven-storey lighthouse nearby was built in 1829. The church at Pointe-aux-Anglais was constructed in 1962, thanks to the efforts of 120 hard-working parishioners who each carried 40 stones a distance of three miles, and is worth a visit to view its impressive bas relief basswood and walnut Stations of the Cross. Watch for the pink blossoms called kalmais near Port-Cartier, once called Shelter Bay, the terminus of several iron ore railways. From this point, it's a short drive through Clark City to Sept-Iles.

The Labrador Route

Through rugged canyons and plunging tunnels, past countless waterfalls and along the shores of the world's largest inland lakes on your way to the iron mines of wilderness Labrador

Sept-Iles to Schefferville and Labrador City/Wabush

Jacques Cartier sailed into Sept-Iles harbour in 1535, pausing only to christen its Round Islands before continuing to what is today Montréal. When the Oblate Father Pierre Babel ventured up the Hamilton (now the Churchill) River to Knob Lake several centuries later, his diary contained the simple entry: "Abundant iron." In 1892, the distinguished scientist, Dr. A.P. Low, explored these upper reaches by dog sled and canoe, but it wasn't until another half-century had passed that further investigations confirmed the Montagnais Indians' stories of widespread ore deposits. The tiny fishing village of Sept-Iles was suddenly transformed. Land surveys to determine a suitable rail route began in 1945, followed by aerial photography of the wild and inhospitable terrain.

Construction started in the fall of 1950 on a railway that would make possible today's gigantic mining industry. Its route lay through forest so impenetrable that there weren't even trappers' trails to guide the crews. Detailed surveys had to be conducted by helicopters hovering at treetop height. Over a period of three years, the longest peacetime airlift in history ferried 170 million tons of machinery and supplies to 13 airstrips in a region where temperatures vary from −55° to 100°F. Two major tunnels were blasted through the rock face, 19 bridges erected across precipitous river valleys and tracks laid across 200 miles of muskeg.

Everything about the Labrador route is larger than life. Menihek Lake is 70 miles long; the Tonkas Falls is 200 feet high. A typical southbound train might be two miles long, consisting of 260 cars carrying 22,000 tons of iron ore, and pulled by five diesel engines. Even the track is special: the original rails, designed to bear extra-heavy loads, weighed 132 pounds a yard. It's also a route with highly flexible scheduling. Only

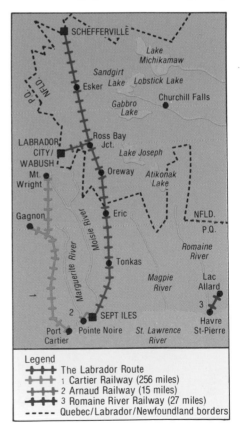

Legend
- ┿┿┿ The Labrador Route
- ┿┿┿ 1 Cartier Railway (256 miles)
- ┿┿┿ 2 Arnaud Railway (15 miles)
- ┿┿┿ 3 Romaine River Railway (27 miles)
- - - - - Quebec/Labrador/Newfoundland borders

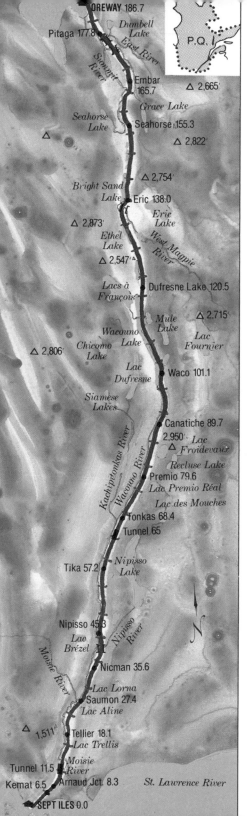

OREWAY 186.7
Dumbell Lake
Pitaga 177.8
East River
P.Q.
Sioumit River
Embar 165.7
△ 2,665'
Grace Lake
Seahorse Lake
Seahorse 155.3
△ 2,822'
△
△ 2,754'
Bright Sand Lake
Eric 138.0
Erie Lake
△ 2,873'
West Magnie River
Ethel Lake
△ 2,547' △
Lacs à François
Dufresne Lake 120.5
Mule Lake
△ 2,715'
Wacouno Lake
Lac Fournier
△ 2,806'
Chicomo Lake
Lac Dufresne
Waco 101.1
Siamese Lakes
Kachipotonkas River
Canatiche 89.7
2,950' Lac Froidevaux
Wacouno River
Recluse Lake
Premio 79.6
Lac Premio Réal
Lac des Mouches
Tonkas 68.4
Tunnel 65
Tika 57.2
Nipisso Lake
N
Nipisso 45.3
Nipisso River
Lac Brézel
Moisie River
Nicman 35.6
Lac Lorna
Saumon 27.4
Lac Aline
△ 1,511'
Tellier 18.1
Lac Trellis
Moisie River
Tunnel 11.5
Kemat 6.5
Arnaud Jct. 8.3
St. Lawrence River
SEPT ILES 0.0

the terminal departure times are strictly adhered to, and the train can run two hours early or late. On Tuesdays, the northbound train delivers supplies to every section gang and work party along the line, while on Friday nights the southbound passenger train is reserved for miners on their way to a wild weekend in Sept-Iles. At Ross Bay Junction, half the train goes to French-speaking Schefferville, running on Eastern Standard time, while the other half proceeds to largely English Labrador City, on Atlantic Standard. Passenger coaches are an odd mix of second-hand units: some from the CPR's Dominion, which ran between Montréal and Vancouver; others from Southern's Crescent, which serviced New York and New Orleans. There's even an aged dome car from the Wabash Cannonball! And if that's not enough, the Labrador route goes into semi-hibernation during winter months, scaling down from 10 full-length runs per day to six locals a week.

The last spike on the Québec, North Shore and Labrador Railway was driven by the noted mine owner, Jules Timmins, on February 13, 1954. In addition to the route from Sept-Iles, there are two lines that parallel the QNSL: the Romaine River Railway, completed in 1950, was built from Havre St-Pierre to tap titanium deposits at Lac Allard, and the Cartier Railway, pushed through from Port Cartier to Gagnon in 1962 and later to the iron deposits at Mount Wright. All this development turned the area Jacques Cartier described as "the land God gave to Cain" into a fully exploited storehouse of mineral wealth.

POINTS OF INTEREST
Sept Iles to Schefferville (Wacouna and Menihek subdivisions)

Mile 0: In downtown Sept-Iles, you can visit a reconstruction of the fort built by Louis Jolliet in 1661, complete with guard tower, chapel, store and stables. Close to the railway station, you'll see two steam-powered locomotives: engine 702, which hauled the ONR's Northland between North Bay and Timmins (see page 111) and was used on the Labrador route only for its blasts of hot steam, which cleared frozen culverts; and engine 48, which hauled pulpwood from Clarke City to Pointe Noire in the days when that area consisted of nothing more than a string of fishing villages linked with the outside world by ship.

Mile 1-27: Passing through stands of black spruce,

A fishing lodge and tunnels line the bank of the Wacouno River at mile 65

you cross a series of terraced rock formations at mile 10, the remains of an ice-age glacier, then enter a 2,197-foot tunnel at mile 11.5, unusual in that its entire length is illuminated. Immediately upon leaving the tunnel, you cross the Moisie River on a 900-foot bridge soaring 155 feet above water level. The next 15 miles along its rock-strewn gorge are marvellously scenic. The train twists and turns along a narrow shelf, across from sheer rock faces 2,000 feet high. Those shimmering bands that look like veins of quartz are actually spidery waterfalls, feeding salmon-filled pools.

Mile 28-55: The Labrador makes frequent stops to drop off visiting sportsmen. Their most luxurious base is the Fishermen's Nest, seen to the west at mile 28. This is the junction of the Moisie and Nipisso rivers, famous for their salmon. At Nicman, to the west, you may see a "floating" work

camp for track gangs, composed of old CPR sleeping cars that once served on the Dominion between Montréal, Toronto and Vancouver. It's moved whenever maintenance is required. To the east, between miles 45 and 55, cliffs loom closer to the train, making the waterfalls (particularly at mile 55 to the west) easier to photograph. Throughout this stretch, watch for helicopters from nearby mines.

Mile 57-71: Now you start to climb in earnest, in a series of sweeping curves that enable you to see the train stretching out ahead of you. It might include boxcars full of groceries, flatbeds with piggyback trailers and even two-tiered auto carriers bound for Labrador City — a boom town with thousands of vehicles but only 30 miles of paved road. You'll also have excellent views of the Wacouno River, especially to the left at mile 64. Note the white-painted fishing lodge just

81

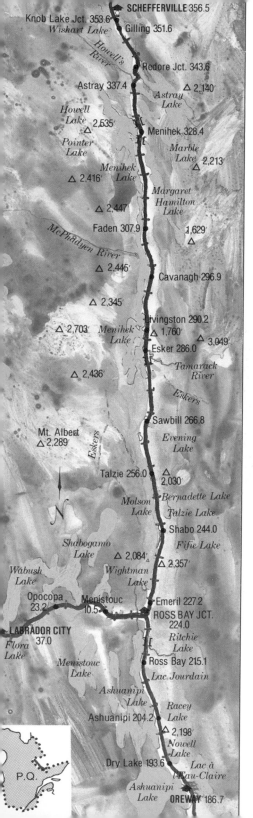

below the entrance to a double tunnel (also lighted) at mile 65. When you emerge 1,047 feet later, you'll have a spectacular view to the west of cliffs, black spruce forest and a 700-foot drop to the river bed. Then, to the west, at mile 68.6, watch for the highlight of your trip — the 200-foot-high Tonkas Falls.

Mile 72-150: Hills become smaller here, and lakes more frequent. At mile 84, there's a huge gravel pit that supplies ballast for the entire railway. Look to the west at miles 77 and 85 to see rapids in the Wacouno River. The first of several great inland lakes appears to the west at mile 100, and extends for 19 miles, as the land flattens out. But you're still climbing, and at mile 148.8 you cross the Québec/Labrador border. This is both the railway's highest point, at 2,066 feet above sea level, and a major watershed, with streams flowing south to the St. Lawrence River or north through the turbines of the Churchill Falls power complex and into the Labrador Sea.

Mile 150-350: Now the trees become more stunted and give way to pale green caribou moss and patches of magenta wildflowers. The terrain for the next 200 miles is largely muskeg — sheer hell for railway builders, but home to roving herds of caribou, which number some 180,000. The tiny settlement at Oreway is an overnight rest stop for freight train crews. At Ross Bay Junction, look west to see a huge glacial boulder. At mile 258, the railway enters the Labrador Trough: a barren wasteland of Precambrian volcanic rock intermingled with granite and serpentine. Esker is a supply stop for the giant Churchill Falls power project; materials travel eastward from here by toll road. A remnant of the airlift that created the railway can be seen to the east at Faden (mile 307.9), in the burned-out shell of a DC-3. The Menihek Dam, which supplies power to Schefferville's mines, is crossed at mile 329.5.

Mile 353-357: At mile 354, you'll have a panoramic view of Schefferville, to the east across Knob Lake. As you approach, remember that an estimated 200 million tons of iron ore exist within a two-mile radius of the town centre.

Ross Bay Junction to Labrador City/Wabush

Mile 0-37: This, too, is an area of fast-flowing rivers and sparkling lakes, much like the scenery between Oreway and Ross Bay. Miles 14 and 25 provide good views of Shabogamo Lake. The twin towns of Labrador City and Wabush lie nestled among hills and lakes, while Smoky Mountain offers the best skiing east of the Laurentians. Nearby is the site of the world's largest open-pit mining operation, which includes a unique electric railway to haul carloads of ore along the west shore of Wabush Lake. It's entirely automated, with special sensors that detect stray caribou on the tracks, and its almost ghostly passage is something to behold.

Passengers on the northbound Labrador can look across Knob Lake at the town of Schefferville

The Labrador Route

Wacouna Subdivision — QNSL Sept Iles/Oreway

This line was built by the Iron Ore Company of Canada between 1950 and 1953.

Miles	Stations	Population	Elev.	Origin of Station Names
0.0	Sept Iles (P.Q.)	35,100	—	The seven islands in the harbour were named by Cartier because they were reminiscent of a place near St. Malo. Formerly called Ichimanipistik (Indian)
6.5	Kemat	—	250	—
8.3	Arnaud Jct.	—	—	Junction with Arnaud Railway to Pointe Noire
18.1	Tellier	—	125	Louis Tellier, MP from 1878 to 1882
27.4	Saumon	—	—	Salmon in nearby Nipisso River
35.6	Nicman	—	225	—
45.3	Nipisso	—	260	Nearby river of same name
57.2	Tika	—	375	Indian for "caribou"
68.4	Tonkas	—	951	Nearby Tonkas Falls
79.6	Premio	—	1,491	—
89.7	Canatiche	—	1,875	—
101.1	Waco	—	1,900	Abbreviation of Wacouna Lake
120.5	Dufresne Lake	—	1,990	Nearby lake
138.0	Eric	—	2,002	—
155.3	Seahorse	—	2,000	Seahorse Lake nearby
165.7	Embar	—	1,875	Abbreviation of Embarrassée River
177.8	Pitaga	—	1,750	—
186.7	Oreway (Lab.)	—	1,700	Iron ore underway

Menihek Subdivision — QNSL Oreway/Schefferville

This line was built by the Iron Ore Company of Canada between 1953 and 1954. The ceremonial "last spike" was driven by Jules Timmins on February 13, 1954.

Miles	Stations	Population	Elev.	Origin of Station Names
186.7	Oreway (Lab.)	—	1,700	(See Wacouna subdivision)
193.6	Dry Lake	—	1,725	Nearby lake that dries up
204.2	Ashuanipi	—	1,750	Indian word meaning "lake with two outlets"
215.1	Ross Bay	—	1,750	Bay of nearby Lake Ashuanipi
224.0	Ross Bay Jct.	123	1,750	Junction with Northern Land Company Limited Railway to Labrador City/Wabush
227.2	Emeril	—	1,760	—
244.0	Shabo	—	1,650	Indian word for "lake of channels"
256.0	Talzie	—	—	—
266.8	Sawbill	—	1,635	Type of duck in the area
286.0	Esker	—	1,610	Esker point in Menihek Lake
290.2	Livingston	—	1,615	Livingston Bay in Menihek Lake
296.9	Cavanagh	—	1,622	—
307.9	Faden	—	1,622	—
328.4	Menihek	—	1,604	Nearby lake and dam
337.4	Astray	—	1,615	Nearby lake
343.6	Redore Jct.	—	—	Junction with line to Redore
351.6	Gilling	—	—	—
353.6	Knob Lake Jct.	—	1,700	Junction with line to iron ore mines at Silver; knoblike mountain
356.5	Schefferville (P.Q.)	3,430	1,705	Mgr. Lionel Scheffer, bishop of Labrador

Wabush Branch — QNSL Ross Bay Jct./Labrador City

This line was built by the Northern Land Company Limited Railway between 1957 and 1960.

Miles	Stations	Population	Elev.	Origin of Station Names
0.0	Ross Bay Jct.	123	1,750	(See Menihek subdivision)
10.5	Menistouc	—	—	—
23.2	Opocopa	—	—	Nearby lake
36.1	Wabush Lake Jct.	—	—	—
37.0	Labrador City/ Wabush	10,169	—	In dispute. Probably from "lavrador" or landholder, title of Joao Fernandes, a Portuguese explorer, and Lavrador in the Azores. Wabush was once known as Carol Lake and is derived from the Amerindian word "waboz," meaning "rabbit"

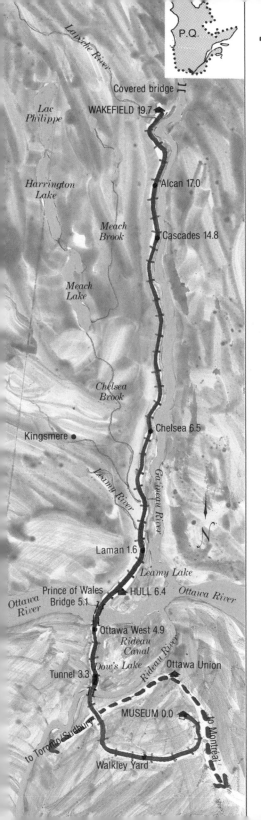

Covered bridge
WAKEFIELD 19.7
Lac Philippe
Harrington Lake
Alcan 17.0
Meach Brook
Cascades 14.8
Meach Lake
Chelsea Brook
Kingsmere
Chelsea 6.5
Leamy River
Gatineau River
N
Laman 1.6
Leamy Lake
Prince of Wales
Ottawa River
Bridge 5.1
HULL 6.4
Ottawa River
Ottawa River
Ottawa West 4.9
Rideau Canal
Rideau River
Tunnel 3.3
Dow's Lake
Ottawa Union
MUSEUM 0.0
to Toronto/Sudbury
to Montreal
Walkley Yard

P.Q.

The Gatineau Route

Ottawa to Wakefield

Ottawa's earliest settlers soon discovered that fortunes were to be made not in farming, but by harvesting the stands of towering white pine that built ships of the British navy. Whole forests that fell under the axes of brawling lumberjacks were floated east to the St. Lawrence ports for shipment overseas. Now you can savour these bygone days with a spectacular ride along the Gatineau River, pulled by a steam locomotive through hills that blaze with colour in the fall.

The Gatineau is powered by engine 1201, built in 1944. It departs from south-central Ottawa, crossing the Rideau River at mile 2.4, then plunging under Dows Lake and the Rideau Canal via a 1,900-foot tunnel — the only one in Canada with signals that warn of flooding. At mile 5.1, you cross the Prince of Wales Bridge over Lemieux Island. To the west are the Little Chaudière Rapids; to the east is a splendid view of the Chaudière Falls, the city of Hull, Québec, and the Parliament Buildings in Ottawa.

North of Laman, you climb Mile Hill, a terraced rock formation left behind by the Champlain Sea 450 million years ago. Ironside (mile 3.0) was the site of the Forsythe Iron Mine, which opened in 1854. North of Chelsea you follow the winding Gatineau River, still packed with floating logs. The most severe congestion occurred at Cascades, where men had to risk their lives to break the jams by hand. Farm Point (mile 16.4), was noted for its quarries; you cross these now-flooded pits on a wooden trestle.

As you approach Wakefield, look east to see the red Gendron covered bridge, measuring 288 feet long. Soon you'll arrive at the former CPR station, where you can enjoy a meal at the Café Pot-au-Feu, go shopping for fresh-baked bread and tourtières, visit the working MacLaren gristmill (1838) and climb a hillside to former prime minister Lester Pearson's simple grave before watching engine 1201 being reversed on a turntable for your return to Ottawa.

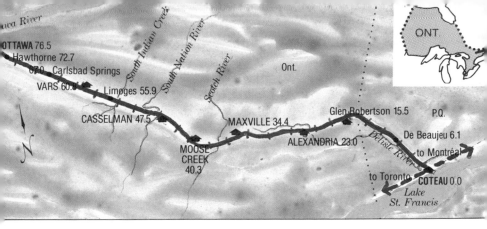

OTTAWA 76.5
Hawthorne 72.7
67.0 Carlsbad Springs
VARS 60.5
Limoges 55.9
CASSELMAN 47.5
MOOSE CREEK 40.3
MAXVILLE 34.4
ALEXANDRIA 23.0
Glen Robertson 15.5
De Beaujeu 6.1
to Montréal
COTEAU 0.0
to Toronto
Lake St. Francis
Ont.
P.Q.
ONT
N
Ottawa River
North Indian Creek
South Indian River
South Nation River
Scotch River
Delisle River

The Laurier and Ottawa Valley Routes

Montréal to Sudbury

For more than 200 years, the Ottawa River was the major link in a chain of waterways joining Montréal and the Great Lakes, via Lake Nipissing and the French River. Etienne Brûlé traveled partway along its length in 1608, returning with Samuel de Champlain in 1613. At Allumette Island, Algonquin Indians warned of hazardous rapids and hostile tribes in the wilderness beyond, but two years later the Frenchmen set out with a party of Huron guides and paddled through to Georgian Bay. Radisson and Groseilliers, Alexander Mackenzie and David Thompson were to follow this same route in their westward explorations; as were the Hudson's Bay and North West Company fur traders who ventured into the vast interior, returning with rich cargoes of beaver, ermine and fox.

Then came the lumber barons, led by Philemon Wright, who founded the city of Hull in 1800. Whole oceans of squared timber came floating down the Madawaska, Petawawa, Bonnechère and Mattawa rivers, then down the Ottawa in great rafts to Québec City. A.K. Egan, H.F. Bryson, E.B. Eddy and J.R. Booth all made fortunes in the lumber trade. Booth was known as "king of the valley." His sawmills were the largest in North America, by 1896 producing a yearly 120 million board feet from holdings that exceeded 7,000 acres.

Permanent settlements didn't appear until construction of the Rideau Canal between 1826 and 1832, but their limestone houses and massive mills were built to last, and can be seen from the train today. The Canada Central Railway erected stone stations all along the line. Some fell into disrepair, or were removed to other sites, but those at Carleton Place and Renfrew survive.

POINTS OF INTEREST
Coteau to Ottawa (Alexandria subdivision)

Note: For points of interest between Montréal and Coteau, see the Lakeshore Route (page 91).

Mile 4-76: Look west at mile 4 to see the stone church at St-Polycarpe. A sign to the north at mile 13 marks the Québec/Ontario border, where town names begin to reflect the British ancestry of the region's first settlers. At mile 22.5, a well-tended golf course appears to the north; the church spires of Alexandria are visible to the south. All along this route you'll see abandoned log houses sitting in the fields. The first is to the south at mile 30, with Greenfield's church in the background. Maxville is the site of the Glengarry Highland Games, the largest such gathering in North America. At mile 40.5, look

85

Stonecliffe 27.7
Moor Lake 15.5
Bass Lake
Deep River
Mackey 19.7
Heart Lake
Wylie 5.3
CHALK RIVER 115.3
Camspur 105.0
Stafford 98.5
Allumette Island
Allumette La
Aylen 45.9
PETAWAWA 103.6
PEMBROKE 93.5
Kath 87.0
Sn R
Petawawa River
ONT.

north to see the town of Moose Creek, with a lovely stone church and cemetery bracketed by tall trees. Casselman's main street is crossed at mile 47.3, followed by a four-span bridge over the South Nation River. The original station at Vars has been removed to a park near Cumberland. Carlsbad Springs once offered relief to arthritis sufferers who came from far and wide to patronize its therapeutic baths.

POINTS OF INTEREST
Carleton Place to Chalk River (Chalk River subdivision)

Mile 17-41: Look south just past the Carleton Place station to the Canadian Wool Growers Factory, once the main repair shop for the Brockville and Ottawa Railway. At mile 17.5 is a beautiful limestone woolen mill, built in 1861. The Mississippi River is crossed at mile 17.6 on a 183-foot bridge, where you'll catch a glimpse of the slate-roofed city hall and St. Andrew's Presbyterian church, with its round stained-glass windows. Carleton Place is noted as the birthplace of A.R. Brown, the WW I air ace who shot down Germany's "Red Baron." Almonte, at mile 23.9, was the home-town of Dr. James Naismith, the inventor of basketball. Look south for its five-sided Wool-stock Mill, built in 1860, standing beside a tumbling waterfall. The countryside from Carleton Place to Pembroke is lush farmland, with sheep grazing in nearby fields. Once, however, it lay beneath the Champlain Sea, an arm of the Atlantic Ocean that extended all the way to Arnprior.

The Mississippi River is crossed again on a 393-foot bridge at mile 32.5; then comes the Madawaska River, crossed on a 319-foot trestle at mile 40.1, with a power dam to the south. To the north you'll see a bridge constructed for the Ottawa, Arnprior and Parry Sound Railway (later absorbed by the CNR), a line financed by J.R.

Crossing the South Nation River near Casselman

Booth to tap the forests of the Madawaska Valley and Algonquin Park. Arnprior's old stone post office, with its distinctive clock tower, is now a lumbering museum. Founded in the early 1800s by a chief of the Clan McNab, who treated the region as his private feudal empire, Arnprior is now the site of the Canadian Civil Defence College and a remarkable underground bunker that's supposed to shelter top-ranked civil servants in the event of nuclear war.

Mile 43-94: The Ottawa River widens into Lac des Chats between miles 43 and 49. Usually this stretch is filled with logging booms, and summer homes can be seen on its banks near Sand Point (mile 46). The settlement on the opposite shore, past a small lighthouse, is Norway Bay, Québec. Look north again between miles 50 and 55 to see several log barns. Renfrew station, to the south at mile 58.8, once served trains of the Kingston and Pembroke Railway, known to its long-suffering employees as the "Kick and Push." A 270-foot bridge crosses the Bonnechère River at mile 59.8; look north to the Renfrew Textiles Mill and the local swimming hole. The distant hills of the Madawaska Valley appear to the south between miles 63 and 64. This section of

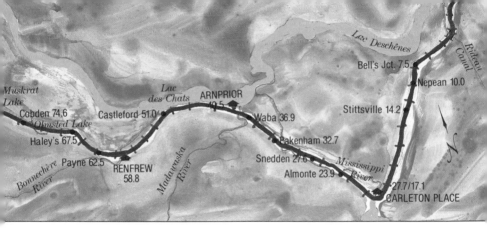

Muskrat Lake

Cobden 74.6
Olmsted Lake
Haley's 67.5
Bonnechère River Payne 62.5
RENFREW 58.8

Castleford 51.0

Lac des Chats

ARNPRIOR 40.5

Madawaska River

Waba 36.9

Pakenham 32.7

Snedden 27.6
Almonte 23.9

Mississippi River

Lac Deschênes

Bell's Jct. 7.5
Nepean 10.0

Stittsville 14.2

Rideau Canal

27.7/17.1
CARLETON PLACE

track parallels the Opeongo Road, a colonization trail, built in the 1850s, which was supposed to run all the way to Lake Superior, but stopped short at Opeongo Lake. A rock cut at mile 64 reveals the huge glacial boulders that thwarted early road builders. Look north between miles 82 and 83 to Muskrat Lake, ringed by attractive summer homes. Allumette Island becomes visible to the north at mile 91. Although the river seems calm from your vantage point, some of Canada's most exciting white water lies just out of sight to the east. Now you approach the outskirts of Pembroke, the first Canadian town to install electric streetlights. The Muskrat River is crossed on a 176-foot bridge at mile 93.6; to the north at mile 94 is the former CPR roundhouse, now occupied by a local industry.

Mile 104-113: The turbulent Petawawa River is crossed at mile 104, just before you enter an artillery range at the Canadian Armed Forces base. Look to the north, and you'll see the reinforced tank crossings on Highway 17. Chalk River is the site of Canada's first nuclear reactor, installed in September 1945 and named ZEEP (for Zero Energy Experimental Pile). Most workers at the plant live seven miles away, in Deep River.

POINTS OF INTEREST
Chalk River to North Bay (North Bay subdivision)

Mile 1-61: Here the terrain becomes more rugged and dotted with lakes; the settlements smaller and farther apart. Bass Lake, at mile 9, is an excellent fishing spot. Look north at mile 19 for a view of the Laurentian Mountains rising in the distance. Construction of the Des Joachims dam, which powers Chalk River's nuclear facility, caused extreme disruption along this stretch of line. The track had to be raised, but the old roadbed is plainly visible to the north between miles 26 and 28. Acres of forest were flooded, creating the driftwood-strewn shoreline of Holden Lake. At mile 33.5 you circle Pine Tree Lake, where a lonely tree remains on a tiny island to the north. The 197-foot bridge over Bissett Creek at mile 38 was once featured in Ripley's "Believe It or Not," when it involved three separate levels. Look for rapids and waterfalls to the south between miles 39 and 40, then look north between miles 50 and 62 to the spot where novice voyageurs were "baptized" on their first trip west. The islands to the north of Aumond Creek,

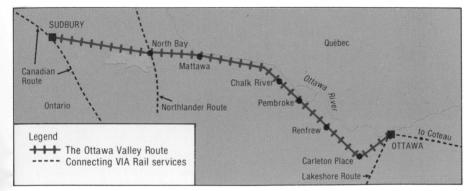

SUDBURY

North Bay

Mattawa

Québec

Canadian Route

Chalk River

Ottawa River

Ontario

Northlander Route

Pembroke

Renfrew

to Coteau

OTTAWA

Legend
+++ The Ottawa Valley Route
----- Connecting VIA Rail services

Carleton Place

Lakeshore Route

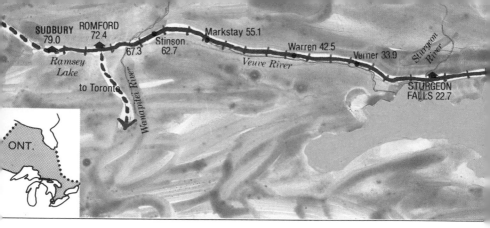

SUDBURY 79.0   ROMFORD 72.4   67.3   Stinson 62.7   Markstay 55.1   Warren 42.5   Verner 33.9   STURGEON FALLS 22.7

Ramsey Lake

to Toronto

Wanapitei River

Veuve River

Sturgeon River

ONT.

Looking north across the Ottawa River at the rugged shore of Québec

(mile 61), served as campgrounds for Champlain and other explorers.

Mile 69-71: Log booms are frequently visible to the north, starting at mile 69. The Ottawa and Mattawa rivers meet at mile 71, a fabulous view captured by Franklin Carmichael, one of the Group

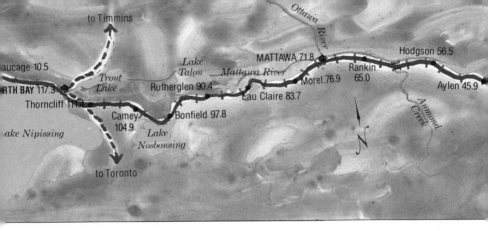

Map labels: to Timmins, Ottawa River, MATTAWA 71.8, Hodgson 56.5, aucage 10.5, Lake Talon, Mattawa River, Rankin 65.0, Trout Lake, Morel. 76.9, RTH BAY 117.3, Rutherglen 90.4, Aylen 45.9, Thorncliff 11, Eau Claire 83.7, Camey 104.9, Bonfield 97.8, Ammond Creek, ake Nipissing, Lake Nosbonsing, to Toronto

of Seven, in a painting now on display in the National Gallery of Canada. In the 1880s, the province of Québec, the Catholic church and the Oblate Fathers decided that colonization of Lake Timiskaming would be spurred by a rail line running north along the Ottawa. Three horse-powered and one steam-driven narrow-gauge railways were built to bypass its rapids — construction that predated the Temiskaming and Northern Ontario Railway from North Bay (see page 112).

Mile 72-117: Nipissing Indian legends termed this wildly beautiful country "the Land of the Sorcerers," and spoke of a man-eating monster that lived in a cave on Lake Talon. Archeologists have discovered strange stone formations nearby, arranged in geometric patterns which they believe to have had religious significance. The valley is part of a 600-million-year-old fracture called the Mattawa Fault. Its towering red cliffs contain an ochre mine. Eau Claire occupies a beautiful setting at mile 83.7; look south here to see rapids and a hillside church. Several beaver dams are visible to the south at the far end of Smith Lake. Rutherglen, at mile 90.4, has a pair of churches facing each other across the track. Look north at mile 94.3 for a glimpse of Lake Talon, then south at mile 97.8 to Bonfield Falls, at the western end of Lake Nosbonsing. The Ontario Northland Railway's main shops are to the north at mile 117, and one of its original steam locomotives, 503, is preserved in Lee Park, to the south at mile 117.3.

Mile 117.3: North Bay holds the world's largest fur auctions five times a year, with sales totaling some $3 million. In 1882, a Methodist clergyman, Reverend Silas Huntington, paddled along Lake Nipissing to the site of today's CPR station and held the city's first church service in a wooden boxcar — an event reenacted 100 years later by parishioners who portaged up from the waterfront.

POINTS OF INTEREST
North Bay to Sudbury (Cartier subdivision)

Mile 1-79: The most spectacular views along this line occur between miles 1 and 13, with Lake Nipissing's waters visible to the south. This huge inland lake, the home of giant pickerel, is 40 miles long by 10 miles wide. Ice-fishing huts dot its surface during the winter months, and in summer the ONR's *Chief Commanda* cruises to the mouth of the French River. Sturgeon Falls was once an important Hudson's Bay Company outpost on the Sturgeon River, crossed at mile 23.8. Now it's noted for a caviar cannery and pulp mills. Then comes a stretch of pleasant farmland spreading on either side of the Veuve River between miles 24 and 61, before you enter the rocky barrens that surround the city of Sudbury. At mile 65, the Inco smokestack, at 1,250 feet the world's tallest, towers on the horizon. The Sudbury Basin — a depression some 35 miles long by 16 miles wide — was formed about 1,700 million years ago when a giant meteorite crashed to earth. Its impact revealed evidence of the region's copper, iron, nickel, gold and platinum deposits, although it wasn't until the late nineteenth century, during construction of the CPR, that these were discovered and exploited.

The Laurier Route

Alexandria Subdivision — CNR Coteau Jct./Ottawa
This line was built by the Montréal and City of Ottawa Junction Railway (later the Canada Atlantic Railway) between 1881 and 1882, and opened for traffic on September 13, 1882. The portion from Hawthorne to Ottawa was relocated in 1966, when the Ottawa area track was rebuilt to accommodate the new Union Station. Passenger trains now running between Montréal and Ottawa use CN's Kingston subdivision between Central Station and Coteau Junction.

Miles	Stations	Population	Elev.	Origin of Station Names
0.0	Coteau Jct. (P.Q.)	—	160	(See Kingston subdivision, page 99)
1.8	Delisle	—	165	Early settler

The southbound Gatineau Steam Train

6.1	De Beaujeu	150	195	G.S. de Beaujeu, seignior of Soulanges
15.5	Glen Robertson (Ont.)	409	261	Scottish glen, named by an early settler
23.0	Alexandria	3,498	—	Rev. Alexander MacDonell, who built the first grist mill. Formerly called Priest's Mills
34.4	Maxville	852	335	Corruption of Macsville, (as so many settlers were "Mac")
40.3	Moose Creek	163	288	Nearby creek
47.5	Casselman	1,422	208	M. Casselman, 1843 pioneer and lumberman, who built a sawmill on the South Nation River
55.9	Limoges	616	—	Limoges, France
60.8	Vars	303	—	—
67.0	Carlsbad Springs	478	—	The mineral springs nearby are reminiscent of a famous Czechoslovakian health spa
72.7	Hawthorne	—	220	(Junction to Ottawa freight yards)
74.5	M & O Junction	—	—	Junction with CPR's Montréal and Ottawa subdivisions
76.5	Ottawa (Ont.)	739,400	212	(See Carleton Place subdivision)

The Ottawa Valley Route

Carleton Place Subdivision — CPR Ottawa/Carleton Place
Chalk River Subdivision — CPR Carleton Place/Chalk River

The line from Ottawa to Carleton Place was opened by the Canada Central Railway in 1870. The line from Carleton Place to Renfrew was opened by the Brockville and Ottawa Railway in 1872, then extended to Pembroke in 1877. The B & O was amalgamated with the Canada Central, which opened the line to Chalk River in 1880.

Miles	Stations	Population	Elev.	Origin of Station Names
0.0	Ottawa(Ont.)	739,400	260	Algonquian tribe named "adawe" (to trade), which controlled the trade on the river. Formerly called By-town, after Colonel John By, builder of the Rideau Canal
7.5	Bell's Jct.	—	—	Hugh Bell, a pioneer, who in 1832 planned the village
10.0	Nepean	—	—	Sir Evan Nepean (1751-1822), under secretary for the colonies
14.2	Stittsville	—	399	Jackson Stitt, who settled in the area in 1818
27.7/ 17.1	Carleton Place	5,020	450	Square in Glasgow, Scotland

23.9	Almonte	3,708	397	Mexican General Juan Almonte (1804-1869)
27.6	Snedden	—	379	—
32.7	Pakenham	350	323	British General Sir Edward M. Pakenham (1778-1815)
36.9	Waba	—	—	—
40.5	Arnprior	6,016	300	The ancestral home of Andrew Buchanan, an early settler in the area
51.0	Castleford	76	307	—
58.8	Renfrew	8,617	417	Renfrewshire, Scotland
62.0	Palmer	—	—	—
62.5	Payne	—	744	—
67.5	Haley's	83	530	Local landowner named Haley
74.6	Cobden	937	475	Richard Cobden (1804-1865), British statesman
80.1	Snake River	—	424	—
87.0	Kathmae	—	—	Kathleen and Mae, daughters of CP Superintendent J.K. Savage
93.5	Pembroke	13,300	381	Sidney Herbert, son of the Earl of Pembroke (1810-1861), secretary to the Admiralty when the name was chosen. Formerly called Sydenham, Moffatt and Miramichie
98.5	Stafford	—	474	Staffordshire, England, home of Sir Charles Bagot, governor-general of Canada from 1842 to 1843
103.6	Petawawa	5,784	376	Indian word meaning "murmuring water"
105.0	Camspur	—	—	—
115.3	Chalk River (Ont.)	1,096	524	Logs were "chalked" or marked in the river here

North Bay Subdivision — CPR Chalk River/North Bay

The segment from Chalk River to Bonfield was built by the Canada Central Railway between 1878 and 1880, and acquired by the CPR in 1881. The segment from Bonfield to North Bay was built by the CPR in 1881.

Miles	Stations	Population	Elev.	Origin of Station Names
0.0	Chalk River (Ont.)	1,096	524	(See Chalk River subdivision)
5.3	Wylie	—	528	James Wylie, member of the Legislative Council of Canada before Confederation in 1867
15.5	Moor Lake	—	666	Early settler called Moor
19.7	Mackey	—	580	Owner of the local lumber company
27.7	Stonecliffe	—	515	Formerly called Rockcliff
45.9	Aylen	—	725	—
56.5	Hodgson	—	506	Local trapper
65.0	Rankin	—	—	Colin Rankin, MP
71.8	Mattawa	2,849	563	Algonquian word meaning "meeting of the waters"
76.9	Morel	—	643	Harry Morel, MP
83.7	Eau Claire	—	591	Nearby "clear water" lake
90.4	Rutherglen	50	789	—
97.8	Bonfield	—	785	James Bonfield, MPP, elected to the Legislature in 1875
104.9	Camey	—	—	First initials of the Dionne quintuplets
111.4	Thorncliff	—	701	Nearby cliff
117.3	North Bay (Ont.)	52,600	659	Bay of nearby Lake Nipissing

Cartier Subdivision — CPR North Bay/Sudbury

This line was built by the CPR and opened in 1883.

Miles	Stations	Population	Elev.	Origin of Station Names
0.0	North Bay (Ont.)	52,600	659	(See North Bay subdivision)
10.5	Beaucage	—	668	Original settler in the area
22.7	Sturgeon Falls	6,400	688	Sturgeon in nearby river
33.9	Verner	877	672	The maiden name of the wife of A. Baker, a general superintendent of the CPR
42.5	Warren	569	689	Dr. Warren, local sawmill owner
55.1	Markstay	375	689	Marks Tey, village in Essex, England
62.7	Stinson	—	864	—
72.4	Romford	—	819	Town in Essex, England
79.0	Sudbury (Ont.)	153,800	855	Town in Suffolk, England

The Lakeshore Route

Along Lake Ontario and the St. Lawrence River on Canada's original intercity rail corridor, past limestone stations, placid countryside and a space-age nuclear facility

Montréal/Ottawa to Toronto

Today you can board an LRC train and travel through one of Canada's most interesting regions in less than four and a half hours; and you can wine and dine in your reclining seat while viewing the landscape in air-conditioned comfort through huge picture windows. On October 27, 1856, passengers on the first trip along this route were faced with quite a different set of circumstances. They departed from either Montréal or Toronto early in the morning, meeting for lunch at Kingston. Each train was powered by one of the Grand Trunk Railway's steam locomotives, which burned a cord of wood every 35 miles and pulled three drafty wooden coaches behind a bright yellow baggage car. The trip took 15 hours and involved 64 stops.

In those days, you'd have peered through small, soot-encrusted windows and a hail of cinders to see sturdy limestone, brick and frame houses, a water-powered generating plant, carefully tended village graveyards, fine old stone stations, passenger steamers on the Rideau and Trent-Severn canal systems and swimmers in long bathing suits frolicking on Fairport Beach. Today, of course, the soot and cinders are gone, but many of the old landmarks remain. New additions include a nuclear power plant, sprawling suburban areas, modern glass and steel stations, apple orchards, cornfields, farms and an international fleet of huge, ocean-going ships sailing majestically along the St. Lawrence Seaway. This route between Québec and Ontario (once called Upper and Lower Canada) is a unique study in contrasts.

POINTS OF INTEREST
Ottawa-Brockville (Beachburg, Smiths Falls and Brockville subdivisions)

For the first few miles out of Ottawa's Union Station, look north to see the skyline, framed by the Gatineau Hills. At mile 5.7, as you cross the Rideau

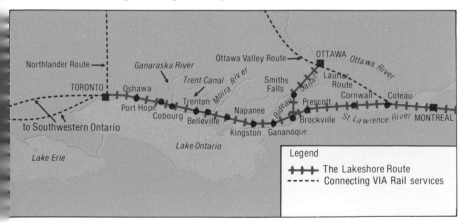

Legend
+++ The Lakeshore Route
----- Connecting VIA Rail services

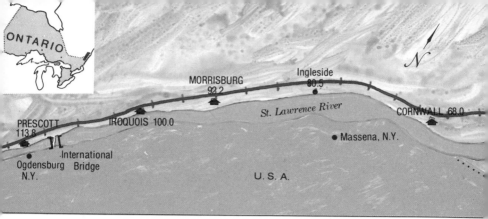

ONTARIO

PRESCOTT 113.8
IROQUOIS 100.0
MORRISBURG 92.2
Ingleside 80.5
CORNWALL 68.0

St. Lawrence River

International
Ogdensburg Bridge
N.Y.

Massena, N.Y.

U. S. A.

N

Etienne Brûlé and his companions at the mouth of the Humber River

Public Archives of Canada C-73635

Canal, look south to where pleasure boats now sail. Once this was the Champlain Sea — a huge, postglacial lake, where archeologists have found the skeletons of ancient marine creatures.

After leaving Smiths Falls, look east at mile 1.1 to see the Hershey Chocolate plant. At mile 1.2 are bridges over the Rideau Canal and river. Construction of the canal was financed by the British government to create a route between Upper and Lower Canada less vulnerable to attack by the United States than the one along the St. Lawrence River. Lieutenant-Colonel John By of the Royal Engineers was in charge of carving a 126-mile route through the largely wilderness area from Kingston to Ottawa (once named Bytown in his honour). Many of the men who built the canal between 1826 and 1832 died of "swamp fever" (thought to be malaria or typhus), because of "noxious fumes" rising from the

Cranberry Marsh. The canal system includes 47 locks at 23 stations, with such exotic names as Black Rapids, Old Slys and Poonamalie Locks.

Just before arriving at Brockville, at mile 27.6, look south to glimpse the portal of a 1,720-foot tunnel that passes under city hall.

POINTS OF INTEREST
Montréal-Brockville (Kingston subdivision)

Mile 20-24: Those pigs and cows you might see to the north at mile 20 are "on campus," at McGill University's experimental farm. Just beyond are fields of corn and a giant arboretum; classrooms, laboratories and student residences lie to the south. At mile 21.4, look north as you cross a 1,370-foot bridge over the Ottawa River. The river was used for two centuries by fur traders, explorers and missionaries as a route between Montréal and the Great Lakes, via Lake Nipissing and the French River. Etienne Brûlé, the first white man to live among the Indians, traveled this route as early as 1608. At mile 24, as you again cross the Ottawa River, look north. In front of the Laurentian Mountains is Lake of Two Mountains, once a stopping place for fur traders heading west and the scene of fierce clashes between Indians and the French.

Parks Canada Brian Morin

A freighter with a cargo of manufactured goods sails down the St. Lawrence River

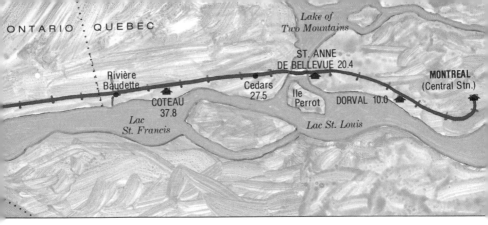

One of the gravestones beside the Blue Church is that of Barbara Heck, the founder of Methodism in North America

Mile 43.6: The peaceful Québec town of Rivière Beaudette is the last before the Québec/Ontario border. At mile 45.1, look north for a small white and red sign that marks the provincial boundary.

Mile 49: The mighty St. Lawrence River, Canada's third longest, flows for 1,900 miles, from Lake Ontario to the Atlantic Ocean, and defines Ontario's southern border with the United States. Between miles 49 and 51, the river can be glimpsed against a backdrop of the Adirondack Mountains.

Mile 65-103: When the St. Lawrence Seaway was built in the 1950s, as a joint project of Canada and the United States, nearly 40 miles of track and seven stations were submerged. At mile 65, the original route through Cornwall, now only a spur, is evident to the south. At mile 80.5 is the new

town of Ingleside, created for the displaced citizens of Aultsville, Farran's Point, Woodland's, Nickinson's Landing and Wales. The original Aultsville station, as well as the other stations' nameboards, is carefully preserved at nearby Upper Canada Village. In 1958, modern glass and brick stations were built on the new route at Morrisburg (mile 92.2) and Iroquois (mile 100). Look south at mile 103 for a glimpse of Iroquois, where 157 buildings and 1,000 residents from several miles around were relocated.

Mile 105-121: Huge tankers and freighters are common sights on this part of the St. Lawrence River. At mile 111, the graceful International Bridge, linking Canada and Ogdensburg, New York, soars over huge grain elevators. At mile

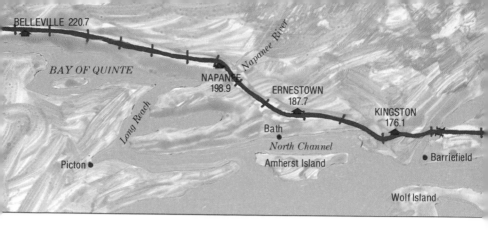

BELLEVILLE 220.7

Napanee River

BAY OF QUINTE

NAPANEE
198.9

Long Reach

ERNESTOWN
187.7

Bath

KINGSTON
176.1

North Channel

Picton •

Amherst Island

• Barriefield

Wolf Island

At Kingston Mills VIA's Canadian crosses the first of 47 locks on the Rideau Canal, which extends from Kingston to Ottawa

112.5, watch for the original tracks of the Bytown and Prescott Railway (now CP), which pass underneath your train. This pioneer railway, opened in 1854, provided the first rail passenger service to Bytown (Ottawa), then a city of 10,000 persons. At mile 113.8, look south to the original stone station at Prescott.

Mile 116.5: The pretty clapboard Blue Church to the south, built in 1845, has always been painted that colour, though no one knows quite why. Barbara Heck, founder of Methodism in North America, is buried in the adjacent graveyard.

Mile 125: To the south is Canada's oldest and most unusual railway tunnel. Completed in 1859, it's the only one in eastern Canada with doors to prevent ice forming on its roof. Closed in the 1960s, it was used for almost 100 years by the Brockville and Ottawa Railway (later CPR) to gain access to the waterfront.

POINTS OF INTEREST
Brockville-Trenton (Kingston subdivision)

Mile 128-141: Here the placid terrain suddenly changes to rugged rock cuts, pine trees and wilderness areas. At mile 128.5, a farmer struggles to raise sheep and chickens on a small farm in the valley to the south. Between miles 131 and 132, and miles 142 and 143, are curved rock cuts and beautiful banks of windswept trees, with not a house in sight. This is how pioneers of the 1850s must have viewed this part of Ontario. At mile 134, the small, neat cemetery for the hamlet of Yonge's Mills is split in two by the tracks.

Mile 155.3: Some additional history for railway buffs: just west of Gananoque station to the south are the tracks of the 6.33-mile-long Thousand Islands Railway (now CN), built in 1889 to link the town of Gananoque on the St. Lawrence River

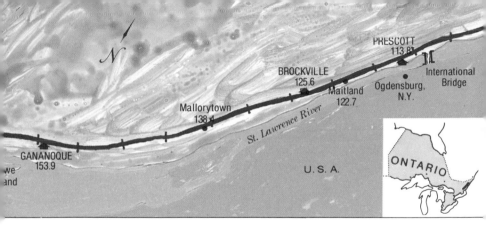

with the Grand Trunk Railway. There were four stops: Cheeseboro, next to a cheese factory; Cemetery (where else in Canada could you take a train to a funeral?); downtown Gananoque, where passengers fished right from the train windows; and, finally, the waterfront station, where holiday-ers could board cruise ships to circle the Thousand Islands. The station is now a restaurant, but modern cruise ships continue to tour the islands.

Mile 169.4: At Kingston Mills the train crosses the Rideau Canal once more. To the north are a waterfall, locks and the Cataraqui River. To the south, you'll see more locks and a rocky gorge.

Mile 171-176: Look south at mile 172 to see the Great Cataraqui River and St. Mark's, an 1844-vintage, Gothic-style church, high on the hill in Barriefield. The church, financed by a grant from the British Admiralty, was established for the early settlers who worked nearby in the Kingston naval yards. At mile 173, you'll pass through a long limestone cut, the stone used in so many

Kingston Mills blockhouse on the Rideau Canal

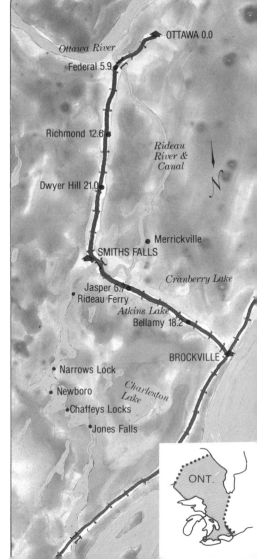

ONTARIO

Rouge River

Whitby 305.0   OSHAWA 302.2   Newtonville 278.3

Frenchman Bay

GUILDWOOD
321.2

TORONTO (Union Stn.)
333.8

L A K E

The town of Napanee has one of the most beautiful settings of any in Ontario

Kingston area homes. The new modern station at Kingston mile 176.1, serves a busy industrial and educational centre that has been, in succession, an Indian village, French fortress, British citadel and the capital of Canada. Kingston was also the home of Sir John A. Macdonald, Canada's first prime minister.

Mile 177: The red roof and thick walls of Kingston Penitentiary are visible to the south. Some of its most famous "guests" include Norman (Red) Ryan, Toronto gang leader and bank robber of the 1920s, who escaped.

Mile 180-194: In this area are good views to the south: sparkling Collins Bay at mile 180; a scarecrow at mile 182; the North Channel and Amherst Island at mile 183; the tall towers of a coal-fired generating plant near Bath, at mile 191; and picturesque farms at the crossing of Big Creek, at mile 193.6.

Mile 198-199: Napanee has one of the most beautiful settings of any Ontario town. Look south across the golf course at mile 198 for a good view.

At mile 198.5, while crossing the Napanee River, look south again. You'll see waterfalls in Springside Park, where in 1780 a sawmill and grist mill formed the nucleus of today's town. The limestone town hall is followed at mile 198.9 by an old and attractive stone station.

Mile 206-214: At mile 206, keep looking south across the Long Reach toward Picton and the mountain at Glenora. On top of this precipice is the unusual Lake-on-the-Mountain (called Onokenoga — Lake of the Gods — by the Hurons), which is 120 feet deep. The Salmon River is crossed at mile 212.1; look south at its small waterfall. Beyond is the ghost town of Milltown, a bustling village with 21 shops in the 1850s. Soon you'll see the Bay of Quinte, with Big Island in the background, at mile 213.7.

Mile 221.1: Early Loyalist settlers established two mills on the Moira River, which helped make Belleville so prosperous that residents petitioned Queen Victoria to designate their city the capital of Canada. She must have said "We are not amused."

Mile 232.2: Look north to see the Trent River, part of a 240-mile-long system of canals and locks that join Lake Ontario to Georgian Bay. Started in 1835, the Trent-Severn waterway traces the centuries-old route of Indians and explorers. Its 45 lock stations were built so barges and steamers could carry timber and passengers past the upper rapids.

POINTS OF INTEREST
Trenton-Toronto (Kingston subdivision)

Mile 233-264: Between Trenton Junction and Cobourg is a "Grandma Moses" landscape: white frame and red brick farmhouses, rolling hills, cornfields and apple orchards. Every so often Highway 2, the heritage route that once formed the only road link between Upper and Lower Canada, comes into view. Lake Ontario, the most eastern of the Great Lakes, and the smallest, with

RT HOPE
270.7

COBOURG
264.0

Grafton 256.1

BRIGHTON 240.8

*Presqu'Ile
Bay*

TRENTON JCT
232.8

*Trent
River*

BELLEVILLE 220.7

River

O N T A R I O

N

The Pickering Nuclear Generating Station looms to the east across Frenchman Bay

a total area of just over 11,200 square miles, is also frequently visible. To the north, at mile 236, is a windmill belonging to a local nursery, followed at mile 260 by the Pentecostal Bible Camp — an ideal spot for meditation right on the shore. Cobourg, at mile 264, is the home town of the internationally famous silent-screen actress Marie Dressler.

Mile 267-275: The views of Lake Ontario become even more spectacular. At mile 267.5, the lake is so close to the train that birds on a nearby sandbar are right outside your window. There you'll see an unusual lighthouse just offshore. At mile 270.3, the train crosses a curved, 1,232-foot trestle over the Ganaraska River, providing a good view of the harbour to the south and Port Hope's churches to the north. This town was first an Indian settlement called Cochingomink, then a trading post called Smith's Creek. Renamed Toronto in 1817, it lost out to an upstart two years later and became Port Hope. Its tree-lined streets feature gracious homes in Georgian, Regency, Victorian Gothic and Italianate architectural styles, some with "Deep South" porches and pillars. Look for the original stone station at mile 270.7. A sandy beach at mile 271 is followed by the clay bluffs of Port Britain at mile 272. One of the most pastoral scenes on this route appears at mile 274.5: a farm, valley with stream, and Lake Ontario in the background.

Mile 276-291: A coal-fired generating plant to the south intrudes upon this peaceful landscape at mile 276, followed by more orchards and cornfields between miles 281 and 284. Watch for a goose farm to the south, at mile 282.

Mile 297-302: Darlington Provincial Park lies in a sylvan setting to the south, at mile 297.5. Just across from the modern Oshawa station, at mile 302, is the sprawling General Motors automobile plant. Robert McLaughlin started doing business on this very site in 1877 when he formed the British Empire's largest carriage works. By 1907, the McLaughlin Motor Car Company was producing some of the best-designed automobiles in Canada, but in 1918, the firm was sold to its present owners. Parkwood Mansion, the McLaughlin family home, with its richly-furnished 55 rooms, gives visitors a rare insight into a bygone era.

Mile 305: Some people believe old railway stations should never die. To the south is the 1903 CN Whitby station, now a gallery for local craftsmen.

Mile 313: The Pickering Nuclear Generating Station, the world's second-largest natural uranium nuclear plant, sits in solitude across Frenchman Bay, at mile 313. Day or night, it's an imposing sight. If you're interested, or just want to become an informed critic, there are impressive displays in the Nuclear Communications Centre. This plant currently produces two million kilowatts of electricity, and is expected to double that output by 1985. Its huge domes stand in sharp contrast to the nearby Pickering Museum, with its circa 1830 log cabin.

Mile 316-333: Watch for sun worshippers on Fairport Beach when crossing the Rouge River at mile 316.1. The next few miles afford sweeping views of Lake Ontario to the south. At mile 318.3, the Scarborough Bluffs loom like stony ghosts in the distance ahead, marking your final approach through Toronto's suburbs to Union Station.

VIA's new LRC (light, rapid, comfortable) train

The original stone station at Prescott

The Lakeshore Route

Beachburg Subdivision — CNR Ottawa/Federal
Smiths Falls Subdivision — CNR Federal/Smiths Falls East
Brockville Subdivision — CPR Smiths Falls/Brockville

The segment from Ottawa to Federal was relocated in 1966 when the new Ottawa station was opened. The segment from Federal to Smiths Falls East was built by the Canadian Northern Ontario Railway, and opened for traffic on December 30, 1913. Passenger trains now running between Ottawa and Toronto use CN's Kingston subdivision between Brockville and Toronto.

Miles	Stations	Population	Elev.	Origin of Station Names
0.0	Ottawa (Ont.)		212	(See Alexandria subdivision. page 90)
3.4	Ellwood Jct.			—
5.2	Wass	739,400		(Junction to Ottawa freight yards)
5.9	Federal			Federal government complex nearby
0.0	Federal	—	—	—
12.6	Richmond	2,667	321	Charles Lennox, third Duke of Richmond
21.0	Dwyer Hill	—		Early settler
34.1	Smiths Falls East		380	Junction between CNR and CPR
0.0	Smiths Falls	9,280	423	Early settler who built a mill on the waterfall
6.7	Jasper	228	—	—
18.2	Bellamy	—	393	—
27.8	Brockville (Ont.)	19,600	281	(See Kingston subdivision)

Kingston Subdivision—CNR Montreal/Toronto

Most of this route was built by the Montreal and Kingston Railway or the Kingston and Toronto Railway, both of which later became the Grand Trunk Railway. The opening dates for traffic on the various lines are as follows: Dorval to Brockville, November 19, 1855; Brockville to Belleville, October 27, 1856; and Belleville to Oshawa, October 7, 1856. Part of the route between Montreal and Dorval is on the Montreal and Lachine Railway, which opened in November 1847.

Miles	Stations	Population	Elev.	Origin of Station Names
0.0	Montreal (P.Q.)	2.8 million	47	Mount Royal (originally called Ville Marie)
10.0	Dorval		86	—
19.6	Caron		123	—
20.4	St. Anne-de-Bellevue		113	—
27.5	Cedars	421	161	Cedar trees in vicinity
37.8	Coteau	869	159	Small hill on portage opposite rapids
38.0	Coteau Jct.	—	160	—
39.8	Coteau-Ouest		—	—
52.4	Garry (Ont.)	—	169	—
65.4	Regis		183	—
68.0	Cornwall	44,500	193	Duke of Cornwall, eldest son of reigning sovereign
69.4	Wesco		220	—
74.0	Bergin	—	—	—
83.4	Crysler	498	246	—
92.2	Morrisburg	2,188	266	Hon. James Morris. Postmaster-General in 1860
100.0	Iroquois	1,278	242	Indian tribe
102.9	Galop	—	300	—
113.8	Prescott	4,975	310	Robert Prescott, Governor-in-Chief of Canada from 1797 to 1807
118.4	Brockem	—	310	—
122.7	Maitland	502	331	Sir Peregrine Maitland, Lt.-Gov. of Upper Canada 1818-1828
125.6	Brockville	19,600	281	Major-General Sir Isaac Brock, Canadian hero of the War of 1812
125.8	Perth	—	—	—
127.4	Lyn		547	—
138.4	Mallory-town	310	338	Mallory Family, United Empire Loyalist pioneers
152.3	Leeds	—	325	F.G. Osborne, 5th Duke of Leeds
153.9	Gananoque	5,103	346	Indian for "rocks rising out of the water" (Thousand Islands)
162.0	Kings	—	354	—
174.9	Queens	—	264	—
176.1	Kingston	92,900	254	Originally "Kingstown" after King George III
187.7	Ernestown	—	325	Prince Ernest Augustus, 5th son of King George III
190.8	Bath	762	358	English city, founded by Romans in 1st century BC
198.9	Napanee	4,844	315	Indian "Nan-pan-nay" (flour) from local milling industry
199.7	Napanee West			
202.0	Mohawk	—	292	—
209.1	Marysville	—	335	—
218.9	Quinte	—	304	Iroquois Indian village called "Quents"
219.2	Wilson	—	555	—
219.5	Belleville East		—	—
220.4	Center	—	—	—
220.7	Belleville	34,900	286	Wife Arabella, of Lt.-Gov. Gore
220.9	Moira	—	—	—
231.7	Trenton	35,200	284	Reversal of "on the Trent." River Trent in England
232.8	Trenton Jct.	—		
240.8	Brighton	3,199	304	Abbreviation of Saxon Bishop Brighthelmstone
256.1	Grafton	349	283	—
264.0	Cobourg	11,300	299	Spouse of Queen Victoria, Prince Albert of Saxe-Cobourg Gotha
267.5	Coport	—	262	—
270.7	Port Hope	9,788	288	Col. Henry Hope, Lt.-Gov. of Quebec 1785-1789
278.3	Newtonville	—	396	—
287.0	Clarke	—	415	—
288.8	Clarke West	—	—	—
299.6	Oshawa East			
302.2	Oshawa	116,425	327	Indian for "carrying place" There was an old portage here from Lake Ontario to Lake Scugog
303.3	Oshawa West			
304.9	Whitby	28,173	277	Seaport in Yorkshire, England
311.4	Pickering Jct.		—	—
312.9	Pickering		291	Town in Yorkshire, England
313.0	Liverpool			—
317.3	Rouge Hill		267	Originally called Port Union
321.2	Guildwood		405	—
323.2	Eglinton		—	—
325.2	Scarborough	2.9 million	543	Town in England with similar craggy cliffs
327.0	Geco		—	—
328.6	Danforth		426	Asa Danforth, builder of the 100 Mile Road to Bay of Quinte in 1800
332.4	Cherry St.		—	—
333.8	Toronto (Ont.)		275	Iroquois Indian "Thoron-to-hen" (timber in the water)

The Tecumseh, International and Maple Leaf Routes

Canada's busiest rail passenger network links Toronto with Southwestern Ontario, taking you through Mennonite farmland or straight to the grandeur of Niagara Falls

The Great Western Railway's groundbreaking ceremony took place at London, Ontario, on October 23, 1849. Having turned the first sod, Colonel Thomas Talbot and his fellow dignitaries enjoyed a banquet that featured 17 sorts of meat, including porcupine. Service began between Hamilton and Niagara Falls in November 1853, reaching London the following month and Windsor in January 1854. Express trains took more than 10 hours to travel the entire route, after which passengers continued by paddlewheel steamer to Detroit.

The Great Western was a luxurious and innovative line that introduced Canada's first postal car with letter-sorting facility (1854), the first parlour cars and sleepers (1860) and the first diners (1876). It also created havoc by building to a five foot, six inch gauge at a time when the standard was four feet, eight and a half inches. In 1864, a third rail was installed to accommodate mixed-gauge trains. Despite horrific switching problems, this continued until the whole system was standardized in 1873.

Today, the Southwestern Ontario services consist of three separate routes: from Toronto to Windsor, Sarnia and Niagara Falls. They carry 5,000 passengers on 19 return trains a day — more than the Toronto-Ottawa and Toronto-Montréal routes combined. Through trains operate to New York and Chicago; intercity trains link with GO Transit's commuter service at Oakville and Georgetown.

Some of Canada's oldest and most interesting stations are still in use along the lines,

at Brantford, Brampton, Guelph and Kitchener. Grimsby's station is a one-of-a-kind Victorian wonder and Georgetown's is an absolute gem, while the washrooms at Dundas and Wyoming have a time-capsule quality all their own. Other stations, such as those at Oakville, London and Windsor, are impressively modern. Many of these routes were also witness to high drama and peculiar superstition. In 1936, the London brewing magnate John Labatt was abducted and taken by train to Muskoka, but released before his kidnappers obtained the $50,000 ransom. Whenever the Toronto Maple Leafs traveled to Chicago, their coach, Punch Imlach, would ride in nothing but the Fisher sleeping car — a fetish that may or may not have improved his team's performance on the ice.

POINTS OF INTEREST
Toronto to London (Oakville and Dundas subdivisions)

Mile 0-37: To the south, at mile 1.1, is historic Fort York, the scene of a bitter battle on April 27, 1813, between the defending garrison and 1,700 American invaders. Between miles 2 and 3, you pass the Canadian National Exhibition, the world's largest annual fair, which has attracted millions of visitors since it began in 1879. Look north between miles 4 and 5 to the 339 wooded acres of High Park. The placid stretch of water is Grenadier Pond, a well-stocked, big-city fishing hole. After crossing the Humber River at mile 5 and Mimico Creek at mile 5.9, look for GO Transit's main shops to the north at mile 6.7. This provincially operated network has been serving commuters since 1967, and you'll see its distinctive green and white bilevel cars between Toron-

The eastbound VIA train crosses the Grand River at Paris, Ontario

to and Oakville. Etobicoke Creek is crossed at mile 9.8. Look south while crossing the Credit River at mile 13.3 to see hopeful fishermen and racing sculls heading downstream to the harbour. Sixteen Mile Creek (sometimes called Oakville Creek) is crossed at mile 21.7 on a 490-foot trestle running 90 feet above the water. In Old Oakville, some two dozen buildings, the earliest dating from the 1830s, remind visitors that the city once boasted a flourishing shipbuilding industry. At mile 25.9, you cross Twelve Mile Creek (Bronte Creek) on a 558-foot bridge, 75 feet high. Look south at Bayview for a glimpse of Hamilton Harbour, with ocean-going vessels and hundreds of pleasure craft side by side.

Mile 0-19: For several miles the train passes through Hamilton's Royal Botanical Gardens — 2,000 acres of lush growth, with the Desjardins

Canal to the south. Look north and you'll see the Canada Crushed Stone plant perched on a high bluff where electric trains haul rock from nearby quarries. Now you begin a climb up the Niagara Escarpment, running along a ridge, through rock cuts and over deep gorges, before arriving in the town of Dundas, set in its sheltered valley with Hamilton's skyline still visible in the distance to the south. Construction of this section of line quite literally bogged down, with an almost bottomless marsh near Lynden taking two years to fill. At mile 18.6, Fairchild Creek is crossed on a 594-foot trestle running 65 feet above the valley floor.

Mile 23-25: Brantford's station, built in 1904, has an aristocratic air, with its tall brick tower and high-domed waiting room. Some historians disagree, but a Brantford designer, Thomas Burn-

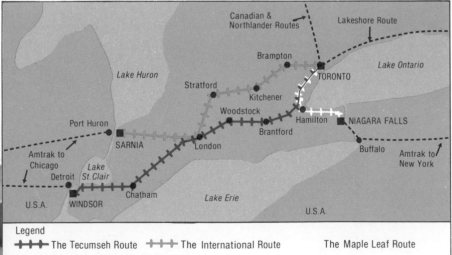

Legend
╋╋╋ The Tecumseh Route   ┿┿┿ The International Route   The Maple Leaf Route
------ Connecting VIA Rail and Amtrak services

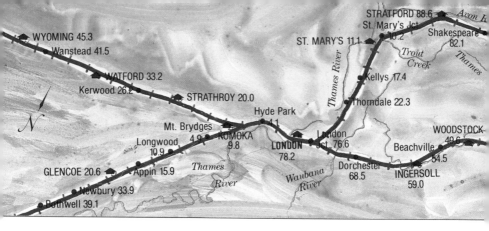

ley, claimed to have produced the world's first sleeping car in 1859 for a special train that carried the Prince of Wales on tour the following year. Painted a royal blue, its interior was fitted with spacious bunks, thick rugs, silk drapes and upholstered chairs. Unfortunately, Burnley failed to patent his invention, losing millions to George Pullman, an American whose name became synonymous with sleeping cars of any description. Brantford is also noted for other events. This is where Alexander Graham Bell developed the telephone in 1874 and completed the first long-distance call on August 10, 1876. His homestead, and Canada's first telephone office, have been maintained as museums. In 1784, the Mohawk chief Joseph Brant led a band of Six Nations Indians from upper New York State to the Grand River Valley, where they were granted land by the Crown for their loyalty to the British during the American Revolution. Her Majesty's Chapel of the Mohawks, built the following year, can still be visited today. Farther south on the Grand River is Chiefswood, the birthplace of Pauline Johnson, the beloved Indian poet. As you leave Brantford, look south at mile 24 to the entrance of Glenhyrst Gardens, a grand 11-room home surrounded by another floral showplace. Just beyond, to the north, an old wooden boxcar serves as a tourist information centre.

Mile 29-78: A sweeping curve between miles 29 and 31 affords superb views of Paris and the Grand River. Look south at mile 29.8 to see track belonging to the Lake Erie and Northern Railway, a former electrified interurban line. The Grand River is crossed at mile 30.1 on a 767-foot trestle, 100 feet high; look south to view a picturesque waterfall. The town of Paris was noted for its plaster of paris deposits and curative sulphur springs. The Nith River is bridged at mile 34. Woodstock's two-storey station was built in 1853 — one of several interesting buildings that include St. Paul's Church (whose bell tower is said to have been used to hold prisoners during the 1837 Rebellion) and the courthouse, whose remarkable limestone façade includes carved monkeys. There's even a statue of a cow, Springbank Snow Countess, honouring her monumental butterfat production over a 17-year lifetime. Several quarries lie to the south near mile 57. Ingersoll, with a station dating from 1878, is famous for its cheese. The first factory was established in 1864, and in 1866 local residents shipped a mammoth 7,300-pound Cheddar to England to advertise their wares. The Waubuno River is crossed at mile 72.2, just before arrival in London, whose tree-lined streets bear very English names (Oxford, Regent and Kensington). So do its bridges (Blackfriars and Westminster), and even its courthouse is a copy of Ireland's Malahide Castle.

Joseph Brant, the Mohawk chief after whom Brantford is named, stands at the Grand River

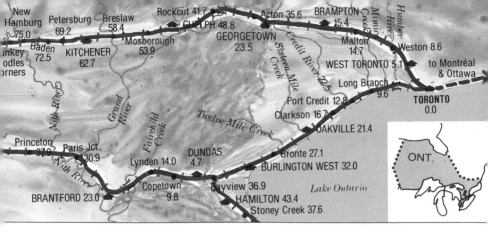

New Hamburg 75.0
Petersburg 69.2
Breslaw 58.4
Rockcut 41.7
GUELPH 48.8
Acton 35.6
BRAMPTON 15.4
Mosborough 53.9
GEORGETOWN 23.5
Malton 14.7
Weston 8.6
Baden 72.5
KITCHENER 62.7
WEST TORONTO 5.1
to Montréal & Ottawa
nkey odles rners
Long Branch 9.6
Credit River 22.5
Port Credit 12.8
Clarkson 16.7
TORONTO 0.0
Princeton 31.0
Paris Jct. 30.9
Lynden 14.0
DUNDAS 4.7
OAKVILLE 21.4
Bronte 27.1
ONT.
Copetown 9.8
Bayview 36.9
BURLINGTON WEST 32.0
Lake Ontario
BRANTFORD 23.0
HAMILTON 43.4
Stoney Creek 37.6
Sixteen Mile Creek
Twelve Mile Creek
Fairchild Creek
Grand River
Nith River
With River
Humber River
Mimic Creek

POINTS OF INTEREST
London to Windsor (Longwood and Chatham subdivisions)

Mile 0-48: The Thames River is bridged at miles 0.4 and 1.4; the second crossing takes place on a 566-foot bridge, 70 feet high. The station at Glencoe, with its stamped-tin interior panels, represents typical 1890s railway architecture. This is the terminus of the Canada Air Line Railway, on which P.T. Barnum's famous elephant, the 13,000-pound Jumbo, fatally collided with a locomotive on September 15, 1885. The Tecumseh route takes its name from a courageous and eloquent leader of the Shawnee tribe who aided Major-General Isaac Brock in defeating the Americans at Fort Detroit during the War of 1812. He died during the battle of Moraviantown, quite near present-day Thamesville, on October 5, 1812. An inscribed boulder commemorates the event, but his actual grave remains unknown. The Thames River is crossed for the final time at mile 47.6.

Mile 60-105: Chatham was "end of the line" for the Underground Railroad, an escape route organized by abolitionists to free American slaves. Now it's the centre of a rich agricultural area that sometimes experiences severe heat waves. The worst occurred in July 1936, when temperatures reached 105° F every day for a week, resulting in many deaths. Starting at mile 76, the Tecumseh follows the shoreline of Lake St. Clair. This district is known as Sun Parlour Country, and enjoys Canada's longest growing season. Watch for fields of corn, soybeans, tomatoes and wheat, peach and cherry orchards, and thriving vineyards. Farther south, giant greenhouses produce exotic houseplants and cacti, as well as oranges, lemons and bananas. Be on the lookout here for migratory birds, winging their way to the Jack Miner Bird Sanctuary at Kingsville, to the south.

Windsor's station is actually located at Walkerville, next to a major distillery. Prohibition in the U.S. brought about an instant boom in the Canadian liquor trade, and the Detroit River was *the* major waterway for illicit traffic. (Today, it remains one of the world's busiest shipping channels, handling more than 16,000 vessels every year.) The original station stood on what is now the waterfront Dieppe Gardens, where you can see steam locomotive 5588, the Spirit of Windsor. For many years, whole trains were carried across to Detroit aboard an iron-hulled ferry named the *Lansdowne*. Along with two Skyview lounge cars that once served on the Ocean route between Montréal and Halifax, it's preserved as part of a restaurant complex on the American side. Now, of course, you can visit Detroit by traveling through the world's only international underwater road tunnel, or over the majestic Ambassador suspension bridge.

POINTS OF INTEREST
Toronto to Sarnia (Weston, Halton, Guelph, Thorndale and Strathroy subdivisions)

Mile 1-17: After passing through Toronto's industrial suburbs, the International crosses the Humber River at mile 9.6. Look south here for views of the Weston Golf and Country Club. To the north, at mile 13.5, is Woodbine Race Track, home since 1956 of the prestigious Queen's Plate, first run in 1860. Mimico Creek is crossed at mile 13.7; to the south you'll see the runways and terminal buildings of Toronto International, Canada's busiest airport.

Mile 15-24: The Brampton station's somewhat stern design is softened by arches, turrets and a large porte-cochère, built to protect passengers arriving in horse-drawn carriages. Brampton is known as "Flower Town"; its commercial greenhouses cover an area as large as 24 football fields. The Credit River is crossed at mile 22.5 on

U.S.A.

DETROIT

WINDSOR 105.6

Tecumseh 99.0

Lake St. Clair

Puce River

Belle River

Belle River 90.0

Essex

Stoney Point 82.0

Jeanette's Creek 75.4

Prairie Siding 69.0

Thames River

Northwood 52.6

CHATHAM 61.6

a limestone bridge built in 1857. This same stone, quarried at nearby Limehouse, was used to build the handsome station at Georgetown. (When the railway reached this point, Georgetown was a tiny village called Hungry Hollow. A day trip to Toronto was a study in endurance, with shaken passengers sitting on benches nailed to the boxcar floors.)

Mile 33-59: Now you enter the scenic Credit Valley, an area noted for its fall colours. Near Rockwood (mile 41.2), are a number of large potholes, the result of granite being ground into softer limestone by retreating glaciers. This same glacial action produced the Eramosa River Valley, crossed on a 532-foot bridge at mile 41. To the north is Rockwood Academy, a boys' boarding school established in 1850. The original CN station has been moved several miles south, to the Halton County Railway, a project that re-creates a portion of the electrified line that once linked Toronto and Guelph. You cross the Speed River at mile 48.5 on a 493-foot bridge; look north here to see a power dam and an attractive park containing CN steam locomotive 6167. Guelph's station, built in 1911, combines Gothic and Italianate architectural styles. Just behind it is the imposing city hall. Guelph was settled in 1827 by English and Scottish immigrants, who built to last; at one time a city bylaw required that every structure on the main street have a limestone façade. Farther west, at mile 58.7, the Grand River is crossed on a 413-foot bridge.

Mile 62-89: Kitchener's red brick station was built in 1897. In those days, its platform was piled high with the maple and beech logs used for firing steam locomotives, and a stagecoach would meet every train, taking passengers north to Elmira. Founded by Pennsylvania Mennonites in 1799, it was originally known as Ebytown, but was renamed Berlin in 1833, after an influx of German settlers. It changed name again in 1916, in honour of Lord Kitchener. Today's most fa-

Public Archives of Canada C-69058

Built in 1856, the City Hall of Guelph, Ontario stands just behind the train station

mous attractions are the huge farmers' market (*the* place for homemade sausages and shoofly pie) and the annual Oktoberfest, a nine-day merry-go-round of beer drinking and oompah bands. With luck, you'll be able to see the dark-clothed Old Order Mennonites, whose customs have changed very little over the years, driving their horse-drawn wagons along the roadways.

The original station at Petersburg (mile 69.2) has been removed to Doon Pioneer Village, near Kitchener. Baden is the birthplace of Sir Adam Beck, founder of Ontario's Hydro-Electric Power Commission and the force behind the early electrified railways. New Hamburg, founded in 1820 by Amish settlers, each year holds a Mennonite relief sale to benefit Third World countries. A few miles to the south is the remarkable community of Punkeydoodles Corners (population 14), where one day every June, thousands of people gather at a specially set-up Post Office to mail letters with this peculiar postmark and thrill to the fast-paced excitement of frog-jumping contests. Look north while crossing the Nith River at mile 75.6 to see if you can spot a hillside tunnel used to age cheese. This is a rich dairy farming region; in fact, the

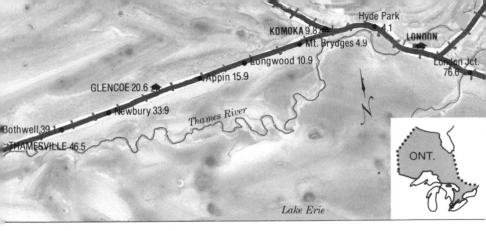

KOMOKA 9.8
Hyde Park 4.1
Mt. Brydges 4.9
LONDON
Longwood 10.9
London Jct. 76.6
Appin 15.9
GLENCOE 20.6
Newbury 33.9
Thames River
Bothwell 39.1
THAMESVILLE 46.5
N
ONT.
Lake Erie

surrounding counties have the highest number of milk cows per square mile in all of North America. At mile 84, look south to the Fryfogel Inn. The first log structure was built by a Swiss immigrant in 1828; the present building, dating from 1845, is made of brick and beam and features colourful exterior murals on the south side.

The Stratford Shakespearean Festival was conceived by Tom Patterson, a local man who in 1952 enlisted the aid of Tyrone Guthrie and mounted the first production (*Richard III*, starring Alec Guinness) the following year. Stratford's huge brick station is appropriately located on Shakespeare Street, a short distance from the Festival Theatre, on the shore of swan-filled Lake Victoria.

Mile 0-31: At one time, St. Mary's Junction had a roundhouse, repair sheds, cattle pens and accommodation for 300 Irish navvies, who maintained the track. Its limestone station was built in 1858 by the same firm responsible for the Lakeshore route's Prescott and Port Hope stations. Thomas Edison worked here as night operator in 1863, but his mind was on his experiments, and when he caused a near-collision

Canada Geese at the Jack Miner Bird Sanctuary

between two trains, he was ingloriously fired. Trout Creek is crossed at mile 11 on an 805-foot bridge; look down and you might see a flock of graceful swans. St. Mary's station was built in 1902 on property owned by the town butcher (whose name, believe it or not, was Mr. Bone). The railway's arrival in 1858 put this tiny village on the map. Its citizens immediately erected a limestone opera house, which staged performances of *Ben Hur*, complete with live chariot races. Look north at mile 26 across Fanshaw Lake to Fanshaw Pioneer Village, containing 22 restored pioneer buildings.

Mile 10-59: A five-mile railway to Petrolia, to the south, at mile 46.3, was financed by local interests during an early oil boom. North America's first commercial well was drilled at nearby Oil Springs in 1858. It was only 14 feet deep and pumped a mere 60 barrels a day, but it spurred a period of vigorous exploration that made Ontarians, for a time, Canada's blue-eyed sheiks.

Before working at St. Mary's Junction, Edison rode the trains between Sarnia and Toronto, selling newspapers in the passenger cars. This, too, proved unsuccessful, and once his experiments set fire to a baggage car. Settled in 1832, and originally called The Rapids, Sarnia remained a minor forest products centre until both the railway and news of oil discoveries arrived in 1858. Today it's the site of vast petrochemical complexes, visible to the south. Just west of the station is the St. Clair Tunnel to the United States — at 6,025 feet, one of the world's longest submarine transport links. Construction began on January 1, 1889, and ended September 19, two years later. Workers drove through blue clay 81 feet under the river bed, using great cylindrical steel shields driven forward by hydraulic rams. The tunnel replaced a rail-ferry service to Port Huron, and many people questioned its $2.7 million cost; but freight traffic increased so dramatically that the entire Toronto-Sarnia line had to

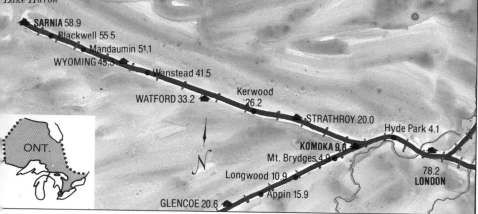

be double-tracked in 1905. It was originally used by special steam locomotives, but ventilation problems led to its electrification in 1906.

POINTS OF INTEREST
Hamilton to Niagara Falls (Grimsby subdivision)

Hamilton: Trains bound for Niagara Falls turn south at Bayview, crossing the old Desjardins Canal at mile 37.6. Look east here for a sweeping view of Hamilton Harbour. Then, at mile 38.5, look west to the 35-room Dundurn Castle, a striking edifice that preserves the elegant life-style of Sir Allan Napier MacNab — lawyer, financier, politician and once president of the Great Western Railway. It's open to the public, and beautifully restored — just one example of the way that Hamilton maintains its many historical properties amid a bustling industrial setting. Hamilton's station, opened in 1930, itself resembles a courthouse or art gallery, with massive front pillars, a huge waiting room and bas-relief etchings that depict several types of CNR steam locomotives.

Mile 37-15: The Niagara Peninsula is eastern Canada's major fruit belt, at its best during May, when peach, apple and cherry trees come into bloom. Its orchards lie between the escarpment to the south and Lake Ontario to the north, irrigated by several streams. Almost 90 percent of Canada's wines are processed in this area, and vineyards line the tracks on either side. At Grimsby (mile 27.4), look south to see the turreted Victorian station, built in 1882. Now it houses a restaurant, and immediately behind it stands the original frame station, dating from 1855. Quarries at Beamsville (mile 23.2), supplied the stone for Sarnia's submarine rail tunnel (page 105) and Montréal's Victoria Jubilee Bridge (page 62). Twenty Mile Creek is crossed on a 15-span, 1,170-foot bridge running 75 feet above

the water at mile 17.7. Look north here across the lake for a view of Toronto's CN Tower, some 35 miles distant. You might also see an owl circling over the surrounding marshes, since Canada's only owl sanctuary is located at nearby Vineland. Sixteen Mile Creek is bridged at mile 15.8 on a 578-foot, seven-span structure, 57 feet high.

Mile 12-7: The buildings to the north at mile 12, on the banks of Twelve Mile Creek, belong to Ridley College, a noted private school. Now you approach the outskirts of St. Catharines, first settled by United Empire Loyalists in 1792. A 512-foot bridge carries the Maple Leaf 94 feet above Twelve Mile Creek at mile 11.2, with views of the city to the north. At mile 10.6, look north again to the Burgoyne Woods, a peaceful and heavily wooded retreat. Mile 9.9 marks your first crossing of the original Welland Canal. It was completed in 1829, with 40 timber locks a mere eight feet deep. The second canal, started in 1842, had 27 slightly larger stone locks; the third, completed in 1887, had eight locks measuring 270 feet long by 45 feet wide. Today's system, built between 1913 and 1932, numbers only eight locks, but they can accommodate vessels up to 730 feet long and 76 feet wide. It runs 27 feet deep and stretches 27 miles between Lakes Erie and Ontario, raising ships 326 feet en route. You cross this present canal at mile 8.5, on a drawbridge over lock four. Since it handles 6,600 ships a year, there's almost certain to be one in view. At mile 7.7, you cross the 1842 canal on a 540-foot bridge.

Mile 6-0: Look north between miles 5 and 3.5 for views of Lake Ontario. The concrete Queenston Power Canal appears at mile 2.1. Built between 1918 and 1921 by Ontario's Hydro-Electric Power Commission, it carried water the 8½ miles from the Upper Niagara River to the Queenston generating plant. A railway was built to remove 13 million tons of earth and rock, with 21 electric locomotives working 24 hours a day. Some of

Bronte 27.1

Lake Ontario

BURLINGTON WEST 32.0

Niagara-on-the-Lake

U.S.A.

DUNDAS 4.7

Stoney Creek 37.6

Winona 32.1

ST. CATHARINES 11.8

to Buffalo and New York

Clifton 4.6

petown .8

HAMILTON 43.4

Beamsville 23.2

Jordan 17.5

Merritton 9.6

NIAGARA FALLS 0.6

GRIMSBY 27.4

Grand River

Twenty Mile Creek
Sixteen Mile Creek
Twelve Mile Creek
Welland Canal
Niagara River

N

The Canadian Falls at Niagara

these vintage engines are still hauling ore at Inco's Sudbury smelter. At mile 0.5, the 1,082-foot bridge over the Whirlpool Rapids soars 250 feet above the swirling waters of the Niagara Gorge. To the north are the Whirlpool Rapids; to the south, Niagara Falls. The world's first suspension bridge was built here in 1848, with its original line carried across by a child's kite. An upper deck was added in 1855, and the whole structure was replaced by the present bridge in 1897 as trains grew heavier and more frequent. No rail mishap has ever occurred at Niagara, but pedestrian and road bridges have had their problems. Gale-force winds destroyed the Falls View Bridge in 1899, and in 1938 the Honeymoon Bridge collapsed, its supports weakened by un-usually severe ice.

Some facts to bear in mind as you look down on Niagara's incredible spectacle: the Canadian falls are 2,200 feet wide and 176 feet high; the American falls, 1,000 by 184 feet. Both are only 12,500 years old, and they're eroding at the rate of some three feet a year. In 1829 a man named Sam Patch jumped twice, but miraculously survived. The circus performer Blondin walked across the gorge on a tightrope in 1859, inspiring many imitators. In 1886 people started trying their luck in barrels. Some enjoyed Patch's good fortune; others did not. Such stunts were outlawed in 1912, and nowadays the only excitement comes from watching this supreme stroke of nature in action.

The Kissing Bridge, just outside West Montrose

The Tecumseh Route

Oakville Subdivision — CNR Toronto/Hamilton

This line was built by the Hamilton and Toronto Railway, and opened for traffic on December 3, 1855.

Miles	Stations	Population	Elev.	Origin of Station Names
0.0	Toronto (Ont.)		275	(See Kingston subdivision, page 99)
1.1	Bathurst St.		—	Bathurst St. crosses overhead
1.8	Cabin "E"		—	—
2.0	Exhibition		—	Site of the Canadian National Exhibition
2.5	Dufferin		—	Dufferin Street crosses overhead (GO station)
6.2	Mimico East		—	—
6.7	Mimico	2.9 million	300	Mississauga Indian word meaning "place of the wild pigeon" (GO station)
8.4	Canpa		—	Abbreviation for Canadian Pacific
9.6	Long Branch		—	Long branch of nearby Etobicoke Creek (GO station)
11.5	Port Credit East		—	—
12.8	Port Credit		266	Once a port at the mouth of the Credit River (GO station)
16.7	Clarkson		322	Early settler Warren Clarkson, who sold his land to the Great Western Railway (GO station)
17.8	Park Royal	—	—	—
19.3	9th Line	—	—	—
20.6	Oakville Yard	—	—	Freight yard for Oakville area
21.4	Oakville	68.950	329	The centre of an oak stave industry when it was named
22.1	Kerr Street	—	—	—
24.7	Oakville West	—	—	(GO station)
27.1	Bronte	2,029	334	Admiral Horatio Nelson, Duke of Bronte (1758-1805)
30.5	Burlington East		328	—
31.5	Burlington		281	A corruption of the name Bridlington, a town in Yorkshire, England. Formerly Wellington Square (GO station)
32.0	Burlington West	536.200	—	—
33.3	Aldershot East		—	—
34.9	Aldershot		—	Early settler from Aldershot, England
36.9	Bayview		—	View of Hamilton Harbour
37.3	Hamilton Jct.		318	—
38.9	Hamilton Yard		—	Freight yard for Hamilton area
39.3	Hamilton (Ont.)		254	George Hamilton (1787-1835), son of Robert Hamilton, who divided his farm into town lots

Dundas Subdivision — CNR Bayview/London

This line was built by the Great Western Railway, and opened for traffic on December 1, 1853.

Miles	Stations	Population	Elev.	Origin of Station Names
0.0	Bayview (Ont.)	—	—	(See Oakville subdivision)
0.4	Hamilton West	—	254	—
4.7	Dundas	19.180	516	Henry Dundas, British naval treasurer from 1783 to 1801
9.8	Copetown	148	755	—
10.9	Copetown West	—	735	—
14.0	Lynden	533	751	Town in Vermont, U.S.A.
21.0	Masseys	—	637	Massey Ferguson plant nearby
22.2	Brant Jct.	—	—	—
22.7	Simpson	—	—	—
23.0	Brantford	83,400	705	Joseph Brant (1742-1807), Mohawk chief and leader of the Six Nations Indians
24.9	Hardy	—	—	Arthur Sturgis Hardy, premier of Ontario from 1898 to 1899
30.9	Paris Jct.	6,715	843	Deposits of plaster of paris in the area. Formerly called Forks of the Grand River
32.6	Paris West	—	—	—
37.9	Princeton	450	934	—
49.6	Woodstock	26,800	947	Town in Oxfordshire, England
54.5	Beachville	988	918	Andrew Beach, an early settler and grist mill owner (1784)
56.2	Munroes	—	—	Named by Colonel Charles Ingersoll, the first postmaster, in 1821, in memory of his father
59.0	Ingersoll	8,200	879	Major Thomas Ingersoll, a United Empire Loyalist. Laura Secord was his half-sister
68.5	Dorchester	2,756	852	Lord Dorchester, previously Sir Guy Carleton (1724-1808), governor of Québec from 1768 to 1778 and governor-in-chief of British North America from 1786 to 1796
76.5	London East		819	—
76.7	London Jct.	279.500	816	—
78.2	London (Ont.)		805	London, England. Named in 1826

Longwood Subdivision — CNR Komoka/Glencoe
Chatham Subdivision — CNR Glencoe/Windsor

This line was built by the Great Western Railway, and opened for traffic on January 27, 1854.

Miles	Stations	Population	Elev.	Origin of Station Names
0.0	Komoka (Ont.)	367	812	(See Strathroy subdivision)
4.9	Mt. Brydges	1,036	—	C.J. Brydges (1827-1889), Grand Trunk Railway general manager from 1861 to 1874
10.9	Longwood	60	735	—
15.9	Appin	175	740	Appin, Scotland, birthplace of first doctor in the area
20.6	Glencoe	1,820	728	Argyllshire, Scotland
27.8	Glencoe	1,820	728	—
33.9	Newbury	388	701	—
39.1	Bothwell	899	688	Town in Scotland
46.5	Thamesville	1,003	621	Thames River runs through town
52.6	Northwood	—	613	—
61.6	Chatham	40,700	598	Town in Kent, England
69.9	Prairie Siding	—	582	—
75.4	Jeanette's Creek	198	580	Early family called Jeanette
82.0	Stoney Point	240	584	A translation of the French name Pointe-aux-Roches
90.0	Belle River	3,250	583	Belle Rivière, a stream that flows into Lake St. Clair
99.3	Tecumseh	5,330	589	Shawnee Indian chief, killed fighting with the British forces at Moraviantown in 1814
101.3	Storage	—	—	Storage point for surplus cars
104.4	George Ave.	—	—	—
105.6	Windsor (Ont.)	246,000	581	Windsor, England, on the River Thames

The International Route

Weston Subdivision — CNR Toronto/Halwest
Halton Subdivision — CNR Halwest/Silver
Guelph Subdivision — CNR Silver/Stratford
Thorndale Subdivision — CNR Stratford/London Jct.

The section from Toronto to Guelph was built by the Toronto and Guelph Railway, and opened for traffic on July 1, 1856. The Guelph to Stratford section was built by the Grand Trunk Railway, and opened for traffic in August 1856. The Stratford to St. Mary's Jct. section built by the Grand Trunk Railway, opened for traffic in October 1858. The section from St. Mary's Jct. to London East was built by the London and Grand Trunk Junction Railway, and opened for traffic in October 1858.

Miles	Stations	Population	Elev.	Origin of Station Names
0.0	Toronto (Ont.)		275	(See Kingston subdivision. page 99)
1.1	Bathurst St.	—		Bathurst St. crosses overhead
1.2	Cabin D	—	—	
2.4	Parkdale		305	Residential section of Toronto
4.0	Bloor		371	Bloor St. crosses underneath
5.1	West Toronto		—	Residential section of Toronto
5.3	Keele		—	Keele Street crosses underneath
8.6	Weston	2.9 million	425	Early English settler from Weston-super-Mare, England
11.0	Etobicoke North		—	From the Amerindian word meaning "a place where alders grow"
12.5	Woodbine East		—	Woodbine racetrack nearby
14.1	Woodbine West		—	
14.7	Malton		549	Town in Yorkshire, England (GO station)
17.0	Halwest		—	
11.1	Halwest		—	
11.6	Bramalea		—	In the "lea" of nearby Brampton (GO station)
14.3	Peel	103.455	—	
15.2	Brampton East		712	—
15.4	Brampton		720	Market town in Cumbria, England and birthplace of John Elliott, an early settler
22.5	Credit		—	Bridge over the Credit River
23.5	Georgetown		846	From 1974 called Halton Hills, after Major William Halton, secretary to Sir Francis Gore, lieutenant-governor of Upper Canada, from 1806 to 1817
24.1	Silver	36.700	—	—
30.0	Silver		—	—
33.8	Limehouse		1,002	—
35.6	Acton		1,198	—
41.7	Rockcut	—	—	Rockcut nearby
48.8	Guelph	75,300	1,067	Family name of Queen Victoria. Named in 1827
49.8	Guelph Jct.	—	1,075	—
53.9	Mosborough	—	1,084	—
58.4	Breslau	715	1,023	East German hometown of a Mennonite settler
62.7	Kitchener	288,000		Field Marshal Lord Kitchener (1850-1916), British hero of the South African War (1899-1902)
69.2	Petersburg	201	1,210	—
72.5	Baden	824	1,156	Named by Jacob Beck, a native of the Grand Duchy of Baden
75.0	New Hamburg	3,628		Hamburg, Germany, home of early settlers
82.1	Shakespeare	287	1,182	William Shakespeare
88.6	Stratford	26,200	1,189	Stratford-on-Avon, England, birthplace of William Shakespeare
0.0	Stratford	26,200	1,189	—
10.2	St. Mary's Jct.	—	—	—

Miles	Stations	Population	Elev.	Origin of Station Names
11.1	St. Mary's	4,040	1,002	Wife of Commissioner T.M. Jones of the Canada Company, founder of the local school
11.5	St. Mary's West	—	—	—
17.4	Kellys	—	—	—
22.3	Thorndale	290	934	—
31.3	London Jct. (Ont.)	—	805	—

Strathroy Subdivision — CNR London/Sarnia

The segment from London to Komoka was built by the Great Western Railway, and opened for traffic on January 27, 1854. The section from Komoka to Sarnia was built by the London and Port Sarnia Railway, and opened for traffic on December 27, 1858.

Miles	Stations	Population	Elev.	Origin of Station Names
0.0	London (Ont.)	279,500	805	(See Dundas subdivision)
4.1	Hyde Park	250	902	Hyde Park in London, England
9.8	Komoka	367	812	From the Amerindian word meaning "where the dead lie" or for "junction"
20.0	Strathroy	7,770	744	From the Gaelic "strathan" (valley) and "ruadh" (reddish). Also, Strathroy, County Antrim, Northern Ireland
26.2	Kerwood	104	768	—
33.2	Watford	1,365	783	Town in Hertfordshire, England
41.5	Wanstead	—	700	—
45.3	Wyoming	1,650	709	Town in Pennsylvania, U.S.A.
46.3	Petrolia Jct.	—	716	Junction with the line to Petrolia
51.1	Mandaumin	—	645	—
55.5	Blackwell	—	601	T.E. Blackwell, general manager of the Grand Trunk Railway
56.3	Modeland	—		—
57.2	Sarnia Yard	—		Freight yard for Sarnia area
57.9	Sarnia Jct.	82,200	—	—
58.9	Sarnia (Ont.)		587	Original Roman name for Guernsey, Channel Islands. Named by the former lieutenant-governor of that island, who visited the area in 1835

The Maple Leaf Route

Grimsby Subdivision — CNR Niagara Falls/Hamilton
Most of this line was built by the Great Western Railway, and opened for traffic on November 10, 1853. The segment between miles 7.0 and 8.5 was built by the Grand Trunk Railway in 1903 to bridge the Welland Canal.

Miles	Stations	Population	Elev.	Origin of Station Names
0.0	Suspension Bridge		—	Bridge over the Niagara River
0.6	Niagara Falls (Ont.)		573	From the Huron Indian word for "thunder of waters resounding with a great noise"
2.6	Clifton	309,500	582	Nearby cliffs of Niagara Canyon
9.6	Merritton		389	Thomas R. Merritt (1824-1906), who founded St. Catharines and promoted the Welland Canal
11.8	St. Catharines		579	Catharine Askin Hamilton, wife of Robert Hamilton and mother of George Hamilton
17.5	Jordan		309	Biblical name given by William Bradt, early magistrate and postmaster
23.2	Beamsville	14,500	297	Jacob Beam, early settler who originally owned the land. Now called Lincoln
27.4	Grimsby	15,565	287	Town in Lincolnshire, England
32.1	Winona	1,217	285	—
37.6	Stoney Creek	30,290	274	—
43.4	Hamilton (Ont.)	536,200	254	George Hamilton (1787-1835), son of Robert Hamilton. (See Oakville subdivision)

The Northlander Route

Canada's most luxurious train winds past Muskoka's fabled resorts, where a restored steamer plies sparkling lakes — then to Temagami and Ontario's gold mining regions

Toronto to Timmins and Kapuskasing

The first steam locomotive built in Ontario slowly chugged out of James Good's Toronto foundry on April 16, 1853, destined for the tracks of the Ontario, Simcoe and Huron Railway. This balloon-stacked 4-4-0 bore the number 2 and was named the Toronto. A month later — hauling two boxcars, a combination baggage and passenger car and a single coach — it rolled northward through the prosperous farming communities of Maple and King to Machell's Corners (now Aurora), making the 30-mile trip in two hours. Conductor John Harvey sold the first ticket for $1 to a shoemaker named Maher. Plaques commemorating this historic run can be found at Toronto's Union Station and the Aurora station. Later the same year, service was extended north to the town of Barrie.

The Muskoka area, north of Orillia, remained largely unsettled until 1815, when the federal government bought the land for $20,000 from the Chippewa Indians, in hopes of luring would-be farmers. But European settlers had barely begun to arrive, drawn by the prospect of free homesteads, when the Toronto was making its maiden run. Colonization roads were built through the rocky bush, followed by steamer routes on major waterways. Washago, at the northern tip of Lake Couchiching, became an important terminus for these hopeful ventures. But all to no avail — the region simply wasn't suitable agricultural land, and the farmers drifted away.

Muskoka's salvation appeared in the unlikely form of W.H. Pratt, an eccentric though far-sighted New Yorker. In 1870, he built a mansion on Lake Rosseau and opened a first-class resort, charging the then outrageous sum of $5 a day, American plan. Rosseau House was enormously popular, drawing guests from as far away as Britain and the Carolinas, and prompting other entrepreneurs to open more luxury inns.

From the mid-1870s, the cream of North

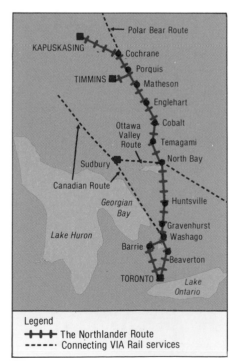

Legend
+++ The Northlander Route
----- Connecting VIA Rail services

The restored *Segwun*, the last remaining steamer run the 100-mile excursion on Lake Muskoka

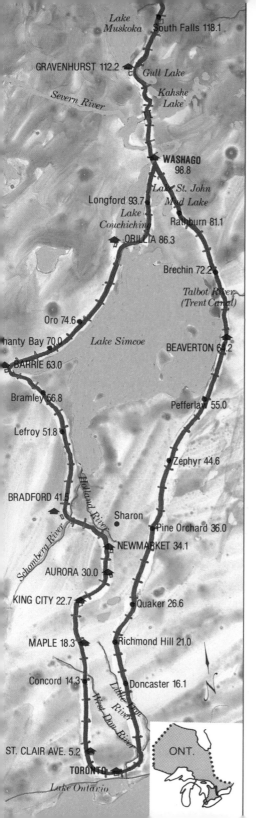

Lake Muskoka   South Falls 118.1

GRAVENHURST 112.2   Gull Lake

Severn River   Kahshe Lake

WASHAGO 98.8

Lake St. John
Longford 93.7   Mud Lake
Lake Couchiching   Rathburn 81.1

ORILLIA 86.3

Brechin 72.2

Talbot River (Trent Canal)

Oro 74.6

Shanty Bay 70.0   Lake Simcoe   BEAVERTON 66.2

BARRIE 63.0

Bramley 56.8   Pefferlaw 55.0

Lefroy 51.8

Zephyr 44.6

BRADFORD 41.5   Holland River

Schomberg River   Sharon
Pine Orchard 36.0
NEWMARKET 34.1

AURORA 30.0

KING CITY 22.7   Quaker 26.6

MAPLE 18.3   Richmond Hill 21.0

Concord 14.3   Doncaster 16.1
Little Don River
West Don River
N

ST. CLAIR AVE. 5.2

TORONTO

Lake Ontario

ONT.

American society arrived by train each summer in parlour or private cars, complete with bevies of servants. One route led to the Muskoka wharf near Gravenhurst, where passengers transferred to steamboats bound for Beaumaris and Port Carling — a cruise you can take today. Another went to the Huntsville wharf, where the world's shortest train conveyed vacationers to the Bigwin Inn, while a third led farther north, direct to the Highland Inn and the Hotel Algonquin in what was later to become Algonquin Provincial Park. These lines were instrumental in forming the nucleus of a tourist industry that's made Muskoka one of Canada's busiest holiday playgrounds.

The Temiskaming and Northern Ontario Railway (now the Ontario Northland) is a "rags to riches" fable come true. When construction began in 1902, sponsored by the provincial government, the line was intended only to serve a small number of farmers along the western shore of Lake Timiskaming. But the next year (or so legend goes) a Cobalt blacksmith, Fred La Rose, threw his hammer at what he thought were a fox's eyes shining in the dark and struck the world's richest vein of silver. By 1907, the railway was running a "Cobalt Special," complete with luxury Pullman sleepers, diners and a library car, the better to service a stream of instant mining millionaires. That same year, a decision was made to extend the line to Cochrane, and four years later a branch line reached Timmins. Gold strikes in Timmins in 1909 and Kirkland Lake in 1912, plus the later discoveries of gold and copper in the Rouyn-Noranda area and asbestos near Matheson, contributed to the region's boom. In 1922, construction began on yet another line, north from Cochrane. It reached the shores of James Bay 10 years later, and today forms the route of the popular Polar Bear Express (page 123).

Today, Toronto is linked with Muskoka and Northern Ontario by two excellent trains. Daylight service to Timmins is provided by the Northlander — perhaps Canada's most luxurious train, featuring European-style compartments, single and double seats with pull-out tables in an open coach section and full dining-car service. These units were previously part of the first-class Trans-Europ

This canal, linking Newmarket to Lake Simcoe, has never been used

Express network, operating as L'Arbalête between Paris and Zurich. Or, if you wish, you can travel overnight to Cochrane and Kapuskasing aboard the Northland, which features both coaches and sleeping car to Kapuskasing as well as a meal-service lounge car to Cochrane. Most northbound and southbound trains use the track on the west side of Lake Simcoe; occasionally a southbound train will use the track on the east side.

POINTS OF INTEREST
Toronto to North Bay (Newmarket subdivision)

Mile 14-34: Some of Ontario's finest farms are located along this stretch, just outside the boundaries of Toronto.

Mile 36: The huge concrete locks to the east on the Little Holland River are part of a canal begun by the Liberal government in 1908. This scheme — which would have linked the town of Newmarket with Lake Simcoe — was halted three years later by a newly elected Conservative regime.

Mile 38-41: Between 1924 and 1928, Professor William H. Day transformed a swampy wasteland into the productive market garden known as Holland Marsh, to the west. Its few uncultivated acres provide nesting grounds for birds rarely seen elsewhere in the province, including yellow rails and Leconte's sparrows. Irrigation is provided by the Schomberg River, crossed at mile 41.5.

Mile 63-67: Kempenfelt Bay, an arm of Lake Simcoe, appears to the east. On winter days thousands of fish huts dot the ice, their hardy occupants hoping for a cold-weather catch. At mile 64, one of the last steam engines to travel this route, CN 1531, is on display in a small park.

Mile 86.5: Orillia was immortalized by Canada's

foremost humourist, Stephen Leacock, who used it as the model for Mariposa in his *Sunshine Sketches of a Little Town.* Local residents were displeased by his gentle satire, but now a yearly festival honours him, and you can see the entrance to his home, now maintained as a museum, on Old Brewery Bay to the west.

Mile 88.4: The swing bridge at Atherley Narrows, between Lakes Simcoe and Couchiching, is the first crossing of the Trent-Severn Waterway, a 240-mile system of rivers and lakes joined by locks, canals and two marine railways. Initiated in the 1830s and completed in 1918, it joins Lake Ontario and Georgian Bay. Although created to carry commercial traffic, it's now used primarily by pleasure boaters.

Mile 89-98: Lake Couchiching is visible to the west between miles 87.5 and 97. Lake St. John, part of the Rama Indian Reserve, can be seen to the east, between miles 93 and 96.

Mile 99-112: Here you'll begin to understand why Muskoka defeated its early farmers. Rolling fields give way to rugged granite dotted with shining lakes — scenery that's at its best in the fall, when the hills are ablaze with colour. Rock cuts appear more frequently, especially between miles 109 and 110. Look east as you approach the outskirts of Gravenhurst to see a barge moored in Gull Lake, where band concerts take place in summertime.

Mile 112.2: Gravenhurst is the hub of the Muskoka region — a 1,600-square-mile paradise containing hundreds of lakes. No wonder that turn-of-the-century socialites and business magnates such as the Rockefellers, Carnegies, Eatons and Seagrams claimed it for their own, occupying whole islands and building grandiose summer homes with enormous boathouses, stables, tennis courts and all the trappings of luxury. Some of these have been destroyed by fire, but many remain on Lake Muskoka's "Millionaires' Row." Occasionally a property is offered for sale, but

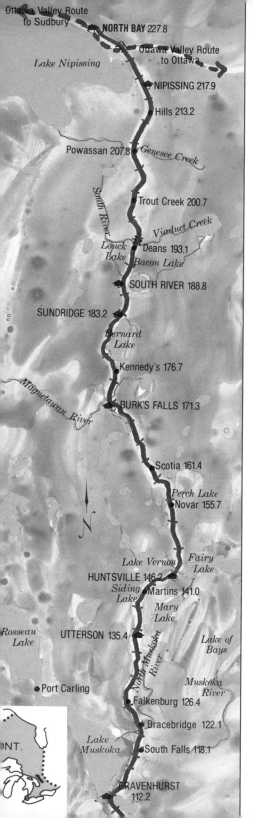

Ottawa Valley Route
to Sudbury
NORTH BAY 227.8

Lake Nipissing

Ottawa Valley Route
to Ottawa

● NIPISSING 217.9

● Hills 213.2

Powassan 207.8   Genesee Creek

South River

● Trout Creek 200.7

Viaduct Creek

Louck Lake   ● Deans 193.1
Bacon Lake

● SOUTH RIVER 188.8

SUNDRIDGE 183.2 ●

Bernard Lake

● Kennedy's 176.7

Magnetawan River

■ BURK'S FALLS 171.3

● Scotia 161.4

Perch Lake
● Novar 155.7

N

Lake Vernon   Fairy Lake
HUNTSVILLE 146.2
Siding   ● Martins 141.0
Lake
Mary Lake

Rosseau Lake   UTTERSON 135.4 ●   Lake of Bays

North Muskoka River

● Port Carling

Muskoka River

● Falkenburg 126.4

● Bracebridge 122.1

Lake Muskoka   ● South Falls 118.1

**GRAVENHURST
112.2**

ONT.

---

prices can start at $500,000. Prestigious resorts remain as well, such as Windermere House, opened in 1869 to serve the influx of well-heeled holidayers.

The best way to appreciate the grandeur that remains is to board the S.S. *Segwun* — the last of 21 excursion ships that once cruised these lakes. Segwun is Ojibwa for "springtime" — but whatever the season, you'll be transported back in time to 1887, the year she was proudly launched. Her dining room features original gumwood paneling and white oak beams, linen tablecloths and the finest silver. Notice the period lamps, velvet drapes and carpeted decks — even the iron rings that tethered rich men's horses — as you listen to the throbbing of her coal-powered engines and haunting three-chime brass whistle.

Mile 120-145: Having crossed the Hawk Rock Viaduct, mile 118.7, look west at mile 121 as you pass over the turbulent south branch of the Muskoka River on a 516-foot bridge running 82 feet above the water. The north branch, following almost immediately, is crossed by a 347-foot span rising 46 feet. These wild streams enabled Bracebridge (mile 122.1), to generate its own electricity in 1894 — the first Ontario town to do so. Prior to that time, they powered several sawmills. Look west to see Woodchester Villa, a peculiar octagonal house with widow's walk, almost hidden amid the trees, then west again at mile 144 for a view of Lake Vernon.

Mile 146.2: Huntsville was once the starting point for a most unusual rail-to-steamboat connection. Trains pulled into Huntsville wharf, and passengers boarded the S.S. *Algonquin* for a cruise along Fairy and Peninsula lakes, joined by a canal. At North Portage, they'd take the Portage Flyer, run by the Huntsville and Lake of Bays Railway Company. Two wheezing steam locomotives pulled a string of former Toronto and Atlantic City streetcars over a narrow-gauge track only 1 1/8 miles long, up the hill to South Portage. It was the world's shortest railway — and, surprisingly, its rolling stock is still on the tracks in Pinafore Park, near St. Thomas, Ontario. Some 15,000 passengers a year rode the Flyer, then boarded the S.S. *Iroquois* at South Portage for a voyage down Lake of Bays to the internationally renowned Bigwin Inn.

Mile 146.9-173: As you cross Lake Vernon's Hunters Bay at mile 146.9, look south to the hills known as Maple Ridge — a spectacular view in autumn. Scotia, at mile 161.4, was once the junction of a rail line leading east into Algonquin Park, a 2,900-square-mile wilderness area that even today remains largely inaccessible except by canoe or hiking trail. A golf course appears to the west at mile 167, followed at mile 171 by the huge old station at Burk's Falls. This was where people would leave to board the steamer *Wanita*,

Maple Ridge provides the backdrop for the Northlander as it leaves Huntsville en route to Timmins

which sailed 35 miles west along the Magnetawan River, whose north branch you'll cross four times between miles 166.1 and 172.3.

Mile 189-218: Now the terrain becomes a series of rolling hills and deep valleys. Look west at mile 189.4 to see a waterfall on the South River. The best view on this stretch is obtained at mile 194, as you cross the 751-foot-long Viaduct Creek trestle. To the west at mile 207, you'll see a hilltop fire tower and a large stand of yellow fir trees, also to the west, near mile 212.

POINTS OF INTEREST
North Bay to Englehart (Temagami subdivision)

Mile 1-70: Construction of the Temiskaming and Northern Ontario Railway officially began in the spring of 1902, when F.R. Latchford, then provincial commissioner of public works, turned the first sod at what is now mile 3.7. Most people believed that the line would merely service a small farming community on Lake Timiskaming, but Latchford argued that "transporting lumber and exploring for minerals could lead to a more lucrative future." Little did he know that fantastically rich veins of silver lay in the path of the

The Portage Flyer and the S.S. *Iroquois* at South Portage, near Huntsville

track gangs. (Because of confusion with the Texas and New Orleans Railway, the T&NO changed its name in 1946, becoming the Ontario Northland. It had, by that time, earned the title "Ontario's Development Road" — and just as well, because it had previously been saddled with the far less flattering nickname "Time No Object.")

Like most other railways at that time, the ONR was built by immigrant labourers, whose presence led to friction with the area's primarily British settlers. (These men lived in boxcars and earned $1 a day, minus meals and accommodation. Train crews received somewhat better pay, and a skilled engineer made more than a member of Parliament.) Local residents were further annoyed by the practice of renaming stations as a form of political patronage. Driftwood City became Monteith (for the provincial minister of agriculture); McDougall's Chute was rechristened Matheson (the provincial treasurer); and mile 138 enshrined a Mr. Englehart, then chairman of the railway board.

On leaving North Bay, the ONR passes through 18 miles of rich agricultural land. The next 50 miles, however, are heavily timbered with red and white pine, black and yellow birch, cedar, hemlock, spruce and maple. Between miles 35 and 65, be on the lookout for beaver, otter and marten in the Temiskaming Game Preserve.

Mile 71-93: Lake Temagami, Cree for "deep water," contains 40 varieties of fish, including lake trout, northern pike, muskellunge and sturgeon. In summertime, its 1,200 tiny islands are a holidayer's dream, and one — Bear Island — was the site of a Hudson's Bay Company trading post, established in the 1870s. This is where an Englishman named George Stansfeld Belaney came in the early 1900s to live among the Indians. He was to achieve worldwide fame as Grey Owl, an advocate of wildlife conservation

ONT.

Jardine 20.9

Round
Lake

Adams Jct. 14.8
Mindoka 12.5

ENGLEHART 138.5

Englehart River

Earlton 128.6

Thornloe 124.8

Uno Park 118.1

NEW LISKEARD 112.7

Lake
Timiskaming

HAILEYBURY 107.5

Latchford 94.2   COBALT 102.8

Bay Lake

Hound
Chute
Lake   Freeman 86.0

Rib
Lake

Owaissa 78.5   Montreal River
Kanichee Lake

Net Lake

TEMAGAMI 71.9   Cassels
Lake Temagami   Lake

Upper   Rabbit
Twin Lake   Lake

Doherty 63.9   Lower   Ont.   P.Q.
Twin
Lake

Redwater 55.8

Mackenzie
Lake

Bown
Lake

Fanny
Bushnell 47.1   Lake

Otter Lake

Osborne 37.6

Jocko Lake

Brûlé Lake

Little
Tomiko   Tomiko 27.5
Lake

Mulock 18.3

NORTH BAY

Feronia 8.9

Lake Nipissing   Trout Lake   Mattawa River

and humane trapping techniques. It wasn't until after his death that his many admirers learned that he was in fact a white man. As you wind along the shore of Rib Lake, to the east between miles 82 and 87, you'll appreciate his description of the area as "a great, lonely land of forest, lake and river where moose, deer, bears and wolves roam free."

Mile 93-95: At mile 93.8 you cross the Montréal River, crawling at 30 mph over a three-span steel bridge. This point marks the southern boundary of both the James Bay Frontier Tourist Region and Ontario's gold and silver mining country. Steam-driven paddlewheelers once carried materials upstream from here to the mines at Elk Lake and Gowganda. In nearby Latchford, the House of Memories Museum contains turn-of-the-century furnishings, geological displays and mining exhibits, while a local park features the world's smallest covered bridge.

Mile 103: On August 7, 1903, here on the shores of Long (now Cobalt) Lake, J.H. McKinley and Ernest Darragh, looking for suitable timber to make railway ties, noticed a metallic gleam along the beach. Their discovery was to become the famous McKinley-Darragh mine, but they were only the first of many to strike it rich. By 1905, some 16 mines were in full swing, and silver bullion worth millions of dollars was stacked on railway baggage carts awaiting shipment to the south. The lure of quick profit, quite predictably, made Cobalt a wide-open town. Roller-coaster streets spread out in a crazy-quilt pattern from the stone railway station. Cheap frame houses sprang up side by side with brothels and bars, and a thriving black market was the order of the day.

Today, the headframes of abandoned mines dot the hillsides surrounding the town. At the north end of Cobalt Lake, look east to see the Right-of-Way mine — so named because its silver holdings ran directly beneath the tracks, with the result that the ONR shared in the profits. (That vein is long since exhausted, but at the Cobalt Northern Ontario Mining Museum, you can view the Prospectors' Hall of Fame, containing a section of the original "silver sidewalk," another vein so rich that it ran along the surface of the ground.) High on a hilltop, also to the east, a fire tower stands guard against a repetition of the blaze that destroyed much of the town in 1977.

Mile 104-113: When the silver boom was at its height, the ONR built a special siding known as Dynamite at mile 104, where cars loaded with high explosives were stored. At mile 107.5, look east to Haileybury and to Lake Timiskaming (Cree for "cold, dry water"). It's 700 feet deep and a fisherman's dream. Today, Haileybury is the centre of the area's municipal government and the site of a mining school, but it was always the more "civilized" community. When mine

A moose roams through Grey Owl's "great, lonely land of forest, lake and river"

Parks Canada

owners came to visit the rough-and-ready camps around Cobalt, they'd be sure to stay at the Matabanick Hotel, whose owner boasted that his establishment was the equal of the grand hostelries of Toronto and Montréal. More good views of the lake appear between miles 108 and 111. For many years, the ONR operated special picnic trains so that its employees could enjoy the lake's fine beaches. Indeed, the whole area was covered with track. A radial electric railway, the Nipissing Central, was built in 1910, offering service between Haileybury and Cobalt on the half-hour. The line was extended north to New Liskeard in 1912, and by 1916 passengers numbered 1.5 million a year. A further extension to Kerr Lake in 1914 handled mainly freight traffic, but the whole system fell into disuse during the Depression and was abandoned in 1935.

Mile 113-137: Now you enter the Great Clay Belt, a huge and surprisingly fertile area where land sold for 50¢ an acre in the early 1900s. This was also the site of a terrible fire on October 4, 1922, which left 6,000 people homeless overnight. A relief train left North Bay, dropping emergency supplies at every siding, and Toronto dispatched 85 streetcars by rail to serve as temporary shelters. Fires remain a constant hazard in the north country, which is one of the reasons why all the railway's wooden trestles have been replaced with steel structures, or packed with solid fill.

(There used to be a wood bridge over the Wabi Creek at mile 119.1, but it collapsed under the weight of passing freight trains.)

Mile 138-139: At mile 138.1, you cross the Englehart River, which flows through Kap-Kig-Iwan Provincial Park, with its two waterfalls, pleasant nature walks and unusual rock formations. At Englehart station you'll want to take a close look at locomotive 701, which hauled the ONR's last steam-powered train from Timmins to North Bay on June 24 and 25, 1957. Built at Kingston in 1921, it's maintained in immaculate condition.

POINTS OF INTEREST
Englehart to Timmins (Ramore subdivision)

Mile 1-25: To lay track across the Clay Belt, the ONR's builders had to bank against landslides, drain countless sinkholes and erect expensive steel bridges, such as the one across the Blanche River, mile 7.4. At mile 12, the terrain changes once again, and rock cuts become more frequent. Mile 25 marks the spot where Harry Oakes discovered gold in 1912. Oakes was a highly colourful character who'd prospected all over the world, and had already filed claims farther north, at Porcupine. But something told him that, at this location, the gold lay much deeper in the ground. His Lake Shore Mining Company set about drilling to a depth of 8,000 feet — a North American record — and extracted $265 million worth of ore before closing in 1968. Oakes was quick to spend his fabulous wealth

117

Kapuskasing Inn, a comfortable place to stay in Northern Ontario

on a château in Kirkland Lake, an English town-house and a palatial estate in the Bahamas. Only the château remains, now housing the Museum of Northern History. The mine headframe was torn down to make way for a shopping centre, the office became a nursing home and the bunk-house, a motel. Oakes became Sir Harry in 1939, but was murdered in the Bahamas in 1943 under highly mysterious circumstances. Still, he spurred a boom in Kirkland Lake that produced the famous "Golden Mile" — 12 gold mines side by side, including the claim staked by W.H. Wright, who put his profits from the Wright-Hargreaves strike to use by purchasing the Toronto *Globe and Mail* and *Empire*, merging them to create *The Globe and Mail*. By 1927, develop-ment had become so widespread that the ONR built a 60-mile branch line from Kirkland Lake to tap the rich copper resources of Rouyn-Noranda. You'll see it diverge at mile 25.6. Be glad you aren't on it, because its rugged con-tours earned it the instant nickname "the Burma Road."

Mile 26-85: Look east at Swastika to a waterfall and an island park, joined by bridge to the mainland. This was the site of the Lucky Cross gold mine, opened in 1911. The former Belleek siding at mile 31.4 was named by an Irishman, pining for his home in the Sligo uplands. Here you cross

the Arctic Divide — from this point all streams flow north to James Bay. Sesekinika Lake lies to the west between miles 35 and 38. Several rivers are crossed in the next 40 miles: Little Wildgoose Creek at mile 58.3; the Watabeag River at mile 70.9, where logjams sometimes make it re-semble a corduroy road, and the Driftwood River at mile 79.3. From its trestle, look west and you'll see the isolated Monteith Correctional Centre. At this very spot, in 1909, eight men stepped off the train and sailed west along the river toward Night Hawk and Porcupine lakes. One of them, Harry Preston, stripped some moss off a conical rock, exposing gold. The claim they filed re-sulted in the famous Dome mine. Several months later, Benny Hollinger, exploring this same area, came upon a vein of gold measuring six feet wide by five feet long — a discovery that would become the Hollinger mine. But disaster was soon to follow these promising events. On July 29, 1916, a freak combination of dry weather, sudden wind and several small brush fires produced a wall of flame eight miles wide that raced toward Cochrane at 40 mph, wiping out the villages of Matheson, Val Gagné and Porquis Junction. Many residents were saved by ONR crews, who steamed bravely through the inferno, but 223 lives were lost before the con-flagration burned itself out. With the first gold

strike at Porcupine, the ONR established a siding at Kelso (mile 83.2), using an old coach as a station. A stage coach departed at seven in the morning, bouncing over a clay-and-log road to Night Hawk Lake, with stops at "halfway houses" — log shacks where passengers could sleep for 50¢ a night. Another 50¢ bought a meal of pork, potatoes, pumpkin pie and strong black tea. No wonder prospectors blessed the railway's arrival in Timmins on July 1, 1911.

Mile 92-117: Look north between miles 92 and 96 for excellent views of Frederick House Lake, or south to McIntosh Lake (miles 92 to 93), and Barbers Bay (mile 95). At mile 96, a long bridge crosses Frederick House River. On July 11, 1911, Porcupine (mile 109.7), was engulfed by yet another tragic fire. The entire town went up in flames as a boxcar full of dynamite exploded at the rail siding. Residents took refuge in the lake, clinging to boats, planks and logs, but 73 people drowned. A cairn erected at Deadman's Point commemorates the tragedy. Farther north, you pass a succession of headframes towering above the trees: the Pamour mine (north at mile 107); Hugh and Reef mines (north at mile 108); Dome mine (south at mile 114); McIntyre mine (north at mile 115) with a 7,400-foot-deep shaft; and Hollinger mine (south at mile 117). There are 1,500 miles of underground tunnels in this one

small area.

Mile 118.7: Timmins, "the city with a heart of gold," is Canada's largest city in area, ever since establishing its 1,260-square-mile municipal boundaries. That's equal to the combined areas of New York, Toronto, Montréal and Winnipeg, and takes in 20 traplines, five mines and 500 lakes. Be sure to visit the Porcupine Outdoor Museum, the Costain mineral collection and the unique Rock Wall, a geological mosaic built into a giant fault.

POINTS OF INTEREST
Porquis to Cochrane to Kapuskasing (Devonshire and Kapuskasing subdivisions)

At Cochrane's Union Station you'll see a steam locomotive and several vintage passenger cars — part of the Cochrane Railway and Pioneer Museum. Many of the household articles on display were retrieved from wells, where they'd been thrown during forest fires. The baggage car features Indian and Inuit artifacts, while other exhibits are dedicated to loggers, trappers and homesteaders. The coach houses a model railroad, a ticket office, telegrapher's equipment and dining car dishes — all enhanced by period photographs. A CN caboose, the traveling hotel for countless railwaymen, is preserved in its original condition. On the station exterior you'll

119

notice a painted polar bear and Canada goose, promoting the Polar Bear route to Moosonee (page 123). The station restaurant is one of the very few remaining in all of Canada, since most were closed with the advent of dining cars. Here you can buy posters showing the Northland and Polar Bear as they appeared in steam-powered days.

Mile 0-69: The Cochrane to Kapuskasing run crosses eight major rivers that flow into James Bay. The track passes through an area settled by French Canadians who arrived with the National Transcontinental Railway, built west from Québec City between 1911 and 1915. Smooth Rock station is the stop for Smooth Rock Falls, 3.3 miles distant. At one time the Mattagami Railroad hauled passengers on this 10-minute trip, charging 15¢ for a ride aboard a wooden coach from the Toronto, Hamilton and Buffalo Railway, pulled by a beautiful black and red steam locomotive that remains on display in the town, at the entrance to the Abitibi-Price paper mill. This engine also saw duty on the Greater Winnipeg Water District Railway (page 149). The Mattagami River is crossed at mile 31.4; look for logs floating downstream toward the mill. The Spruce Falls Power and Paper Company complex is visible to the south at mile 69. It supplies newsprint for *The New York Times* and pulp for the makers of Kleenex tissues. The mill is powered by a dam at Smoky Falls, 50 miles to the north. Its construction required the creation of a private railway, the Smoky Line. The town of Kapuskasing is noted for its severe winter temperatures, which is why General Motors maintains a centre here to test its vehicles in cold-weather conditions. The brick station sells rail, bus and air tickets under the same roof, and houses a travel agency. Right next door you can visit the Ron Morel Memorial Museum. It consists of a steam locomotive, several vintage passenger cars and a caboose that serves as information centre. One car depicts Kapuskasing's early days, the other features relics from every station between Cochrane and Hearst, including a complete ticket office, track tools, silver and glassware, oil lamps and a model railway display.

The Mattagami Railroad steam engine

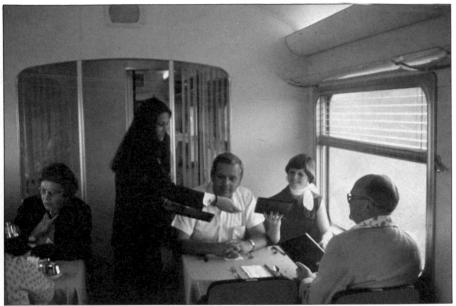

The Northlander dining room, sun-filled and comfortable

The Northlander Route

Newmarket Subdivision — CNR Toronto/Washago/North Bay

This route is an amalgamation of various railways that later became part of the Canadian Northern Ontario Railway. The Toronto to Allandale segment was built by the Toronto, Simcoe and Lake Huron Union Railway, and opened on October 11, 1853. The Allandale to Barrie segment was built by the Northern Railway of Canada, and opened on June 10, 1859. The Barrie to Gravenhurst segment was built by the Toronto, Simcoe and Muskoka Junction Railway between 1872 and 1875, and opened in November 1875. The segment from Gravenhurst to Nipissing Junction was built by the Northern and Pacific Junction, and opened on June 30, 1885.

Miles	Stations	Population	Elev.	Origin of Station Names
0.0	Toronto (Ont.)	} 2.9 million	275	(See Kingston subdivision, page 99)
2.4	Parkdale		323	—
5.2	St. Clair Ave.		453	—
8.1	Downsview		612	—
10.4	Airbase		681	—
12.9	Snider		700	—
14.3	Concord	1,061	661	—
18.3	Maple	2,026	847	—
22.7	King City	1,864	983	In dispute. Either John King, under secretary of state, or Sir Richard King, an admiral in the British navy
27.5	Cherry	—	1,008	—
30.0	Aurora	14,249	918	Goddess of the morning
34.1	Newmarket	24,795	800	Town in Suffolk, England
41.5	Bradford	3,390	753	Town in Yorkshire, England
51.8	Lefroy	277	800	—
56.8	Bramley	—	916	—
63.0	Barrie	57,000	766	Commodore Robert Barrie, a British naval officer, who, in 1828, inspected the naval depots of the Great Lakes
70.0	Shanty Bay	—	848	—
74.6	Oro	—	820	Spanish word for gold; after Rio del Oro, a town in Spanish Territory on the west coast of Africa. In the 1820s, Oro township was suggested as a place for liberated slaves, hence an African name was thought appropriate
86.3	Orillia	24,300	754	In dispute. Either from an old Spanish word for the shore or bank of a river, or from the Amerindian word "orelia" for a berry growing in the surrounding bush
93.7	Longford	129	764	County and town in Ireland
98.8	Washago	332	729	From the Indian word "wash-a-go-min," meaning "sparkling waters"
112.2	Gravenhurst	7,986	851	This English town, which only existed in the author's mind, is featured in "Bracebridge Hall," a tale by Washington Irving (1783-1859)
118.1	South Falls	—	937	—
122.1	Bracebridge	8,428	848	From Washington Irving's tale "Bracebridge Hall." Also the name of a parish in Lincolnshire, England
126.4	Falkenburg	—	990	—
135.4	Utterson	184	1,071	—
141.0	Martins	—	1,043	—
146.2	Huntsville	11,400	987	George Hunt, first white settler, who arrived in 1858
155.7	Novar	241	1,107	—
161.4	Scotia	58	1,120	—
171.3	Burks Falls	871	1,006	David Francis Burk, an early settler
176.7	Kennedy's	—	1,152	—
183.2	Sundridge	692	1,134	Town in Kent, England
188.8	South River	1,094	1,193	—
193.1	Deans	—	1,229	—

Miles	Stations	Population	Elev.	Origin of Station Names
200.7	Trout Creek	623	1,087	—
207.8	Powassan	1,238	890	From an Ojibway word meaning "the big bend," due to a bend in the river
213.2	Hills	—	922	—
217.9	Nipissing	160	793	From the Ojibway word "nipisisinan," meaning "little body of water" (in comparison with the Great Lakes)
218.5	Derland	—	775	—
225.6	Transfer Yard	—	775	—
227.8	North Bay (Ont.)	52,600	659	Bay of nearby Lake Nipissing

Bala Subdivision — CNR Toronto/Washago

This line was built by the James Bay Railway, and opened for traffic on November 6, 1909. The segment from Don to Rosedale was built by the Toronto Belt Line Railway in 1892.

Miles	Stations	Population	Elev.	Origin of Station Names
0.0	Toronto (Ont.)	2.9 million	275	(See Kingston subdivision, page 99)
2.0	Don		—	Nearby Don River
3.6	Rosedale		—	Residential section of Toronto noted for its flower gardens
11.3	Oriole		—	Flocks of orioles are common in the region (GO station)
14.1	Old Cummer		—	(GO station)
15.4	Doncaster South		—	—
16.1	Doncaster		—	—
18.3	Langstaff		—	(GO station)
21.0	Richmond Hill		817	Charles Gordon Lennox, fourth Duke of Richmond, governor-in-chief of British North America from 1818 to 1819
22.2	Elgin	—	432	Lord Elgin, governor-general of Canada from 1847 to 1854
26.6	Quaker	—	—	Quaker religious settlement nearby
36.0	Pine Orchard	72	—	Orchards nearby
44.6	Zephyr	261	767	—
55.0	Pefferlaw	184	—	—
64.2	Beaverton	1,737	761	Beaver River nearby
72.2	Brechin East	267	745	Early settler (1860)
81.1	Rathburn	—	—	—
88.9	Washago (Ont.)	332	728	Indian word meaning "sparkling waters"

Temagami Subdivision — ONR North Bay/Englehart

This line was built by the Temiskaming and Northern Ontario Railway between 1902 and 1908. The segment from North Bay to New Liskeard was opened on January 16, 1905; the segment from New Liskeard to Englehart was opened on November 30, 1908.

Miles	Stations	Population	Elev.	Origin of Station Names
1.6	North Bay (Ont.)	52,600	659	(See Newmarket subdivision)
8.9	Feronia	—	—	—
18.3	Mulock	—	—	Sir William Mulock, Toronto member of the King's Privy Council
27.5	Tomiko	—	795	—
37.6	Osborne	—	—	—
47.1	Bushnell	—	—	—
55.8	Redwater	—	—	—
63.9	Doherty	—	—	In dispute. Either C.J. Doherty, minister of justice and attorney-general from 1911 to 1917 or Manning Doherty, minister of agriculture from 1919 to 1923
71.9	Temagami	721	964	Indian word meaning "deep water"
73.5	Rock Jct.	—	1,280	Junction with line to the Sherman Mine
78.5	Owaissa	—	—	—
86.0	Freeman	—	—	A. Freeman, ONR general manager
94.2	Latchford	457	—	F.R. Latchford, who played an important part in the early days of the ONR
102.4	Coleman	—	—	A.P. Coleman, geologist in the early 1900s
102.8	Cobalt	2,056	—	Large deposits nearby
107.5	Haileybury	4,939	—	Haileybury College, England,

the school of Charles C. Farr, town founder

112.7	New Liskeard	5,601	—	Liskeard, town in Cornwall, England
118.1	Uno Park	103	—	—
124.8	Thornloe	151	—	—
128.6	Earlton	1,008	—	Earl, son of the first postmaster, A.E. Brasher
138.5	Englehart (Ont.)	1,767	—	J.L. Englehart, petroleum pioneer and former chairman of the ONR

Ramore Subdivision — ONR Englehart/Timmins
Devonshire Subdivision — ONR Porquis/Cochrane

This line was built by the Temiskaming and Northern Ontario Railway between 1905 and 1908, and opened for traffic on November 30, 1908.

Miles	Stations	Population	Elev.	Origin of Station Names
0.0	Englehart (Ont.)	1,767	—	(See Temagami subdivision)
12.5	Mindoka	—	—	—
14.8	Adams Jct.	—	—	Junction with line to the Adams Mine
20.9	Jardine	—	—	A. Jardine, an ONR general manager in the 1950s
25.6	Swastika Jct.	—	—	Junction with line to the mines at Kirkland Lake and Rouyn/Noranda
26.0	Swastika	935	—	Ontario Geographic Name Board files say the name is for "the good luck charm on a lady's necklace"
34.7	Steele	—	741	—
44.3	Bourkes	56	—	—
56.2	Ramore	332	—	—
66.4	Matheson	826	—	A.J. Matheson (1842-1913), provincial treasurer and MPP for South Lanark
76.4	Val Gagne	250	—	—
85.7	Porquis	237	—	—
102.8	Keyson	—	—	—
104.0	Kidd	—	—	George Nelson Kidd, MPP for Carleton at the turn of the century
109.7	Porcupine	1,213	—	Island nearby shaped like a porcupine
112.4	South Porcupine	5,144	—	—
118.7	Timmins (Ont.)	45,300	—	Noah A. Timmins (1867-1936), president of the Hollinger Consolidated Gold Mine Ltd., the richest gold mine in the western hemisphere
0.0	Porquis	237	—	—
0.8	Welsh	—	431	—
4.6	Nellie Lake	—	—	—
12.6	Potter	—	—	—
28.2	Cochrane (Ont.)	4,974	—	Francis Cochrane, Ontario minister of Lands and Forests in 1908, who became federal minister of Railways and Canals in the Borden Cabinet in 1911

Kapuskasing Subdivision — CNR Cochrane/Kapuskasing

This line was built by the National Transcontinental Railway between 1911 and 1915, and opened for traffic on June 1, 1915.

Miles	Stations	Population	Elev.	Origin of Station Names
0.0	Cochrane (Ont.)	4,974	—	(See Devonshire subdivision)
0.4	Cochrane Jct.	—	—	Junction with ONR to Moosonee
6.3	Frederick	—	—	—
8.4	Buskegau	—	—	—
11.8	Hunta	—	—	—
17.3	Driftwood	—	—	—
30.3	Smooth Rock	2,373	—	Smooth rocks in Mattagami River
41.7	Strickland	—	—	—
49.7	Fauquier	511	—	Railway contractor
55.9	Moonbeam	627	—	After Moonbeam Creek, where it is alleged that "twinkling lights from the sky fell like moonbeams into the creek"
69.4	Kapuskasing (Ont.)	12,400	—	Cree word for "branch of the river" or "where the river bends"

The Polar Bear Route

North from Cochrane to Moosonee, Ontario's only salt-water port, and a three-centuries-old fur-trading settlement on the shore of James Bay

Cochrane to Moosonee

Moose Factory was the first British settlement in Ontario, founded in 1673 as a Hudson's Bay Company trading post. But the town of Moosonee wasn't connected to the south by rail until July 15, 1932, when not one but *three* last spikes marked the completion of a 10-year project. The first, made of silver, was driven by Mr. Justice F.R. Latchford, who'd turned the first sod on the North Bay to New Liskeard line 30 years before. The second, composed of everyday iron, was left to George W. Lee, chairman of the Railway Commission. The third, in ceremonial gold, was hammered home by G.S. Henry, then premier of Ontario.

Platform marker for the Polar Bear Express

Today's rail line to Moosonee follows the Abitibi and Moose rivers — a canoe route traveled by Chevalier Pierre de Troyes when in 1686, he raided and captured the HBC fort just across the river in what is now Moose Factory. It wasn't until 1730 that Britain permanently reestablished its post, settling in for more than 200 years and growing rich on furs and sealskins. The community, such as it was, remained cut off from the outside world except by sea. But by the turn of the century, Ontario had begun to sense the need for an ocean port, and the Polar Bear edged toward reality.

There are, in fact, *two* Polar Bears. The Big Bear runs in summer only, offering a same-day return, with brief stops en route for taking photographs and several hours to explore the end of the line. It features a diner, a bar car that's frequently the scene of impromptu dances and singalongs and hostesses who provide informative com-

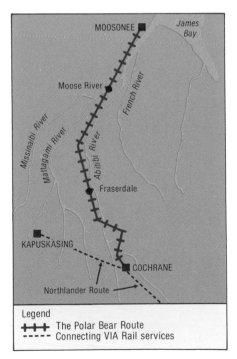

Legend
+++ The Polar Bear Route
----- Connecting VIA Rail services

Indian village on the shore at Moose River

mentary. The Little Bear, on the other hand, is a mixed train — part freight, part passenger — that operates three days a week throughout the year. It includes a restaurant car, but this is a working train, and you may find yourself stopping everywhere, anytime. Freight and mail to this wilderness area are addressed simply to a given milepost, and trackside deliveries are announced by sharp blasts of the whistle. Your fellow passengers might include Cree Indians, Inuit, hunters, fishermen, nurses, military personnel, Ontario Hydro workers, trappers, missionaries, bush pilots and miners. Kids treat the train as a mobile candy store, jumping aboard at bushland stops to buy treats. The Little Bear involves an overnight stay in Moosonee, where accommodation is limited, so you *must* reserve early. And don't forget a heavy sweater (even in summertime), all the insect repellent you can carry and plenty of film.

Or there's a third option: Ontario Northland's Polar Bear Package Tour. This includes a hotel in Moosonee and a wilderness excursion along the Moose River to the tidewaters of James Bay — a memorable trip through a land where canoes, dog teams and snowmobiles are everyday transportation; where "skyscrapers" mean two-storey buildings; where trapping remains a major industry; where streets are unpaved and sidewalks don't exist; where a mini-summer brings out the world's worst mosquitoes;

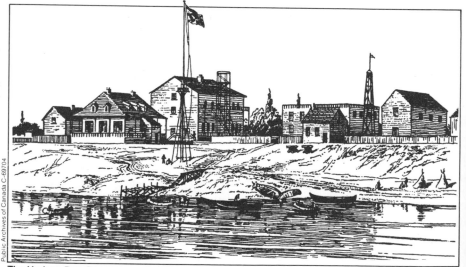

The Hudson Bay Company post at Moose Factory, 1854

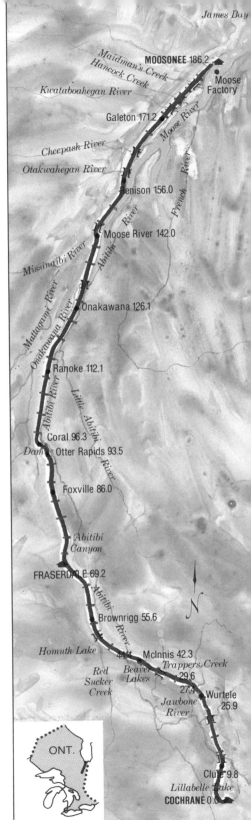

where "bilingualism" refers to English and Cree; where you can watch six-foot ocean tides and fabulous northern lights dance in the night sky. There is one disappointment: the term Polar Bear is a misnomer, since the nearest such animal roams the tundra more than 100 miles to the north.

POINTS OF INTEREST
Cochrane to Moosonee (island Falls subdivision)

Mile 1-30: On leaving Cochrane, you pass through the northern fringe of the Great Clay Belt, a fertile farming district where white daisies, goldenrod, cattails and lavender fireweed spring up beside the track. At mile 4.5, look east across Lillabelle Lake to Cochrane's airport, where planes can land on both runway and water before crossing the Abitibi River at mile 11. Then watch for the Ontario Paper Company's logging operations at Gardiner Lake mile 18.6.

Mile 43-70: The distinctive tower at mile 43 is one of eight built by the ONR to bring colour television, radio, telephone, telex and other communication services to northern communities. The Abitibi River is crossed again at mile 44.4, where a dam to the east powers the Abitibi-Price Paper Mill at Iroquois Falls. Its black spruce pulpwood will be transformed into salt cake and methyl alcohol as well as newsprint. The area between miles 49.3 and 53 was ravaged by a forest fire in 1976. Some 30,000 acres burned out of control for two weeks, until the flames were extinguished by water bombers. At mile 60, another fire caused similar devastation the following year. Fraserdale marks the end of the highway from Smooth Rock Falls. From this point, ONR track becomes the only means of land transport. A spur line used to run east from here for three miles to the Abitibi Canyon generating station, carrying a strange orange and black, self-powered car nicknamed the Island Falls Express. Ontario Hydro maintains several power stations throughout the Moose River Basin. Others will appear at Otter Rapids, mile 93.5, and up the Mattagami River at Kipling, Harmon and Little Long Rapids. Watch for the high voltage transmission lines cutting through the forest on their way to southern Ontario.

Mile 70-94: This stretch of track used to be traveled by the RailBug: a bright orange Volkswagen Beetle and trailer, specially adapted to bump along the right-of-way hauling ill or injured workers from the Otter Rapids power plant to the Fraserdale hospital. Between miles 72 and 77, you curve along the Abitibi River, an excellent spot for photographs. Watch for the looming domes of a Canadian Armed Forces radar station at Relay mile 80. Then, at mile 93.5, look east to the Otter Rapids generating station. Like other far northern plants, it's completely auto-mated, controlled by signals sent from a 300-foot-high antenna, 24 miles distant.

Mile 94-140: Now you enter the James Bay Beaches, or Hudson Bay Lowlands, an 800-mile-long, 250-mile-wide stretch of muskeg. Once this area was completely underwater, and it remains a vast bog, dotted with ancient (and very stunted) spruce, poplar and tamarack trees. Only the riverbanks can sustain normal growth. Coral Rapids, to the east at mile 96.3, is slated for future hydroelectric development, and dia-monds have been discovered nearby. The area around Onakawana is rich in lignite — a peatlike substance that was steam-dried and used to fuel an ONR locomotive in 1941. The experiment proved unsuccessful, but lignite may yet serve as a source of low-cost energy. To the east, near mile 111, are the Nine Mile Rapids; then come the Blacksmith Rapids at mile 127. When cross-ing Medicine Creek at mile 137.8, note the remarkable "upside-down" bridge, with its steel girders on top. In the spring, when the river is high, and the thaw begins, the lack of girders allows the fast flowing ice to pass easily under-neath. You'll see similar bridges at Kwataboa-hegan River (mile 174), Hancock Creek (mile 176.5) and Maidman's Creek (mile 180.2).

Mile 141-143: Look west near mile 142 to the picturesque settlement of Moose River. First come a cluster of houses and a school, sepa-rated by a bay from an Indian village, complete with tepees. Just before you cross the bridge, look back to see a fine, sandy beach. The Moose River is half a mile wide at this point, cut in two by Murray Island. The 1,800-foot bridge (the ONR's longest) is a triumph of engineering skill, com-pleted during the Depression at the immense cost of $1 million. Construction involved closing off one channel at a time so that concrete could be poured and the huge steel supports built.

Mile 144-186: The Otakwahegan River is crossed at mile 157.6 — one of 28 streams that join the Moose River as it rushes to the sea. Large depos-its of gypsum and pottery clay have been discov-ered near the Cheepash River at mile 162. As you approach mile 180, you'll spot Moosonee's red and white water tower rising in the distance ahead.

Mile 186.2: Moosonee is both the end of steel and the gateway to Canada's Arctic. The station posts a list of distances from here to the most remote northern settlements. This isn't a picture-postcard town, but a tough community that struggles to survive in a land where tempera-tures plunge to -50° F. Be careful as you walk the streets: nobody requires a driver's licence, and you might see 10-year-olds weaving down the main drag in pickup trucks. You can't even jump on a sidewalk to escape, because there aren't any! The buildings are strictly practical: walking along First Street to the waterfront, compare the

modern education centre with its neighbours, a frame boarding house and café straight out of the 1920s. You can shop for arctic crafts at the Hudson's Bay store (which still does a roaring trade in raw furs), or you can patronize local kids, who display their wares on blankets. Be sure to visit the cathedral of the Oblate Fathers and the Revillon Frères Museum, commemorating the French fur traders who preceded the HBC.

Some days the waterfront can resemble an Arctic Dunkirk with the arrival of 22-foot-long Rupert's House motor-powered canoes, operated by local Indians, who will transport you to Moose Factory. If you're lucky, you might pass a school of frolicking beluga whales. Moose Factory's ultramodern hospital cares for residents from all across the northland. Watch for a tepee where Indian women bake sticks of bannock (the "bread of the north") over an open fire. Visit St. Thomas' Anglican Church, built in 1864, which went sailing off during a spring flood some years ago. It can't be properly an-chored in the rocky ground, so holes were drilled in its floor to prevent it floating away again. Take time to appreciate its stained-glass windows, Cree hymn books, beaded moosehide altar cloths and the sign outside, which reads, "Pal, you're welcome." Stroll through its tiny grave-yard before seeing the HBC trading post and the company's former staff house, built by ship-wrights in the 1830s. Don't miss Museum Park, with a restored log fort and one of the province's oldest wooden buildings, a 1740 blacksmith shop. And, before you leave, plan to visit Fossil and Ship Sands islands. The former is a mecca for serious rockhounds; the latter, the site of a bird sanctuary where flocks of geese gather in the tidal flats before migrating south.

The Polar Bear Route

Island Falls Subdivision — ONR Cochrane/Moosonee
This line was built by the Temiskaming and Northern Ontario Railway between 1922 and 1932, and opened for traffic on July 15, 1932.

Miles	Stations	Population	Elev.	Origin of Station Names
0.0	Cochrane (Ont.)	4,974	—	(See Devonshire subdivision, page 122)
0.3	Cochrane Jct.	—	—	Junction with CNR to Kapus-kasing
9.8	Clute	—	—	Judge R.C. Clute from Picton, an early settler
25.9	Wurtele	—	835	—
42.3	McInnis	—	777	—
55.6	Brownrigg	—	—	—
69.2	Fraserdale	215	780	—
86.0	Foxville	—	—	—
93.5	Otter Rapids	528	—	Rapids in nearby Abitibi River
96.3	Coral	—	—	—
112.1	Ranoke	—	—	—
126.1	Onakawana	—	—	Indian word describing the lignite coal deposits nearby
142.0	Moose River	—	140	Crossing of wide river at this point
156.0	Renison	—	—	—
171.2	Galeton	—	75	—
186.2	Moosonee (Ont.)	975	33	Indian word "moosoneek," meaning "home of the moose"

Indian tepees at Moose Factory

Displaying fossils in Moose Factory

St. Thomas' Anglican Church

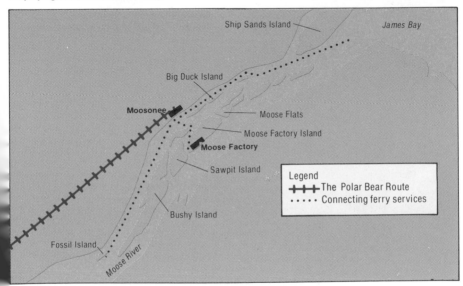

Ship Sands Island

James Bay

Big Duck Island

Moosonee

Moose Flats

Moose Factory Island

Moose Factory

Sawpit Island

Bushy Island

Fossil Island

Moose River

Legend
╂╂╂ The Polar Bear Route
...... Connecting ferry services

The Agawa/Black Bear Route

A never-to-be-forgotten journey through the most striking scenery east of the Rockies — a riot of colour in the fall, a winter wonderland aboard the Snow Train

Sault Ste. Marie to Hearst

Sault Ste. Marie was discovered in 1622 by Etienne Brûlé, the first white man to reach Lake Superior. Before long, Jesuit missionaries were reporting rich copper deposits in the district's Precambrian rock, prompting the French to dispatch Louis Jolliet on a geological exploration in 1669. In 1771, following the British conquest, boats were built at a site just above the St. Mary's rapids, and by 1799 the first crude lock had been constructed by North West Company traders. This is where the voyageurs' canoes would come speeding through en route to the fur-rich wilderness beyond. (The locks you see today — which handle more tonnage than the Suez and Panama canals combined — were completed in 1885 on the American side; the single Canadian lock opened for business 10 years later.)

By 1899, a man named Francis H. Clergue had foreseen the Soo's industrial potential, and obtained a charter for a railway linking the city's Algoma Steel plant with the iron mines at Michipicoten. Clergue had previously laid track in Bangor, Maine, up Mount Washington and across Persia. The prospect of having to conquer the Canadian Shield failed to dampen his enthusiasm.

Construction of the Algoma Central and Hudson Bay Railway (the name was shortened for accuracy's sake in 1965) began in 1901. The original idea was to extend the line to Hudson Bay, spurring colonization along the way, but a combination of muskeg, rock, blackflies and freezing temperatures defeated this grand design. Hawk Junction

(the turnoff to the mines) was reached in 1911, but it wasn't until October 13, 1914 that the first passenger train rolled into Hearst.

For several years, the railway's operations bordered on the surreal. Timetables were best used to wrap fish. If a female passenger's hat blew off, the conductor would

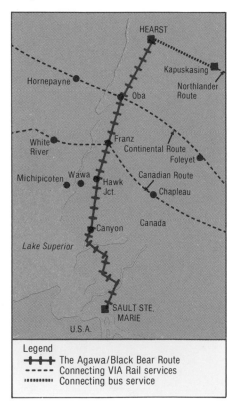

Legend
+++ The Agawa/Black Bear Route
----- Connecting VIA Rail services
•••••••••• Connecting bus service

ck Beaver Falls cascades into Agawa Canyon

ONT.
Kwagama Hill 2,091′
CANYON 113.8
Black Beaver Lake
Agawa River
Little Agawa River
Frater 102.6
Speckled Trout Lake
Little Agawa Lake
Montréal Hill
Hubert Lake
Lake Superior
Hubert 95.5
Montréal River
Montréal River
Montréal Falls 92.3
Regent 88.7
Big Pike Lake
Big Pike Creek
Rand Lake
1,984′
Rand 85.0
Batchawana River
Batchawana 79.8
Mongoose Lake
MONGOOSE 75.0
Wart Lake
Summit 72.9
Batchawana River
Spruce Lake
Spruce Lake 71.0
Pangis 69.0
Tribble Lake
Harmony River
Batchawana Mountain 2,142′
Gavor Lake
Mekatina 64.6
1,600′
Pine Lake 62.0
Trout Lake 57.0
Alva Lake
Mashkode 56.2
Trout Lake
Chippewa River
Chippewa River
Ogidaki 48.1
Ogidaki Lake
Ogidaki Mountain 2,183′
Lake Superior
Achigan Lake
Little Achigan Lake
Achigan 41.8
Achigan Creek
Achigan Creek
N
Wabos 35.9
SEARCHMONT 31.5
Goulais River
Mt. Searchmont 1,875′
Northland 24.7
Goulais 30.7
Goulais River
Bellvue Valley 20
Northland Lake
Island Lake
Heyden 14.1
Heyden Lake
Crystal Lake
Odena 9.5
Steelton 2.0
SAULT STE MARIE 0.0

Morning mist rises over Ogidaki Lake

back up to retrieve it. Women and the clergy were barricaded in rear coaches to keep them away from hard-drinking lumberjacks, and crews were hired largely on the basis of their fighting skills.

That's all changed, but the Black Bear remains one of the last great romantic train rides in North America. It's been a magnet for such diverse personalities as the Prince of Wales, actress Helen Hayes and several of the Group of Seven painters. Even country singer Stompin' Tom Connors recorded a song about true love frustrated by a railway that, in the past, gained several unflattering nicknames. Early passengers knew in their bones that ACHB *really* meant "All Curves and Hard Bumps," and it *still* might signify "All Curves and High Bridges." Today's 296-mile run crosses more than 200 bridges and trestles, but there's not a single tunnel, with the result that the line sometimes resembles a corkscrew. (It's also been rumoured that the station names were produced by a Welshman speaking Russian with an Aberdeen accent.) And even though today's trains are totally modern — the ACR made its conversion from steam to diesel in 1952, the first Canadian railway to do so — there's still a wild side, revealed by a look into the baggage car. It might contain a moose carcass, bearskins, catches of fish, outboard motors and canoes. The train still forms this area's major link with the outside world, and stops anytime for anyone standing on the line in the middle of nowhere.

Several different excursions are operated on the ACR year-round. The most popular is the one-day Wilderness Train Tour, run-

ning daily between June and mid-October, which takes 3 1/2 hours each way, with two hours to explore the Agawa Canyon. January through March, the Snow Train runs on Saturdays and Sundays from the Soo to Eton and back. You pass through the canyon — transformed into a winter wonderland — but because of the cold, there's no stop. Finally, if you'd like to cover the entire route, there's the two-day Tour of the Line, including overnight accommodation in Hearst. Plan to book early, because these trips are extremely popular. In 1952, only 765 people ventured as far as Agawa. By 1981, this number had risen to 106,000 with a further 10,000 riding the Snow Train and 2,500 going to the end of the line.

POINTS OF INTEREST
Sault Ste. Marie to Agawa Canyon

Mile 1-5: As you leave the station, look south to see the Canadian lock in the St. Mary's River, cutting through Whitefish Island. The first of 16 water steps in the St. Lawrence Seaway System, it measures 900 feet. Farther south are the four American locks, ranging up to 1,350 feet. Most tonnage here is iron ore and grain, bound for points all over the world. You'll also see the mammoth Great Lakes Power plant, the Abitibi Paper mill with its huge stacks of pulpwood and, soaring overhead, the mile-long International Bridge to the U.S.A. As you curve north, look west to view the sprawling works of the Algoma Steel Corporation, still the railway's major customer. Just beyond, to the east, are the ACR's own shops, with an unusual covered turntable.

Mile 14-25: At Heyden, a small farming and lumbering community, you lose sight of the Trans-Canada Highway to the west. It hugs the shore of

Lake Superior, and you won't glimpse it again for 85 miles. At mile 15.5, as the train curves around a rocky promontory, the cottages along Island Lake come into view to the east. The 810-foot Bellevue Valley trestle at mile 20 rises 100 feet above the trees — a magnificent viewpoint in the fall, when the whole valley seems aflame. In early morning, however, it's often shrouded in fog. Until 1916, there was a 1,150-foot wooden trestle at this point, with a natural cold water spring at the north end, where trains made an unofficial stop, allowing the crews time for refreshment while passengers drank in the scenery. A short distance up the track, tiny Northland's only claim to fame stems from the day in 1920 when a special train carrying Edward, Prince of Wales (the future Duke of Windsor), stopped so that he could practise target shooting from his private car. The prince was apparently a terrible marksman — most of his bullets missed the hastily positioned tin cans and went plopping into Northland Lake.

Mile 27-32: The Goulais River Valley, a farming area first settled in 1882, lies just to the west at mile 27. Watch for circling ravens overhead and swamp orchids along the river banks. To the east, at mile 31, you can see the 700-foot trails of the Searchmont Valley ski resort. In the old days, this is where crews would offer a free ride to local residents who brought them buckets of beer from a trackside bar while the train offloaded its mail.

Mile 42-61: Achigan Lake, to the east between miles 43 and 45, has fine sandy beaches and excellent trout fishing. At mile 47, look east to Ogidaki Lake, with Ogidaki Mountain in the background. A barrel used to be moored just off-shore — a target for the baggageman, whose aim was equal to Prince Edward's, with the result that the barrel survived for 10 years. Indian legends from this picturesque area were appropriated by

The northbound Snow Train curves along the Batchawana Canyon

Henry Wadsworth Longfellow, and formed the basis of his epic poem *Song of Hiawatha*. Look for a large tree to the west as you cross the Chippewa River at mile 51. Lumberjacks heading for the Soo would wait here for the southbound train and, on their return, would be placed beneath its branches to sober up before stumbling back to camp. The aptly named Trout Lake curves to the east between miles 57 and 61 — a good stretch for photographs. The Department of Lands and Forests (now the Ministry of Natural Resources), once maintained a base here for its fire patrol aircraft, but the buildings have been converted to summer cottages.

Mile 62-76: Look for massive glacial boulders in Pine Lake to the east at mile 62; then, at Mekatina (mile 64.6), for the lakeside cottage that used to be a "message cabin" — a log structure occupied by a railway employee who would convey information to passing trains. Its occupant didn't need

to stray too far; he was literally able to fish from his desk. A peaceful lodge lies to the west at mile 71, and Mongoose Lake, shaped like its namesake, becomes visible to the east between miles 74 and 76.

Mile 80-93: After crossing the Batchawana River at mile 80, the train begins a steep, twisting climb from the valley floor. This area served as inspiration for J.E.H. MacDonald, one of the Group of Seven, whose *Batchawana Rapids* (1920) is housed in the National Gallery of Canada. Along with Frank Johnston and Lawren Harris, he traveled the ACR in 1918, riding aboard a specially outfitted boxcar — a trip that produced such masterworks as *The Solemn Land* and *Wild River*. Mile 92.5 features one of the ACR's most-photographed locations: the 1,550-foot steel trestle curving eastward over the Montréal River, designed by the New York firm of Boller and Hodge and erected by the Canadian Bridge

133

Company in 1911. Consisting of 14 tower girders, one of which stands on an island in mid-stream, it commands a view of a power dam that supplies electricity to the Soo. The train inches across at 20 mph, allowing ample time to appreciate a view that so delighted the Prince of Wales in 1920 that he pulled the emergency cord to halt his progress, nearly causing a collision with a following train. To the east, a fishing lodge offers testimony to the fact that the river is renowned for its walleye and pike.

Mile 97-114: At mile 97, you pass the railway's highest point — 1,589 feet — before reaching Speckled Trout Lake, to the east at mile 99. At Frater, look west for a view of the Trans-Canada Highway snaking its way along Lake Superior's Agawa Bay. Then you begin a descent to Agawa Canyon, dropping 500 feet over 10 miles, past Kwagama Hill and along the Agawa River. This is perhaps the most spectacular scenery east of the Rockies, and at its best in the fall, when the hills are ablaze with colour. At mile 104, there used to be an impressive wooden trestle more than 1,100 feet long, but like similar structures elsewhere, it was filled in to reduce the risk of fire. The canyon

floor is reached at mile 112. Keep your camera ready as you cross the river so as to capture views of Bridal Veil and Black Beaver falls. The former cascades down in several separate streams, forming massive ice sculptures at the base in wintertime.

Mile 113.8: If you're stopping at the canyon, the most noticeable feature — aside from its fabulous view — is the lack of sound. Only the wind and occasional bird calls disturb the silence. A climb up Lookout Trail allows you to photograph acres of spruce, aspen, birch, maple and balsam. The air is clean and fragrant; the river winds quietly below. You can also walk to Black Beaver and Bridal Veil falls, eat a riverside picnic lunch (there aren't any on-site food outlets, but you can buy provisions aboard the train) and try your hand at fishing in a trout-filled pool. For a more detailed description of the canyon and environs, see the map below.

Agawa Canyon to Hearst

Mile 115-132: The train continues through the rugged canyon, in places only 50 feet wide. Mile 118.5 marks the stop for Kwagama Lake Lodge.

Agawa Canyon Park

1 Park attendant's quarters
2 Picnic area: tables and benches in a well-developed setting. **2a** More tables, scattered through a more rustic area
3 Picnic shelters: with several covered tables
4 Water pumps
5 Play areas: swings, slides and log climbers for children; horseshoe pitches for older athletes
6 Women's washrooms
7 Men's washrooms
8 Lookout Trail: this walkway leads through a natural setting along the base of the canyon wall to an intermediate lookout (**8a**) providing good views of the canyon. Most people can manage this walk with ease. A steep climb up the canyon wall leads to the upper lookout (**8b**), which offers a truly magnificent view. This is a favourite spot for photographers, but the ascent is rigorous, and small children should be carefully watched. Please note that due to a year-round fire hazard, no smoking is permitted on the trail
9 Black Beaver Falls: a pleasant and not particularly strenuous walk
10 Bridal Veil Falls: a somewhat longer walk — allow 45 minutes there and back
11 Agawa River: several fishing holes (ask for exact locations on site) are filled with speckled trout
12 Rock slides: look for posted descriptions of the canyon's distinctive geological formations

Legend
+ + + The Agawa/ Black Bear route
- - - - Walking route

atching from the Lookout as the Black Bear pulls into Agawa Canyon station

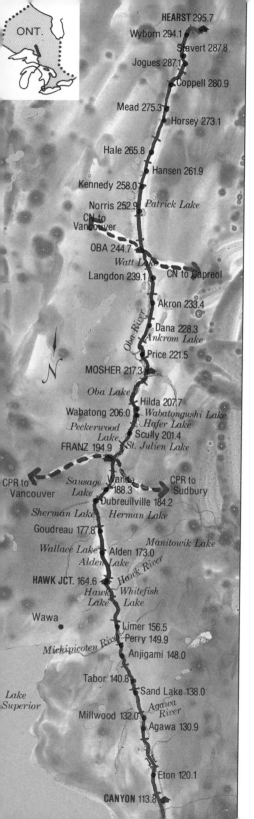

Its winter guests ski nine miles in, while their baggage travels by snowmobile. At mile 122, you cross the "Chinese Bridge," built in the 1940s for the Nationalist Chinese by a Montréal firm. Mao Tse-tung canceled the order when he gained power, and the ACR snapped up the pieces at a bargain price. Between miles 122 and 136, the track forms the eastern boundary of Lake Superior Provincial Park, a 600-square-mile wilderness home to moose, white-tailed deer, hare, beaver, muskrat, red fox, mink and wolf.

Mile 136-165: The Sand River flows southwest to Superior from Sand Lake (mile 136), providing a popular canoe route through the park. At Tabor, watch for a trackside pond where crews sometimes toss breadcrumbs to the fish. At mile 151, there's a large gravel pit that supplies ballast for the ACR. The Michipicoten River, at mile 153, was once a fur traders' canoe route between Lake Superior and James Bay. At Hawk Junction, a 26-mile branch line heads west to the Josephine and Helen mines, the town of Wawa and the harbour at Michipicoten. This is a scheduled service stop, and your chance to enjoy a snack at the Black Bear Restaurant immediately behind the station.

Mile 170-244: This is a largely unpopulated area dotted with small lakes and stands of jackpine. Hobon Lake lies to the east between miles 191 and 195. At Franz, the Black Bear intersects with the CPR track that carries VIA's famous Canadian west toward Vancouver. Franz also features an enclosed and heated water tank, necessary because steam locomotives needed topping up every 50 or 60 miles. Thousands of these structures used to dot Canada's rail lines, leading to the expression "tank towns." At mile 210, the Black Bear crosses the Arctic Watershed, the point at which rivers flow either north to James Bay or south to Lake Superior. Oba Lake is visible to the west between miles 210 and 216. At mile 212.7, the train slows to 25 mph to cross a 1,302-foot trestle that's actually a floating bridge over Hoodoo Bay. Its wooden pilings are buoyed up by a sea of soggy mud that would suck down steel girders overnight. Look west at Tatnall (mile 215.5) and you might see the bright yellow pontoon planes used for fire spotting. At Mosher, you'll notice a small spur track that's used by the Newaygo Timber Company for loading pulpwood. Near mile 242, look east across Watt Lake to see the Continental route (page 138), which meets the Black Bear at Oba.

Mile 245-296: Here the countryside gradually changes to clay-based farming soil. The Mattawitchewan River is crossed on a 700-foot bridge at mile 269. The town of Hearst, at the end of the line, takes great pride in its title "The Moose Capital of Canada." It's still a frontier community in many respects, with five busy sawmills constituting its major industry. From here, it's an easy bus ride east to Kapuskasing, northern terminal of the Northlander Route (see page 110).

Mosher is typical of the lumbering towns at the north end of the Algoma Central run

The Agawa/Black Bear Route

Soo Subdivision — ACR Sault Ste. Marie/Hawk Jct.
This line was built between 1900 and 1912 by the Algoma Central & Hudson Bay Railway. Mashkode was reached in 1903; Mile 68 in 1908; and Montreal Falls in 1911.

Miles	Stations	Population	Elev.	Origin of Station Names
0.0	Sault Ste. Marie (Ont.)	81,200	600	Cataract or falls of St. Mary, named by Jesuit missionaries
2.0	Steelton	—	—	Algoma steel plant
9.5	Odena	—	—	—
14.1	Heyden	—	1,071	Near Heyden Lake
24.7	Northland	—	1,080	Near Northland Lake
30.7	Goulais	—	—	Near Goulais River
31.5	Searchmont	123	780	Near Mt. Searchmont ski area
35.9	Wabos	—	944	Indian for "rabbit"
41.8	Achigan	—	1,112	Near Lake Achigan
48.1	Ogidaki	—	1,227	Near Ogidaki Lake
56.2	Mashkode	—	1,143	—
57.0	Trout Lake	—	1,034	—
62.0	Pine Lake	—	1,279	—
64.6	Mekatina	—	1,453	—
69.0	Pangis	—	—	Near Pangis Lake
71.0	Spruce Lake	—	978	—
72.9	Summit	—	1,413	Near the summit of the rail line
75.0	Mongoose	—	—	Near Mongoose Lake
79.8	Batchawana	—	1,022	Indian word "obatchiwanang," meaning "at the current of the strait"
85.0	Rand	—	—	Near Rand Lake
88.7	Regent	—	1,338	—
92.3	Montreal Falls	—	1,278	Falls on the Montreal River, which was named after the city of Montreal
93.0	Mile 93	—	—	—
95.5	Hubert	—	1,514	Near Hubert Lake
102.6	Frater	—	1,462	T. Frater, president of the Algoma Eastern Railway in 1914
113.8	Canyon	—	937	Agawa Canyon
120.1	Eton	—	1,031	Eton College, England
122.5	Mile 122½	—	—	—
130.9	Agawa	—	1,110	Indian word meaning "bending shore"
132.0	Millwood	—	—	Log-loading area
138.0	Sand Lake	—	1,231	—
140.8	Tabor	—	1,261	—
148.0	Anjigami	—	1,174	Near Anjigami Lake
149.9	Perry	—	989	George Perry (1818-91), MPP for North Oxford from 1867 to 1872, and sheriff of Oxford County from 1873 to 1891
156.5	Limer	—	1,062	Limerick, a county and town in Ireland
164.6	Hawk Jct. (Ont.)	375	1,040	Near Hawk Lake

Northern Subdivision — ACR Hawk Jct./Hearst
This line was built between 1913 and 1914, and opened for traffic in November 1914.

Miles	Stations	Population	Elev.	Origin of Station Names
164.6	Hawk Jct. (Ont.)	375	1,040	(See Soo subdivision)
173.0	Alden	—	1,173	Near Alden Lake
177.8	Goudreau	135	1,212	Goudreau pyrite deposits in area
184.2	Dubreuilville	381	—	—
188.3	Wanda	—	1,168	—
194.9	Franz	20	1,216	W. G. Franz, general superintendent of Algoma Steel in the early 1900s
201.4	Scully	—	1,210	Near Scully Lake
206.0	Wabatong	—	—	—
207.7	Hilda	—	1,142	—
210.0	Mile 210	—	—	—
212.0	Mile 212	—	—	—
217.3	Mosher	—	1,141	—
221.5	Price	—	1,173	—
228.3	Dana	—	1,102	G.A. Dana, MPP for Brockville in the 1890s
233.4	Akron	—	1,079	Near Akron Lakes
239.1	Langdon	—	1,099	Near Langdon Lake
244.7	Oba	75	1,070	Near Oba River
252.9	Norris	—	1,037	Near Norris River
258.0	Kennedy	—	1,027	T.J. Kennedy, ACR general superintendent from 1910 to 1915
261.9	Hansen	—	—	—
265.8	Hale	—	1,026	—
273.1	Horsey	—	926	—
275.3	Mead	—	926	—
280.9	Coppell	213	902	ACR official
287.1	Jogues	77	—	Isaac Jogues founded the mission at Sault Ste. Marie
287.8	Stavert	—	834	—
294.1	Wyborn	—	—	—
294.7	Hearst Jct.	—	—	Junction with CNR
295.7	Hearst (Ont.)	5,195	847	Sir William Hearst (1864-1941), premier of Ontario, noted for his enactment of the infamous Ontario Temperance Act during World War I

The Continental Route

A voyage across the isolated interior of Northern Ontario and Manitoba, past luxury resorts, rustic villages and crystal-clear fishing lakes

Capreol to Winnipeg

The Continental Limited was the pride of the newly formed Canadian National Railways when it made its maiden run on December 12, 1920, from Montreal to Vancouver, covering the 2,944 miles in 112 hours. It consisted of first-class coaches, tourist and standard sleepers, colonist cars, a diner and a special compartment observation lounge equipped with library and buffet. Patrons enjoyed private smoking areas, Thermos bottles of iced water, four o'clock tea and a unique entertainment offered by no other railway in the world: the novelty of radio broadcasts. (The Continental was also one of the first trains to provide open observation cars through the Rocky Mountains.)

Another unusual feature of the Continental was its routing: over what is today Ontario Northland track from North Bay to Cochrane, then along the National Trans-

continental Railway route to Winnipeg. A companion train, the National, traveled over the Canadian Northern Railway track from Toronto to Winnipeg via Longlac, Fort William and Port Arthur (now Thunder Bay) and Fort Frances. These routes would change in 1924, with the completion of the Longlac-Nakina cutoff.

Today's 931-mile route from Capreol to Winnipeg takes you straight across the rugged vastness of the Canadian Shield. When the glaciers receded 10,000 years ago, they left behind a region gouged and scarred by giant holes that became sparkling, fish-filled lakes — an area rich in mineral, forest and hydroelectric wealth, but a railway builder's nightmare. Construction of the Canadian Northern and NTR involved 21,000 laborers and took 15 years. Countless lakes had to be avoided, and 240 rivers bridged under the most adverse conditions.

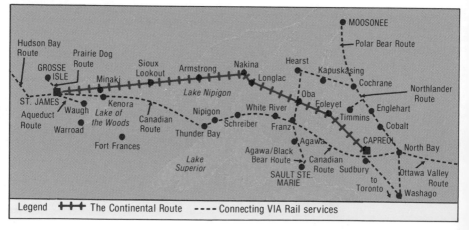

Legend   ┼┼┼ The Continental Route   ---- Connecting VIA Rail services

To lay one 358-mile section of track, engineers surveyed more than 9,100 miles of possible route before obtaining an acceptable alignment. One surveyor described the territory as "a monstrous terrain, empty wasteland as savage as any on the planet, where rocky ribs burst through to scanty soil as in a decayed skeleton. Intervening hollows hold muskeg swamps which gulp down yards of fill before providing firm footing for a roadbed."

Today's traveler can still appreciate these herculean tasks, because the area is little changed. It's also served almost entirely by rail, since highway construction proved equally daunting. Most merchandise, from mail to milk, arrives aboard the train. On-line towns vary in population from nine (Ycliff) to 2,495 (Sioux Lookout); timetables list regular stops at lake resorts, hidden away in the almost impenetrable bush. Lakes and rivers are colourfully, sometimes mysteriously, named: by Indians (Minisinakwa Lake) and for fish (Jackfish River), animals (Otter Lake), people (Gzowski Lake), birds (Pelican Lake), geographic features (Spine Lake) or shape (Boomerang Lake).

POINTS OF INTEREST
Capreol to Hornepayne (Ruel Subdivision)

Mile 0: The Sudbury Basin — a depression approximately 35 miles long and 16 miles wide — was formed about 1,700 million years ago when a giant meteorite crashed to earth. Its impact revealed evidence of the region's copper, iron, nickel, gold and platinum deposits, but it wasn't until the late 1800s, during construction of the railways, that these were discovered and exploited. A century of smelting has made the Sudbury area's fortune as nickel capital of the world, but it's also denuded the landscape and rendered many lakes too acidic (because of sulfur dioxide in the rainfall) to sustain marine life. More stringent pollution controls and reforestation programs have mended some of the damage, but much of the countryside still presents a barren, almost lunar, appearance. In Prescott Park, near Capreol Station, you'll see a 12-ton fragment of another enormous meteorite, a railway handcar used by track section gangs and steam locomotive 6077, which once hauled the Continental Limited on your present-day route as far as Hornepayne.

Mile 1-20: Here you follow the Vermilion River, crossing it four times. Watch for a dam to the north at mile 8.5, rapids to the north at mile 12.5 and to the south two miles farther on.

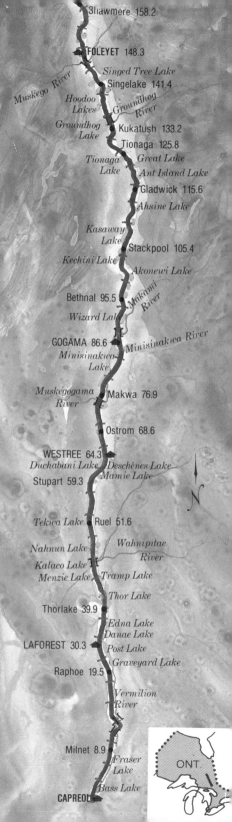

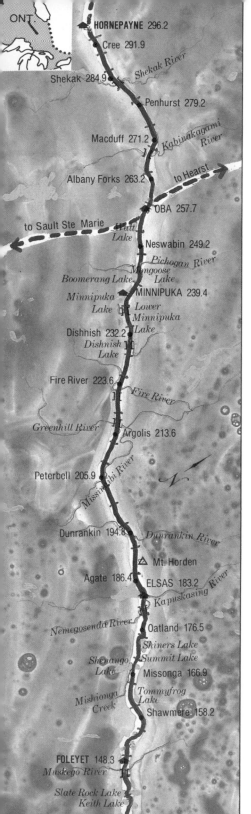

ONT

HORNEPAYNE 296.2
Cree 291.9
Shekak River
Shekak 284.9
Penhurst 279.2
Macduff 271.2
Kabinakagami River
Albany Forks 263.2
to Hearst
OBA 257.7
to Sault Ste Marie
Wataii Lake
Neswabin 249.2
Pichogan River
Mongoose Lake
Boomerang Lake
MINNIPUKA 239.4
Minnipuka Lake
Lower Minnipuka Lake
Dishnish 232.2
Dishnish Lake
Fire River 223.6
Fire River
Greenhill River
Argolis 213.6
Peterbell 205.9
Missinaibi River
Dunrankin 194.8
Dunrankin River
Mt. Horden
Agate 186.4
ELSAS 183.2
Kapuskasing River
Nemegosenda River
Oatland 176.5
Shiners Lake
Shenango Lake
Summit Lake
Missonga 166.9
Mishionga Creek
Tommyfrog Lake
Shawmere 158.2
FOLEYET 148.3
Muskego River
Slate Rock Lake
Keith Lake

Mile 20-133: The world's longest "schoolyard" extended from Capreol to Foleyet — the route of a unique "schoolhouse on wheels," with stops at Raphoe, Laforest, Ruel, Ostrom, Bethnal, Stackpool and Kukatush. The "schoolhouse" consisted of one car that was picked up by a freight or passenger train, taken to one of the above sidings, left for four days while the teacher gave the lessons and then picked up and towed to the next stop. Six other cars serviced the CN, CP and ON railway lines in the same way. The students were the children of local Indians, trappers, lumbermen and railway employees; the teachers, who lived on board, left their pupils enough homework to keep them busy until the car returned. This wilderness educational system was conceived in 1926 by Fred Sloman, who taught in the north for 39 years. It's highly fitting that the only remaining schoolhouse is preserved at Sloman Memorial Park in Clinton, Ontario.

Mile 86-89: Gogama, on Minisinakwa Lake, is a typical on-line community: a wilderness logging and mining town that also caters to fishermen and moose hunters. Here, as in many northern settlements, you'll see spur tracks for loading pulpwood. Just outside the town, at mile 88.6, you cross the Makami River.

Mile 134.7: Here the Groundhog River is spanned by a 1,134-foot bridge.

Mile 148.3: Foleyet is a small lumbering community noted for its superb moose and bear hunting.

Mile 166-189: Wonderful views appear at Missonga (Shenango Lake to the south), mile 174 (Shiners Lake to the north) and Elsas (Kapuskasing Lake to the south). All these are situated on curves, allowing you to photograph both train and water. Look north at mile 189 to see a fire tower on 1,489-foot Mount Horden.

Mile 194.8: Look south as you enter Dunrankin for three small white crosses, marking the graves of CN employees killed in 1964 when an eastbound freight ran into the Super Continental.

Mile 183-257: Here the track forms the northern boundary of the 7,000-square-mile Chapleau Game Preserve, the world's second-largest such

St. Barnabas' Church, at the Allanwater Bridge

sanctuary. Its lakes and rivers shelter mink, otter, beaver, lynx, moose, bear and wildfowl. Look north at mile 213.6, when crossing the Greenhill River, to view the Trestle Rapids. Between miles 239 and 242, you travel along Minnipuka Lake.

Mile 257.7: Oba is the junction of the Algoma Central Railway from Sault Ste. Marie to Hearst (see page 128). Passengers facing a tedious wait in the days of less reliable schedules were known to seek refuge in the local hotel.

Mile 296.2: Hornepayne is located in the heart of a huge wilderness area. Nearby fishing camps feature walleye, speckled trout and northern pike, while hunters can pursue geese, ducks, partridge, moose and bear. The downtown centre is a model for northern development, combining schools, shopping, office space and sports facilities under one roof.

POINTS OF INTEREST

Hornepayne to Armstrong (Caramat subdivision)

Mile 42-46: Another fire tower can be seen to the south near Hillsport, at mile 42.3, as well as a rail line that transports copper ore from Manitouwadge. At mile 45.6, you cross the Little White Otter River — where the last spike of this section of the CNR track was driven by its president, Sir William Mackenzie on January 1, 1914, in a ceremony that lasted only 10 minutes, due to the terrible cold. The completion of this second transcontinental railway was instrumental in opening up Ontario's northland.

Mile 77.6: An abandoned sawmill appears to the south across Caramat Lake. Such facilities were set up to log a specific area, then moved to another location, but this one was left behind.

Mile 100-101: Long Lake is one of Canada's largest inland bodies of water, extending 45 miles south of Longlac townsite. This was a canoe route for the *coureurs de bois* who paddled between Lake Superior and Hudson Bay, so Longlac became both a major trading centre and the scene of bitter rivalry between the Hudson's Bay and North West companies. Today it serves the region's forest industry with several plywood and flakeboard plants. As you circle the lake, look west to a beautiful white church situated on a point of land.

Mile 112-120: Photographic opportunities abound as the train twists and turns past several lakes.

Mile 131.6: Nakina is a supply centre for the area's hunting and fishing lodges, some of which offer ice-fishing, snowmobiling and cross-country skiing during the winter months. In summer, there's nothing tastier than a shore lunch of fresh-caught fish, cooked over an open fire.

Mile 193-222: Look north at mile 193 to see the power dam on Clod Lake. Between miles 209 and 213, Lake Nipigon's Ombabika Bay appears to the south. Your best view can be had at mile 209.9, as the train crosses the Jackfish Creek Via-

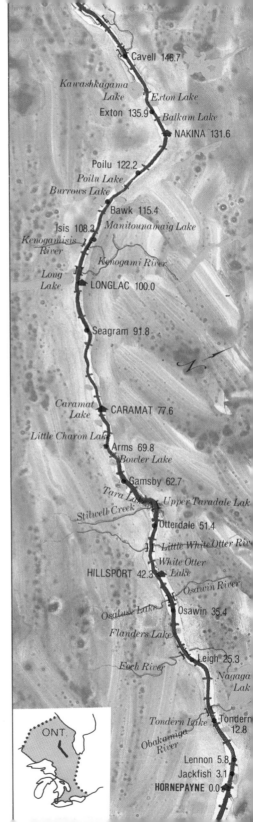

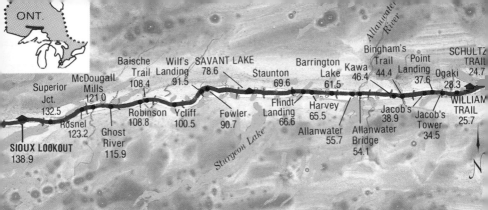

ONT.

					SCHULTZ
		Baische	Wilf's SAVANT LAKE	Bingham's	TRAIL
		Trail	Landing 78.6	Trail	24.7
	McDougall	108.4	91.5 Staunton	44.4 Point
Superior	Mills		69.6 Barrington Kawa	Landing Ogaki
Jct.	121.0		Lake 46.4	37.6 28.3
132.5		Robinson Ycliff	61.5	Jacob's WILLIAM
	Rosnel	108.8 100.5 Fowler	Flindt Harvey	38.9 TRAIL
	123.2	90.7	Landing 65.5	Jacob's 25.7
SIOUX LOOKOUT	Ghost		66.6	Tower
138.9	River		Allanwater Allanwater	34.5
	115.9		55.7 Bridge	
			54.1	

Allanwater River

Sturgeon Lake

N

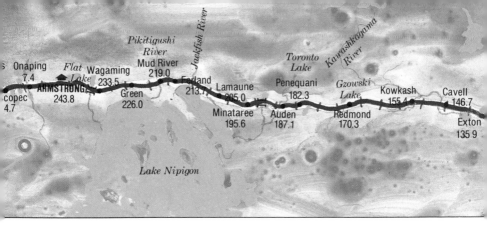

duct, a 798-foot bridge running 74 feet above water level. The bright yellow St. Joseph's Indian Church lies to the north at mile 213, followed at mile 219.1 by the 362-foot Mud River Viaduct. The sluggish waters 60 feet below don't sound much more inviting by their Indian name, Pikitigushi. To the south you'll notice several log cabins, with Lake Nipigon in the background. This is northern Ontario's largest lake, 1,870 square miles, and dotted with hundreds of tiny islands once occupied by the Ojibway indians. Haystack Mountain looms to the north at mile 221.

POINTS OF INTEREST

Armstrong to Sioux Lookout (Allanwater subdivision)

Mile 20-56: A typical station appears, to the west, at mile 24.7. If you miss it there are nine more just like it in the next 95 miles. To the north near mile 55, St. Barnabas Anglican Church ministers to 35 parishioners. By the way, you've now crossed into the Central time zone.

Mile 66-79: Look north at mile 66.5 to the settlement of Flindt Landing on an island in Heathcote Lake. It's connected to the station by a bridge, and you can practically see the fish jumping. At Savant Lake, just to the north, there's a striking contrast between the modern houses in the foreground and the older log cabins farther away. Then comes Sturgeon Lake, which abounds in walleye, northern pike and lake trout.

Mile 120.3: Look north here to a lovely old mill on McDougall Bay — a potentially wonderful restoration project for some northern entrepreneur.

Mile 133-139: You cross the Sturgeon River at mile 133.3 on a 458-foot bridge, then curve along Abram Lake for several miles before arriving at Sioux Lookout, with its impressive mock-Tudor station. To the west across Pelican Lake lie the Sioux Mountains, once the home of an Ojibway

Steam locomotive 6077 shares display space with a meteorite in the park at Capreol

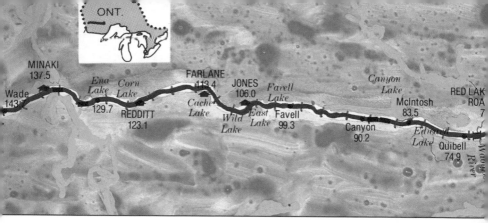

ONT.

MINAKI
137.5
Ena Lake
Corn Lake
FARLANE
113.4
JONES
106.0
Farell Lake
Canyon Lake
RED LAK
ROA
7
Wade
143
129.7
REDDITT
123.1
Cache Lake
Wild Lake
East Lake
Favell
99.3
McIntosh
83.5
Canyon
90.2
Edward Lake
Quibell
74.9

tribe who used this vantage point to spot the arrival of raiding parties of American Sioux — hence the town's very descriptive name.

POINTS OF INTEREST
Sioux Lookout to Winnipeg (Redditt subdivision)
Mile 1-16: Pelican Lake is crossed at mile 1.3 on a 272-foot bridge. At Hudson, a plaque commemorates the early bush pilots who flew supplies from Lost Lake north to Red Lake during the 1926 gold rush. A thousand men staked 3,500 claims, and 15 mines produced $360 million in precious metal.

Mile 41-74: Here you're about to pass through several tunnels that pierce the rugged rock outcroppings. The first is at mile 41.5, cutting through a 325-foot-wide ridge. You cross the Wabigoon River at mile 73.6; look south for a glimpse of the falls beneath the bridge.

Mile 83-106: Marvelous views appear to the north along Canyon Lake, which is particularly attractive at sunrise. Two 525-foot tunnels slice through the red-tinged rock, at miles 88.2 and 89.7, as you twist along the cliffside.

Mile 113-158: This area has had special weekend passenger service for 60 years. Back in the Roaring '20s, the Minaki Campers' Special — complete with dining, parlour and buffet-parlour cars — left Winnipeg late Friday afternoon and at noon on Saturday, returning Sunday evening. Today, it's easy to understand why this route has always been so popular. One CN vice-president — a regular patron during his working days — attained Valhalla when he retired. He purchased his favourite car, moved it to a high point of land overlooking his favourite lake, and spent the rest of his days in quiet rapture. See if you can spot it as you roll along! You'll definitely notice that stations such as Farlane and Malachi are much nicer than those between Armstrong and Sioux Lookout. At miles 130.4 and 135.3, you pass through two more tunnels, 556 and 613 feet long. Look north at mile 137, as you cross the Winnipeg

River over a 407-foot bridge, for a glimpse of Minaki Lodge, once a CN "hotel of distinction." Its day rate in the 1920s was a princely $5, including all meals and passage from the station on a private motor launch. The 1927 log structure, with its magnificent stone fireplace, overlooks one of Ontario's most beautiful vacation spots, with fishing, hunting, boating and canoeing close at hand. It's recently been renovated by the provincial government, so you'll be able to see it in all its former glory. The $5 price tag, alas, is a thing of the past.

Mile 159-182: Look to the north at mile 160 to view a cascading waterfall, and again at mile 162.2 for the boundary marker between Ontario and Manitoba. For the next 20 miles you cross Whiteshell Provincial Park, a protected wilderness area containing 200 lakes. Pierre de la Vérendrye first reached this area in 1733 on his way to the Red River. Each year thousands of waterfowl that migrate along the Mississippi flyway stop here for wild rice — long a staple of the local Indian diet, and in recent years a sought-after gourmet delicacy.

Mile 183-252: The Canadian route is crossed at mile 183.2 as the land suddenly changes from rock and scrub bush to marshy flatlands and sugar beet fields. Look north while crossing the Whitemouth River at mile 196.2 for a view of the onion-domed church and its adjacent graveyard. By the time you're at mile 230, the prairies have begun in earnest, and stretch westward for some 900 miles. At mile 243.4, you cross the 29-mile Red River Floodway on a 903-foot bridge. This huge diversion canal was built to prevent a repetition of the 1950 flood that forced the evacuation of 70,000 Winnipegers. And finally, as you approach the city centre, the Seine River is crossed by a 368-foot bridge at mile 250.5, followed by a 790-foot span over the Red River at mile 251.5. For a description of Winnipeg's history, please see page 43 of the *Scenic Rail Guide to Western Canada*.

Sunset colours the waters of Poilu Lak

N

Taggart Lake
Spine Lake
Alder Lake
Webster Bay
Lost Lake
SIOUX LOOKOUT 0.0
Pelican Lake

Norse Lake
Amesdale 50.9
Good Lake
Sundial Lake
Webster 20.7
Lily Lake Pelican 6.2

Butler Lake
Niddrie 57.8
Walsh Lake
Sunstrum 31.8
Hudson 12.6

Morgan 65.5
Rosamond Lake
Richan 45.5
Millidge 39.4
Vermilion Lake

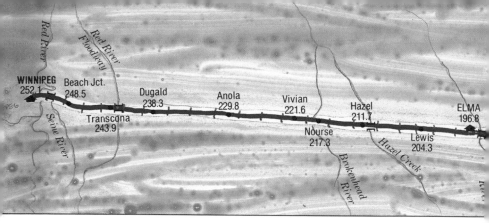

WINNIPEG 252.1	Beach Jct. 248.5	Dugald 238.3	Anola 229.8	Vivian 221.6	Hazel 211.7	ELMA 196.8
	Transcona 243.9			Nourse 217.3	Lewis 204.3	

Miles	Station	Pop.	Elev.	Origin
176.5	Oatland	—	1,085	—
183.2	Elsas	—	1,049	—
186.4	Agate	—	1,038	—
194.8	Dunrankin	—	1,067	—
205.9	Peterbell	128	1,023	—
213.6	Argolis	—	1,026	—
223.6	Fire River	—	997	—
232.2	Dishnish	—.	1,062	—
239.4	Minnipuka	—	1,105	—
249.2	Neswabin	—	1,139	—
257.7	Oba	75	1,077	—
263.2	Albany Forks		1,110	—
271.2	Macduff	—	1,075	—
279.2	Penhurst	—	1,050	—
284.9	Shekak	—	992	—
291.9	Cree	—	—	—
294.4	Wicksteed	—	941	—
296.2	Hornepayne	1,594	1,074	R.M. Hornepayne, one of the builders of the Canadian Northern line

The mock Tudor-style station at Sioux Lookout

The Continental Route

Ruel Subdivision — CNR Capreol/Hornepayne

This line was built by the Canadian Northern Ontario Railway between 1908 and 1915, and opened for traffic on October 15, 1915.

Miles	Stations	Population	Elev.	Origin of Station Names
0.0	Capreol (Ont.)	3,471	993	Frederick Chase Capreol, Toronto businessman and railway promoter, who helped to ensure the construction of the Ontario, Simcoe & Huron Railway in the 1850s
8.9	Milnet	—	1,073	—
19.5	Raphoe	—	1,219	—
30.3	Laforest	—	1,265	—
39.9	Thorlake	—	1,345	—
51.6	Ruel	—	1,335	—
59.3	Stupart	—	1,305	—
64.3	Westree	92	1,315	—
68.6	Ostrom	—	1,315	—
76.9	Makwa	—	1,225	—
86.6	Gogama	639	1,155	Indian word meaning "leaping fish"
95.5	Bethnal	—	1,197	—
105.4	Stackpool	—	1,245	—
115.6	Gladwick	—	1,268	—
125.8	Tionaga	—	1,243	—
133.2	Kukatush	—	1,132	—
141.4	Singelake	—	1,104	—
148.3	Foleyet (Ont.)	504	1,069	Legend has it that Sir Donald Mann wanted to name the station Foley after a railway contractor. When told the name already existed, he cried, "I'll name that station Foley yet!"
158.2	Shawmere	—	1,035	—
166.9	Missonga	—	1,165	—

Caramat Subdivision — CNR Hornepayne/Armstrong

The segment from Hornepayne to Longlac was built by the Canadian Northern Ontario Railway, and opened for traffic on October 15, 1915. The segment from Nakina to Armstrong was built by the National Transcontinental Railway, and opened on June 1, 1915. The link between Longlac and Nakina was opened on December 19, 1923 by the National Transcontinental Railway.

Miles	Stations	Population	Elev.	Origin of Station Names
0.0	Hornepayne (Ont.)	1,594	1,074	(See Ruel subdivision)
3.1	Jackfish	—	1,080	Nearby lake
5.8	Lennon	—	1,085	—
12.8	Tondern	—	1,112	—
25.3	Leigh	—	—	—
35.4	Osawin	—	1,072	—
42.3	Hillsport	—	—	A.J. Hills, general superintendent of the CNR lines between Hawkesbury and Ottawa
51.4	Otterdale	—	—	—
62.7	Gamsby	—	1,113	—
69.8	Arms	—	1,091	—
77.6	Caramat	462	1,104	—
91.8	Seagram	—	1,097	—
100.0	Longlac	1,125	1,035	Named after the lake on whose shore it stands
101.1	Longlac Jct.	—	1,035	—
108.3	Isis	—	1,090	—
115.4	Bawk	—	1,063	—
122.2	Poilu	—	—	—
131.6	Nakina	627	1,052	—
135.9	Exton	—	1,039	—
146.7	Cavell	—	1,082	Nurse Edith Cavell, who, in 1915, was shot by the Germans in Brussels for helping Allied prisoners to escape
155.4	Kowkash	64	1,054	From Kowaskagama, the Indian name of the river that flows through the region

146

Miles	Stations	Population	Elev.	Origin of Station Names
170.3	Redmond	—	1,127	—
182.3	Penequani	—	1,051	—
187.1	Auden	—	—	Principal of Upper Canada College, Toronto from 1902 to 1917
195.6	Minataree	—	1,093	—
205.0	Lamaune	—	1,009	—
213.7	Ferland	—	967	—
219.0	Mud River	—	—	—
226.0	Green	—	—	—
233.5	Wagaming	—	—	—
243.8	Armstrong (Ont.)	1,631	1,119	Sam Armstrong, MPP for Parry Sound

Allanwater Subdivision—CNR Armstrong-Sioux Lookout

This line, built by the Canadian Northern Ontario Railway between 1908 and 1915, was opened for traffic on June 1, 1915.

Miles	Stations	Population	Elev.	Origin of Station Names
0.0	Armstrong	1,631	1,119	(See Caramat subdivision)
7.4	Onaping	—	1,251	Cree word meaning "red paint" or "vermilion"
14.7	Pascopee	—	1,257	—
21.1	Collins	60	1,263	—
24.7	Schultz's Trail	—	—	Lake resort
25.7	Williams' Trail	—	—	Lake resort
28.3	Ogaki	—	1,301	—
34.5	Jacobs Tower	—	—	Lake resort
37.6	Point Landing	—	—	Lake resort
38.9	Jacobs	—	1,346	—
44.4	Bingham's Trail	—	—	Lake resort
46.4	Kawa	—	1,367	—
54.1	Allanwater Bridge	—	—	—
55.7	Allanwater	35	1,357	—
61.5	Barrington Lake	—	—	Lake resort
65.5	Harvey	—	1,375	—
66.6	Flindt Landing	—	1,365	Lake resort
69.6	Staunton	—	1,396	—
78.6	Savant Lake	186	1,424	—
90.7	Fowler	—	1,371	—
91.5	Wilf's Landing	—	—	Lake resort
00.5	Ycliff	9	1,320	—
08.4	Baische Trail	—	—	Lake resort
08.8	Robinson	—	1,210	—
15.9	Ghost River	—	1,228	—
21.0	McDougall Mills	—	—	Lake resort
23.2	Rosnel	—	1,205	—
32.5	Superior Jct.	—	1,210	—
38.9	Sioux Lookout	2,495	1,195	Hill from which the Ojibway watched the river for raiding parties of Sioux warriors

Redditt Subdivision — CNR Sioux Lookout/Winnipeg

This line was built by the National Transcontinental Railway, and opened for traffic on June 1, 1915.

Miles	Stations	Population	Elev.	Origin of Station Names
0.0	Sioux Lookout (Ont.)	2,495	1,195	(See Allanwater subdivision)
6.2	Pelican	—	1,212	—
12.6	Hudson	655	1,175	—
20.7	Webster	—	1,253	—
31.8	Sunstrum	—	1,311	—
39.4	Millidge	—	1,326	—
45.5	Richan	—	1,295	—
50.5	Carroll Jct.	—	1,293	Peter Carroll, who surveyed the area in the 1820s
50.9	Amesdale	—	1,297	—
57.8	Niddrie	—	1,347	—
65.5	Morgan	—	1,288	—
71.3	Red Lake Road	91	1,189	—
74.9	Quibell	—	1,146	—
83.5	McIntosh	—	1,247	—
90.2	Canyon	—	1,239	—
99.3	Favell	—	1,236	—
106.0	Jones	—	1,292	Jonas Jones, judge of the Queen's Bench, in 1837
113.4	Farlane	33	1,203	—
123.1	Redditt	—	1,089	—
129.7	Ena Lake	—	—	—
137.5	Minaki	358	—	Indian word meaning "beautiful country"
140.4	McNulty	—	—	—
143.7	Wade	—	—	—
149.8	Hardy	—	—	—
150.9	Ottermere	—	—	—
153.2	Malachi	—	—	—
159.2	White	—	727	—
160.6	Rice Lake	—	614	—
164.2	Winnitoba (Man.)	—	—	—
166.6	Ophir	—	—	—
175.0	Decimal	—	—	—
179.7	Brereton Lake	—	—	—
181.8	Indigo	—	—	—
187.1	Hoctor	—	—	—
196.8	Elma	110	—	—
204.3	Lewis	—	—	—
211.7	Hazel	—	—	—
217.3	Nourse	—	—	—
221.6	Vivian	333	990	—
229.8	Anola	—	845	—
238.3	Dugald	236	—	—
243.9	Transcona	—	—	—
246.7	Plessis Road	—	—	—
248.5	Beach Jct.	—	—	—
251.3	Terminal Cut-Off	585.900	—	—
252.1	Winnipeg (Man.)		757	From Cree 'Winnipiy' meaning "murky water"

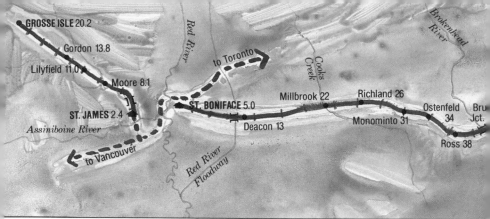

The Prairie Dog Central steams north from Winnipeg to Grosse Isle

The Prairie Dog Route

St. James to Grosse Isle

The Prairie Dog Central steam train is a genuine echo of the past — a survivor of the many excursion trains that puffed their way north to Grand, Victoria and Winnipeg beaches in the early 1900s. Its wooden coaches, built between 1901 and 1913, feature magnificent walnut, oak and mahogany interiors. Passengers sit on wicker seats and enjoy "prairie air conditioning" — open windows and the occasional flying cinder — while the steam whistle and clanging bell provide a properly nostalgic background.

The train's star performer is steam engine

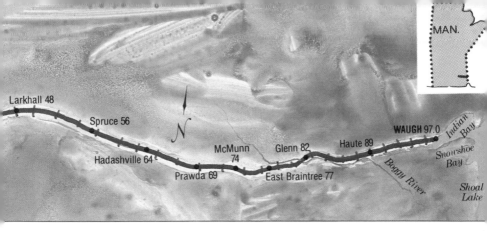

3, Scottish-built in 1882. Hundreds of these classic locomotives hauled Canadian passenger trains for more than 75 years. Engine 3 saw duty between 1918 and 1962 on the Winnipeg City Hydro Tramway, between Lac du Bonnet and Pointe du Bois. In its first 36 years of service, it hauled CPR passenger trains between Fort William and Kenora. The train continues to run, from June to September (Sundays only), thanks to the Vintage Locomotive Society, a group of Winnipeg train enthusiasts who are assisted by qualified CN personnel.

POINTS OF INTEREST

Mile 3-5: While leaving Winnipeg's industrial area, look west for a glimpse of aircraft taking off from the international airport. What a contrast between jumbo jets and your stately Edwardian progress!

Mile 6-8: The CPR main line runs immediately to the north and is crossed at mile 7.8. Watch for the mile-long grain trains with their multihued cylindrical hopper cars.

Mile 9-20: Rolling across the pancake-flat countryside, look sharp for black-tailed prairie dogs. These delightful rodents sit up and bark, live underground in tunneled colonies, and usually frolic throughout the morning, then again in late afternoon. You'll also want a photograph of the vast fields of yellow sunflowers, which are converted into vegetable oil. At Gordon, watch for several grain elevators to the north of the tracks. Just beyond them, in the distance, you'll see a bright red caboose in a farmer's field, performing final duty as a chicken coop.

Mile 20.2: There's plenty of time at Grosse Isle to stretch your legs, lie on the grass and watch the locomotive being turned around for your return trip to Winnipeg.

The Aqueduct Route
St. Boniface to Waugh (Indian Bay)

The Greater Winnipeg Water District Railway is a most unusual line with a unique purpose. Back in 1912, Winnipeg was known as "the Chicago of the North" — a bustling city of 175,000 with a population quadrupling by the decade. Its water supply came from artesian wells and the Red and Assiniboine rivers, but was far too hard, ruining boilers and delicate fabrics alike. A radical solution — a 98-mile-long aqueduct under the barren stretches of eastern Manitoba to Ontario's Shoal Lake — was hotly debated and finally approved by city council.

The GWWD was built to construct the aqueduct. Its last spike was driven by Winnipeg's Mayor Deacon in December 1914, and the $13-million aqueduct was formally opened five years later by the Prince of Wales. The aqueduct, which carries 80 million gallons of pure water per day by simple gravity flow, consists mainly of a nine-foot-wide, 10-foot-high arched trough. At first it was inspected by employees who paddled its length in canoes, but now the system is periodically drained and checked by a bicyclist who wields a flashlight and dictates notes into his portable tape recorder.

A mixed train leaving St. Boniface en route to Waugh

GWWD trains are a breed apart: a combination baggage-passenger car; a streamlined CPR coach; and a second CPR coach — all powered by a tiny diesel locomotive.

POINTS OF INTEREST

Mile 5: This is your actual starting point, although the GWWD railway's tracks are measured from the McPhillips water reservoir farther to the west. The classic sandstone station resembles those in rural England; inside are pictures of early rolling stock and bygone schedules.

Mile 12: A concrete trestle crosses the 29-mile-long Red River Floodway, constructed after the disastrous flood of 1950, which forced 70,000 Winnipegers from their homes.

Mile 43: As you cross a stretch of muskeg and peat bog, look south down a spur line to the nearby quarry. The oddly shaped freight cars are designed to carry gravel, the railway's main traffic today. (It wasn't always so. During the Great Depression, special trains took welfare recipients to gather firewood for the poor. The supplies they cut and stacked lasted until 1952.)

Mile 45-62. Here you pass through the Sandilands Provincial Forest, once the shoreline of glacial Lake Agassiz. This ecologically fragile area became officially protected in 1923. Its tamarack and cedar groves are the home of deer, beaver, lynx, wolf and bear.

Mile 64: A Manitoba Forestry Association training area near Hadashville teaches conservation, reforestation and fire prevention techniques — necessary skills, since parts of the forest bear the scars of a fire that claimed three lives in 1955.

Mile 97: On arrival at Indian Bay, you'll see why early visitors compared the wooded slopes and rocky shores of Shoal Lake to Scotland's Loch Katrine. Here you can admire well-trimmed lawns and carefully tended trees, search for Indian artifacts or fish for giant trout.

The Prairie Dog Route

CNR St. James/Grosse Isle

The segment from St. James to mile 5.3 was built by the Northern Extension Railway, and opened on June 16, 1907; the segment from mile 5.3 to Moore was built by the Canadian Northern Railway, and opened on October 13, 1913; the segment from Moore to Grosse Isle was built by the Winnipeg and Hudson Bay Railway, and opened on December 8, 1904. The Prairie Dog Central now operates over CN's Oak Point subdivision.

Miles	Stations	Population	Elev.	Origin of Station Names
2.4	St. James (Man.)	(Suburb of Winnipeg)	764	
8.1	Moore	—	—	Local landowner
11.0	Lilyfield	—	—	Orange lilies growing nearby
13.8	Gordon	—	—	J. Gordon, CN lease specialist
20.2	Grosse Isle (Man.)	—	—	Large wooded tract of land surrounded by swamp

The Aqueduct Route

GWWD (Greater Winnipeg Water District) — St. Boniface/Waugh

This line was built in 1914 by the City of Winnipeg to facilitate maintenance of an aqueduct and to help colonize the area.

Miles	Stations	Population	Elev.	Origin of Station Names
5.0	St. Boniface (Man.)	(Suburb of Winnipeg)	756	English Christian missionary (680-755). called the Apostle of Germany
13.0	Deacon	—	—	Thomas R. Deacon, once mayor of Winnipeg
22.0	Millbrook	—	—	
26.0	Richland	—	—	Good loam soil in the area
31.0	Monominto	—	—	Earl of Minto, governor-general of Canada from 1898 to 1904
34.0	Ostenfeld	—	—	
38.0	Ross	89	—	Roderick Ross, Hudson's Bay Company factor
43.0	Bruce Jct.	—	—	—
48.0	Larkhall	—	—	—
56.0	Sadlow (Spruce)	—	—	Stands of spruce trees nearby
64.0	Hadashville	—	—	Charles Hadash, postmaster
69.0	Prawda	—	—	—
74.0	McMunn	—	—	—
77.0	East Braintree	—	—	Originally called Braintree
80.0	Wye	—	—	A railway term, describing the "Y"-shaped track, which enables trains to be turned
82.0	Glenn	—	—	—
89.0	Haute	—	—	—
97.0	Indian Bay (Waugh) (Man.)	—	—	R.D. Waugh, mayor of Winnipeg from 1912 to 1915

The Hudson Bay Route

North across vast stretches of tundra from The Pas to Churchill, land of the polar bear, past native villages, swiftly flowing rivers and mammoth power projects

The Pas to Churchill

The 1,055 miles the Hudson Bay travels from Winnipeg to Churchill is one of the most diverse, wild and desolate stretches of track in Canada. The first half of the trip from Winnipeg to The Pas rolls through an area of prosperous farms and busy towns comparable to those in the southern portion of the prairie provinces. North of The Pas, however, a completely different world presents itself: a land where instead of highways are hundreds of lakes and rivers teeming with fish and cascading rapids; where Cree and Chipewyan Indians carry youngsters in moss bags; where Inuit still earn a living hunting and fishing; where cormorants, swans and ptarmigan (partridge) fly overhead; and where polar bears are as common as raccoons are in southern regions. Stunted trees stand in perpetually frozen muskeg; telegraph poles require tripods to remain upright; only arctic moss covers the Barren Lands.

The earliest explorations of the Hudson Bay area were carried out by adventurers in the pay of English merchants seeking a northern trade route to the Orient. Between 1576 and 1616 parties headed by Martin Frobisher, John Davis, Henry Hudson and William Baffin ventured to the region, but success eluded them. Hudson, after whom the bay was named, died in his attempt, cast adrift in June 1611 by his mutinous crew after a winter spent locked in the ice of James Bay.

It wasn't until more than 50 years after Baffin's last voyage that exploration efforts were renewed. This time, though, it was not the fabled route to China's riches that was

being sought, but expansion of the lucrative fur trade. Central figures in this venture were Pierre Radisson and his brother-in-law Médard Chouart, sieur des Groseilliers, two

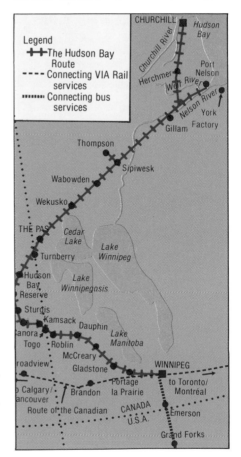

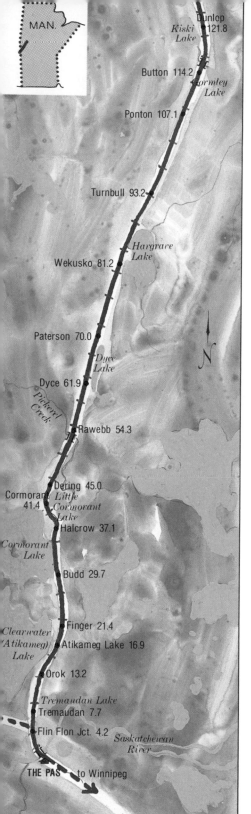

MAN.

Dunlop 121.8
Kiski Lake
Button 114.2
Gormley Lake
Ponton 107.1
Turnbull 93.2
Hargrave Lake
Wekusko 81.2
Paterson 70.0
Dyce Lake
Dyce 61.9
Pickerel Creek
Rawebb 54.3
Dering 45.0
Cormorant 41.4
Little Cormorant Lake
Halcrow 37.1
Cormorant Lake
Budd 29.7
Finger 21.4
Clearwater (Atikameg) Lake
Atikameg Lake 16.9
Orok 13.2
Tremaudan Lake
Tremaudan 7.7
Flin Flon Jct. 4.2
Saskatchewan River
THE PAS   to Winnipeg

N

Frenchmen disaffected with their country after New France officials seized their furs and fined them following a successful expedition to Lake Superior in 1659. The men went to England to seek backers for a voyage to a "Bay to the North" they had been told by Cree Indians was accessible by sea. By 1668 they had succeeded in convincing a group of London businessmen, Prince Rupert among them, of the worth of such a venture and in June set off in two ships. That carrying Radisson was damaged and had to turn back, but Groseilliers continued in the *Nonsuch*, in late September reaching what was named Rupert River, on James Bay. Here Charles Fort (later renamed Rupert's House) was established and during the winter Groseilliers made contact with the Indians of the area; by the following summer he was able to return to England with a quantity of furs, proving the value of the Hudson Bay route. This success led to the formation in 1670 of "The Governor and Company of Adventurers of England trading into Hudson's Bay" — the formal name of the Hudson's Bay Company to this day — which was granted title to Rupert's Land, a massive area comprised of all territories draining into the bay.

The company quickly expanded its operations in Hudson and James bays: Moose Factory and forts Nelson, Churchill, Albany and Severn were completed less than 20 years after the charter was granted. This sudden growth was not unopposed. The French, who had previously monopolized the fur trade, reacted to the threat the HBC represented in 1682 by creating the Compagnie du Nord, which used military strength to combat the company's power. All forts changed hands, in some cases several times, during the next three decades, until the Treaty of Utrecht permanently returned control of Hudson Bay to the English.

A new period of rivalry, often violent, began with the formation of the North West Company in 1783 — a situation that was not resolved until the two merged under the name of the Hudson's Bay Company in 1821.

In 1877 the Winnipeg and Hudson Bay Railway and Steamship Company received its charter and work began on October 9, 1886, after the first sod was turned at Winnipeg. Nevertheless, the track did not reach

Passengers boarding the Hudson Bay at The Pas

The Pas until 1908, Pikwitonei until 1918 and Churchill until March 29, 1929. The Hudson Bay Railway became part of Canadian National Railways on September 5, 1951.

A trip on the Hudson Bay Railway is a trip into history, into an area described by Canadian poet E. J. Pratt as a "great lone land." It is a journey that has much to offer the sportsman, naturalist and historian.

POINTS OF INTEREST

The Pas to Wabowden (Wekusko subdivision)
Mile 0: The Pas is famous for its furs, fish and forests. One of the oldest settlements in Manitoba, it served as a fur trading and supply centre for the developing northern frontier. The Hudson Bay

Sieur d'Iberville, on his ship, *The Pelican*, near Fort Nelson in September, 1697

stops long enough for you to see some of the sights: the Anglican Church of the Messiah, built in 1840, contains some furnishings made by carpenters on a relief expedition looking for Sir John Franklin, as well as hand-hewn pews and a plaque with the Ten Commandments in Cree; a cairn honours Henry Kelsey, the first white man to see the Canadian prairies (1690) and one of the few explorers of the time to keep a journal; the Little Northern Museum, opened in 1958 by naturalist Sam Waller, who has spent years in the area and is known as The Pas' Pierre Berton, displays Inuit miniature ivory carvings as well as Waller's private collection. The Pas Indian Reserve surrounds the town and in the Otineka Mall you can purchase beautiful hand-tooled moosehide mukluks, beaded jackets, moccasins and down parkas. The first grain grown in western Canada was planted along the Carrot River Valley in 1753 by Captain Louis de la Corne; today some 135,000 acres of rich soil produce bumper crops. During the annual Northern Manitoba Trappers' Festival, held each February, trappers, traders, miners, lumberjacks and Indians get together for log throwing, bannock baking, muskrat skinning, tree felling, fiddling, jigging, moose calling, a 150-mile dog derby and the choosing of a Fur Queen. In August, Opasquia Indian Days feature native dancing, bow-and-arrow contests and knife, hatchet and spear throwing.

Mile 0-42: At mile 0.6 the Hudson Bay rumbles across the Saskatchewan River. To the south, along the river bank, are The Pas Indian Reserve and the small Church of the Messiah, part of an old Anglican mission. If the sun is shining, look for a beautiful stained-glass window placed above the altar in 1940 to commemorate the church's centennial. CN's 242-mile line to Cranberry Portage and Lynn Lake diverges to the west at mile 4.2 if you have time, take this mixed train (mostly freight, with one coach), that con-

153

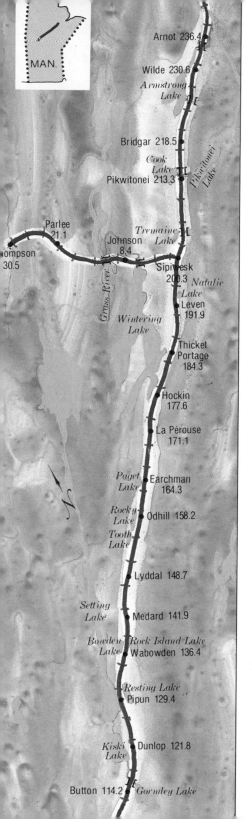

MAN.

Arnot 236.4

Wilde 230.6
*Armstrong
Lake*

Bridgar 218.5
*Cook
Lake*
Pikwitonei 213.3
*Pikwitonei
Lake*

Parlee
21.1
*Tremaine
Lake*
Johnson
8.4
ompson
30.5
Sipiwesk
200.3 *Natalie
Lake*
Leven
191.9
*Wintering
Lake*
Grass River
Thicket
Portage
184.3

Hockin
177.6

La Pérouse
171.1

*Paget
Lake* Earchman
164.3

*Rocky
Lake* Odhill 158.2
*Tooth
Lake*

Lyddal 148.7

*Setting
Lake* Medard 141.9

*Bowden Rock Island Lake
Lake* Wabowden 136.4

Resting Lake
Pipun 129.4

*Kiski
Lake* Dunlop 121.8

Button 114.2 *Gormley Lake*

nects with the Hudson Bay at The Pas: the scenery is spectacular. The trip takes more than 10 hours each way, however, so pack a picnic. At mile 9, the lake district begins, most of it accessible only by rail. Budd honours Henry Budd, who in 1853 became the first native to be ordained as an Anglican minister in western Canada. Cormorant Lake, to the west between miles 31 and 35, harbours a waterfowl sanctuary and several resorts. Halcrow was named in honour of the Halcrow family, two generations of whom carried on fur trading for the Hudson's Bay Company between The Pas and Hudson Bay. Watch for a pink marble quarry to the west. at mile 39.

Mile 41.4: The site of the first settlement of any size along the Hudson Bay Railway, Cormorant has two stores and two churches. The population includes Inuit, Indian and descendants of French, Scottish and Central European settlers.

Mile 54-70: Rawebb, mile 54.3, honours Ralph H. Webb, mayor of Winnipeg from 1925 to 1927 and again from 1930 to 1934, who helped promote the formation of the Hudson Bay Railway. Paterson, at mile 70, was named after General Robert Walter Paterson, president of the "On-to-the-Bay Association," formed in 1924, which also lobbied for completion of this rail route.

Mile 81.2: Wekusko is one of the few northern towns on this line linked to another town by road. From here a road leads 35 miles west to the mining settlement of Snow Lake, the first mining town to be developed under a section of the Local Government District Act, passed in 1945, to provide for the orderly development of mining areas and eliminate the "Tin Towns" characteristic of early mining sites.

Mile 90-130: The limestone formations seen from I he Pas change at mile 90 to shallow muskeg and small tracts of clay.

Mile 136.4: Shortly before reaching Wabowden, the surface of the country becomes somewhat rolling. Here the Laurentian rock is covered with clay, about 50 to 75 percent of which is arable, as the land was once part of lake beds. Wabowden, situated between two small lakes, contains a branch of the Brandon Experimental Farm, where wheat, oats and vegetables are grown. The town's most important role is as a distribution centre for towns in northern Manitoba.

POINTS OF INTEREST
Wabowden to Sipiwesk (Thicket subdivision)

Mile 177-185: Hockin, mile 177.6, is named in memory of Corporal G.H. Hocking of the North West Mounted Police, killed in 1897 by Almighty Voice, who had been sought for two years for the murder of another policeman. He and two accomplices surprised a Mountie search party, of which Hocking was a member, and in the ensuing gunfight Hocking and all three Indians died. Thicket Portage, mile 184.3, previously called

Franklin Portage and one of the oldest inhabited spots of the area, was used by Sir John Franklin during an expedition in the early nineteenth century. Thirty-mile-long Landing Lake, just south of the station, is connected by stream to Nelson River. Early fur traders used to travel from Norway House on Lake Winnipeg to Nelson House on the Burntwood River, crossing the present railway route at Thicket Portage.

POINTS OF INTEREST

Sipiwesk to Thompson (Thompson subdivision)

The track now jogs over to Thompson, connected to the Hudson Bay Railway at Sipiwesk by a 30.5-mile CN branch line initially built to serve the International Nickel Company — indeed, the three stations between here and Thompson are all named for Inco executives. At mile 6.5, the train crosses the Wintering River, then, at mile 12.9, the Grass River. Thompson, right in the geographic centre of Manitoba, has superseded The Pas as the supply and equipment distribution centre for goods and services to the vast north country. The glacial deposits of sand, boulders and clay that surround the city hold enormous mineral wealth, and the Burntwood River has the capacity to produce abundant hydroelectric power. Thompson, Manitoba's nickel capital, has grown solidly since Inco's 1957 decision to establish an extensive nickel mining and refining operation there.

POINTS OF INTEREST

Sipiwesk to Gillam (Thicket subdivision)

Mile 200-235: Back on the main line, bridges and rivers predominate. At mile 204, the train crosses a stream connecting West Tremaine, Middle Tremaine and East Tremaine lakes. The Pikwitonei River, bridged at mile 213.5, connects Pikwitonei Lake to Cook Lake and the Grass River system. During the construction of the Hudson Bay Railway, this served as the contractor's headquarters. Between mile 214 and Gillam, watch for Indians carrying their young children in moss bags. Wilde, at mile 230.6, honours NWMP Sergeant W.B. Wilde, who in 1896 tried to arrest a Blood Indian named Charcoal for murder. Charcoal fled and was tracked by Sergeant Wilde, two constables and two Indian scouts. They sighted him at Pincher Creek and gave chase on horseback. Wilde went ahead and tried unsuccessfully to grab Charcoal singlehanded, but was killed. A few weeks later, after a tip from Charcoal's brother, the police arrested him and he was later executed.

Mile 240.9: Here the train crosses the Nelson River for the first time — at the Manitou Rapids, where the river is narrow and contained in a semi-canyon. Manitou Rapids (in Cree, "Devil Rapids") are so named because the water here is extremely hazardous for canoeists. Although the water appears quite smooth, whirlpools and "boilers"

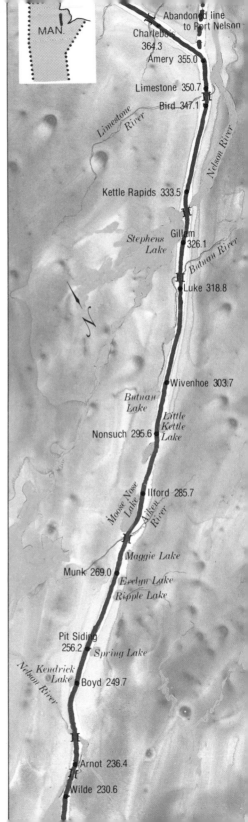

MAN.

Abandoned line
to Port Nelson

Charlebo 364.3

Amery 355.0

Limestone 350.7

Bird 347.1

Limestone River

Nelson River

Kettle Rapids 333.5

Stephens Lake

Gillam 326.1

Butnau River

Luke 318.8

Wivenhoe 303.7

Butnau Lake

Little Kettle Lake

Nonsuch 295.6

Moose Nose Lake

Aiken River

Ilford 285.7

Maggie Lake

Munk 269.0

Evelyn Lake

Ripple Lake

Pit Siding 256.2

Spring Lake

Kendrick Lake

Nelson River

Boyd 249.7

Arnot 236.4

Wilde 230.6

Ice breaking up in Hudson Bay at Cape Merry, near Churchill

can develop suddenly as the waters of the English, Winnipeg, Red, Assiniboine, and North and South Saskatchewan rivers are forced through this channel; in fact, the immense watershed lying between Lake Superior and the Rocky Mountains and extending as far south as the Missouri River drains to the sea through this gorge.

Mile 241-319: Here the land is flat, more muskeg than clay, and trees are much less frequent. At mile 259.9 once stood a siding called Garraway, after Garraway's Coffee House in London, where the first sale of Hudson's Bay Company furs was held in 1671. At mile 278.6, the tiny community of Landing River, on the Split Lake Reserve, is renowned for exquisite beadwork done by its women. Ilford, at mile 285.7, is the railhead for winter freighting operations to Knee Lake mining area and God's Lake goldfields, 130 miles away by trail. Thousands of tons of freight, mining machinery, explosives and supplies are still hauled by tractor over winter trails to the mining field.

Mile 326.1: Five miles south of the Kettle Rapids crossing of the Nelson River, Gillam is a thriving, modern community. In February 1966, when Manitoba Hydro began construction of the Kettle Generating Station nearby, Gillam's population was 356. By the time Kettle became fully operational in 1974, the population had topped 3,000. Gillam was named after Zachariah and Benjamin Gillam, father and son, both sea captains and traders in the area in the late seventeenth century.

POINTS OF INTEREST

Gillam to Churchill (Herchmer subdivision)

Mile 330-350: To the north, near mile 330, is the Kettle Generating Station on the Nelson River, the dam of which forms Stephens Lake. Kettle, the largest generating station in Manitoba, has a 1.3-million kilowatt capability, more than all other hydro stations in Manitoba combined. Hydro-electric power from Kettle is transmitted three miles to the Radisson Converter Station, where it

is converted to direct current for transmission southward to Winnipeg. The Radisson station, the northern terminus of one of the world's longest transmission lines, transmits power via two 565-mile-long lines. The southern end of the DC transmission system is Dorsey Converter Station at Rosser, near Winnipeg, where the power is converted back to alternating current (AC) for conventional transmission and distribution. At mile 331.5, where the Nelson River is crossed, the railway line leaves the Laurentian Plateau of the Canadian Shield and enters the lowland and coastal plain that stretches to Hudson Bay. At mile 337, to the east, is the Long Spruce Generating Station. Along the next few miles are the Long Spruce Rapids, where it's not unusual to catch speckled trout weighing up to six pounds. The Limestone River is crossed at mile 349.8; watch for the rapids to the east, just after the bridge.

Mile 355-435: At Amery, mile 355, the railway line turns sharply and heads straight toward Churchill. To the east, at mile 356, can be seen an abandoned railway right of way to Port Nelson. the only trace of HBR indecision. Unable to decide whether the terminal on Hudson Bay should be Port Nelson or Churchill, the company built a huge 17-span, 2,640-foot bridge and 11 miles of track from the cutoff at Odley to Port Nelson before World War I, but in the end never ran a train on the line. From this point, the perpetually frozen muskeg is sparsely treed with stunted spruce and tamarack. Muskeg is usually about six feet deep, with clay and boulders underneath. The frost extends down often to a depth of more than 40 feet. Large tree roots, walrus tusks and skulls have been found in the frozen ground. The rails for this part of the line were laid in the cold winter of 1928-29 and the ballast was put under them the following summer. Telegraph lines here are supported by three poles tied together to form a tripod. The Weir River, noted for its speckled trout, is crossed at mile 373. Here you are likely to see flocks of arctic ptarmigan, which, like rabbits, change from winter white to summer brown. Also watch for clay and brick dome-shaped Dutch ovens used by CN's railway construction gangs during 1928 and 1929 to cook bread, beans and bacon. Back, at mile 434.4, was named for George Back, a Royal Navy officer who traveled with Sir John Franklin's party to Hudson Bay from 1819 to 1822, one of the few early explorers who chronicled his travels in this area.

Mile 440-509: Between miles 440 and 480, the Hudson Bay crosses the Barren Lands, an area devoid of all trees and growth except for arctic moss. Near Bylot, at mile 485.2, great areas of moss have been stripped from the soil and shipped to Churchill to insulate surface water mains (permafrost prevents the mains from being buried). Tidal, at mile 501.7, is the farthest inland point reached by the tide from Hudson Bay. The town of Churchill can first be sighted ahead, at mile 503.

Mile 509.8: This northern outpost, often called the "Polar Bear Capital of the World," was discovered by Jens Munk, a Dane who left Copenhagen on May 30, 1619. His two ships, the frigate *Unicorn*, carrying 48 men, and the sloop *Lamprey*, with 16 men, landed in Churchill on September 7. Both boats wintered four and a half miles up the harbour from the entrance at what is now known as Munk Cove. Shortly after Christmas, scurvy broke out and when the ice broke up in the spring, only Munk and two men were alive; they sailed from Churchill on July 16, 1620, and returned to Denmark on September 21.

In 1688, the Hudson's Bay Company built its first fort at Churchill, but it was destroyed by fire. The present stone Prince of Wales Fort, directly across from the harbour entrance, was started by Samuel Hearne in 1733, completed in 1744 and lost to the French under Jean François de Galaup, comte de la Pérouse in 1782 — 11 years to build, and lost in an hour. A dozen or so cannon remain where they were left by the French after the looting of the stronghold.

The mouth of the Churchill River is bottle-shaped, with the neck opening to the sea, thus creating a magnificent and natural landlocked harbour, with 30 feet of water at the dock at low tide.

You'll have a day to spend in Churchill seeing the sights before the train returns. There's lots to do: see where Munk and his men were based; buy ivory, fur and parkas in the stores; visit the wireless station that handles much of the North Atlantic air communications; watch beluga whales feeding as the tide falls; pick gooseberries and black currants planted by the British forces some 200 years ago; and have a picnic or dine in one of the town's restaurants. Then at night you can board your train for the 22-hour journey back to Winnipeg.

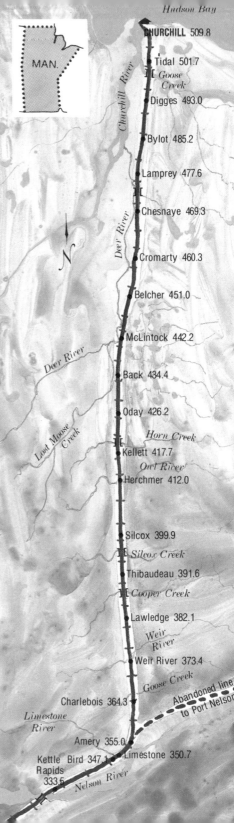

Hudson Bay

MAN.

Churchill River

CHURCHILL 509.8
Tidal 501.7
Goose Creek
Digges 493.0
Bylot 485.2
Lamprey 477.6
Chesnaye 469.3
Cromarty 460.3
Belcher 451.0
McLintock 442.2
Back 434.4
Oday 426.2
Horn Creek
Kellett 417.7
Owl River
Herchmer 412.0
Silcox 399.9
Silcox Creek
Thibaudeau 391.6
Cooper Creek
Lawledge 382.1
Weir River
Weir River 373.4
Goose Creek
Charlebois 364.3
Abandoned line to Port Nelson
Limestone River
Amery 355.0
Kettle Bird 347.1
Rapids 333.5
Limestone 350.7
Nelson River
Deer River
Deer River
Lost Moose Creek

N

A wild dog roams the rocks at Churchill

The Hudson Bay—Winnipeg/Churchill

Gladstone Subdivision—CNR
Portage la Prairie/Dauphin

The Portage to Beaver segment was built by Portage and North Western Railway between 1889 and 1890. Beaver to Gladstone was built by Canadian Northern Railway and opened for traffic on December 4, 1901. Gladstone to Dauphin was built by Lake Manitoba Railway and Canal Company and opened for traffic on January 3, 1897.

Miles	Stations	Population	Elev.	Origin of Station Names
0.0	Portage la Prairie (Man.)	12,500	854	—
0.5	Delta Jct.	—	—	—
9.9	Rignold	—	841	Previously called Ridgeway
18.6	Beaver	—	862	—
23.2	Katrime	—	—	A misspelling of Loch Katrine (Scotland)
31.2	Golden Stream	—	—	Nearby stream
36.5	Gladstone	976	884	Four-time British Prime Minister
50.3	Plumas	300	927	Plumas County, California
54.6	Colby	—	—	Early settler's family
59.1	Tenby	—	—	Town in Wales
63.8	Glenella	195	—	Ella Williams, relative of Sir Donald Mann, one of the founders of the Canadian Northern Railway
72.5	Glencairn	—	954	Town in South Africa
82.9	Neepawa Jct.	—	1,209	—
83.9	McCreary	614	992	William F. McCreary, M.P. for Selkirk
92.4	Laurier	225	965	Sir Wilfrid Laurier, seventh Prime Minister of Canada
100.8	Makinak	105	972	Cree word for "turtle"
108.1	Ochre River	321	929	Nearby river (yellow marl in riverbed)
121.7	Dauphin (Man.)	9,105	957	Fort (1742) named for Dauphin of France

Togo Subdivision—CNR Dauphin/Canora

The Dauphin to North Junction portion was built by the Lake Manitoba Railway and Canal Company and opened for traffic on January 3, 1817. North Junction to Canora was built by the Canadian Northern Railway between 1902 and 1905 and opened for traffic on January 27, 1905.

Miles	Stations	Population	Elev.	Origin of Station Names
0.0	Dauphin (Man.)	9,105	957	See Gladstone subdivision
2.8	North Jct.	—	—	—
11.4	Ashville	—	1,129	—
20.0	Gilbert Plains	847	1,314	Indian trader Gilbert Ross
24.1	Dutton	—	—	W.P. Dutton, Winnipeg contractor
29.5	Grandview	1,013	1,431	Great views in the area
37.0	Meharry	—	—	Local character nickname (Me Harry)
45.3	Shortdale	—	—	Nearby Short Creek
50.7	Bield	—	—	Gaelic word for "shelter"
54.7	Shevlin	—	—	—
62.6	Roblin	1,971	—	Hon. Sir Rodmond Roblin
74.5	Makaroff	62	—	Vice Admiral Serge Makaroff of Russia
79.5	Togo (Sask.)	197	—	Admiral Heihachiro Togo of Japan (Russo-Japanese War)
88.0	Runnymede	120	—	Site of signing of English Magna Carta, 1215
94.8	Cote	—	—	Hon. J.L. Cote, surveyor of the town site
100.9	Kamsack	2,726	—	Local Indian Chief Kamsack
109.3	Veregin	140	—	Doukhobor spiritual leader
117.5	Mikado	160	—	Gilbert and Sullivan operetta
121.2	Ross Jct.	—	—	Roderick Ross, Hudson's Bay Co. factor
124.9	Canora (Sask.)	2,689	—	After Canadian Northern Railway

Assiniboine Subdivision—CNR Canora/Hudson Bay

The Canora to Sturgis Junction section, built by the Canadian Northern Branch Lines Co., was opened for traffic on September 7, 1915.

Miles	Stations	Population	Elev.	Origin of Station Names
0.0	Canora (Sask.)	2,689	—	See Togo subdivision
7.8	Amsterdam	—	—	Home of the first settler from the Netherlands
14.1	Tadmore	—	—	—
17.5	Hassan	—	—	Town in Lebanon
21.2	Sturgis Jct.	—	—	—
22.0	Sturgis	705	—	North Dakota, home town of the first postmaster
23.5	Lilian	—	—	—
29.5	Lady Lake	—	—	Titled lady from Britain on the first air flight
32.5	Hinchliffe	—	—	Pilot of the first trans-Atlantic flight
39.7	Endeavour	220	—	Plane name of the first trans-Atlantic flight
44.7	Usherville	—	—	—
53.4	Tall Pines	—	—	Grove of trees in area
63.1	Reserve	187	—	Nearby forest reserve
72.1	Bertwell	—	—	First storekeeper, Bert Webb
78.1	Clemenceau	—	—	G. Glemenceau, French Prime Minister during World War I
82.6	Akosane	—	—	Cree for "well done"
92.2	Mutchler	—	—	—
93.7	Hudson Bay (Sask.)	2,280	—	Originally called "Etomami," Indian for "three rivers join together"

Turnberry Subdivision—CNR Hudson Bay/The Pas

This line was built by the Canadian Northern Railway and

opened for traffic on February 10, 1910.

Miles	Stations	Population	Elev.	Origin of Station Names
0.0	Hudson Bay (Sask.)	2,280	—	See Assiniboine subdivision
8.8	Wachee	—	—	—
17.9	Ceba	—	—	—
27.2	Chemong	—	—	—
35.2	Otosquen	—	—	Indian name
43.2	Cantyre	—	—	—
50.6	Turnberry	—	—	—
60.5	Whithorn	—	—	Bleached buffalo horn
68.3	Westray	—	910	Westray Island, Scotland (Orkney Islands)
77.8	Freshford	—	885	—
86.5	The Pas South	—	—	—
88.1	The Pas (Man.)	6,600	881	Indian word Opasquiaow, meaning "water converging to a narrows with spruce-treed high lands." Also French Le Pas, meaning narrow passage

Wekusko Subdivision—CNR The Pas/Wabowden

This line was built by the Hudson Bay Railway and opened for traffic on October 9, 1918.

Miles	Stations	Population	Elev.	Origin of Station Names
0.0	The Pas (Man.)	6,600	881	See Turnberry subdivision
4.2	Flin Flon Jct.	—	—	—
7.7	Tremaudan	—	—	Founder of The Pas Herald newspaper
13.2	Orok	—	—	Dr. Orok, first representative to the Manitoba Legislature
16.9	Atikameg Lake	—	—	Indian for "deer of the lake"
21.4	Finger	—	—	Pioneer lumberman
29.7	Budd	—	—	H. Budd, Anglican missionary to the Indians
37.1	Halcrow	—	—	HBC officer
41.4	Cormorant	—	—	Nearby lake frequented by crow ducks
45.0	Dering	—	—	—
54.3	Rawebb	—	—	Ritt Webb, Mayor of Winnipeg
61.9	Dyce	—	—	Village in Scotland
70.0	Paterson	—	872	General Paterson, railway promoter
81.2	Wekusko	51	924	Cree for "herb lake"
93.2	Turnbull	—	857	T. Turnbull, railway location engineer
107.1	Ponton	—	863	Dominion land surveyor
114.2	Button	—	769	Capt. T. Button, English navigator and explorer
121.8	Dunlop	—	768	W.D. Dunlop, resident of Yorkton
129.4	Pipun	—	771	Cree for "winter"
136.4	Wabowden (Man.)	284	767	W.A. Bowden, Chief Engineer of the Department of Railways and Canals. Formerly called Setting Lake.

Thicket Subdivision—CNR Wabowden/Gillam

This line was built by the Hudson Bay Railway and opened for traffic to mile 332 on October 9, 1918.

Miles	Stations	Population	Elev.	Origin of Station Names
136.4	Wabowden (Man.)	284	767	See Wekusko subdivision
141.9	Médard	—	741	Médard des Groseilliers. French explorer
148.7	Lyddal	—	744	William Lyddal, Governor of Rupert's Land
158.2	Odhill	—	720	O.D. Hill, Melfort lawyer
164.3	Earchman	—	726	Hudson Bay Railway engineer
171.1	La Pérouse	—	687	French admiral who captured Fort Prince of Wales
177.6	Hockin	—	653	G.H. Hockin, RCMP corporal
184.3	Thicket Portage	—	—	Translation of Cree name
191.9	Leven	—	656	—
199.8	Thompson Jct.	—	—	The point where the Hudson Bay Railway line to Churchill meets the CN line to Thompson
200.3	Sipiwesk	—	687	Cree for "beautiful vista"
212.1	Matago	—	636	Cree for "limestone"
213.3	Pikwitonei	84	—	Cree for "broken mouth"

Miles	Stations	Population	Elev.	Origin of Station Names
218.5	Bridgar	—	665	Governor of Hudson's Bay Co. post at Fort Nelson
230.6	Wilde	—	678	NWMP sergeant W.B. Wilde
236.4	Arnot	—	641	Man in charge of railway war supply
249.7	Boyd	—	711	First Canadian to fly to Britain
256.2	Pit Siding	—	—	—
269.0	Munk	—	—	Jens Munk, a Norwegian who discovered Churchill harbour in 1619
285.7	Ilford	165	629	Town in England
295.6	Nonsuch	—	—	Hudson's Bay Company ship (1668)
303.7	Wivenhoe	—	515	Hudson's Bay Company ship (1668)
318.8	Luke	—	—	Luke Clemens, brother of Mark Twain (Samuel Clemens), mail carrier and trader
326.1	Gillam (Man.)	356	453	Father and son sea captains at the time of Pierre Radisson (1640-1710), an explorer and one of the founders of the Hudson's Bay Co.

Thompson Subdivision—CNR Thompson Jct./Thompson

This line was opened in October 1957 to serve the new International Nickel Co. mine.

Miles	Stations	Population	Elev.	Origin of Station Names
0.0	Thompson Jct. (Man.)	—	—	See Thicket subdivision
8.4	Johnson	—	—	International Nickel Co. (Inco) executive
21.1	Parlee	—	—	Inco executive
29.7	Wingate	—	—	Inco executive
30.5	Thompson (Man.)	16,700	—	William Thompson, early settler and first postmaster. Previously called Tobacco River.

Herchmer Subdivision—CNR Gillam/Churchill

Built by the Hudson Bay Railway, this line was opened for through traffic from The Pas on September 13, 1929.

Miles	Stations	Population	Elev.	Origin of Station Names
326.1	Gillam (Man.)	356	453	See Thicket subdivision
333.5	Kettle Rapids	—	412	Nearby rapids on Nelson River
347.1	Bird	—	289	Dr. Bird, first in Red River Settlement
350.7	Limestone	—	—	Nearby river and rapids
355.0	Amery	—	309	L.C.M.S. Amery, British Secretary for the Dominion
364.3	Charlebois	—	—	Catholic Bishop of Keewatin
373.4	Weir River	—	—	Nearby river
382.1	Lawledge	—	—	F.M. Lawledge, engineer of the Hudson Bay Railway
391.6	Thibaudeau	—	—	Original railway route surveyor
399.9	Silcox	—	—	Division engineer on Hudson Bay Railway
412.0	Herchmer	—	345	RCMP Commissioner Lawrence Herchmer
417.7	Kellett	—	—	Captain of R.H.M. Resolute
426.2	Oday	—	—	J.O. Day, civil engineer of Hudson Bay Railway
434.4	Back	—	—	Royal Navy officer with Sir John Franklin, an Arctic explorer who died searching for the Northwest Passage
442.2	McLintock	—	278	Royal Navy captain with Sir John Franklin
451.0	Belcher	—	—	Captain of H.M.S. Assistance
460.3	Cromarty	—	232	HBC factor at Fort Severn
469.3	Chesnaye	—	181	Quebec fur trader Aubert de la Chesnaye
477.6	Lamprey	—	115	Ship of Jens Munk, which arrived in Churchill in 1619
485.2	Bylot	—	77	Robert Bylot, crew member on Hudson's ship Discovery
493.0	Digges	—	53	English merchant who financed Henry Hudson's travels
501.7	Tidal	—	25	Tide from Hudson Bay reaches this point
509.8	Churchill (Man.)	1,678	25	John Churchill, Duke of Marlborough

Index